The Asian Modern

Hong Kong University Press thanks Xu Bing for writing the Press's name in his Square Word Calligraphy for the covers of its books. For further information, see p. iv.

The Asian Modern

Culture, Capitalist Development, Singapore

C. J. W.-L. Wee

香港大學出版社
Hong Kong University Press

Hong Kong University Press
14/F Hing Wai Centre
7 Tin Wan Praya Road
Aberdeen
Hong Kong

ISBN 978-962-209-859-6

Secure On-line Ordering
http:// www.hkupress.org

British Library Cataloguing-in-Publication Data
A catalogue record for this book is available from the British Library.

Printed and bound by Condor Production Co. Ltd., in Hong Kong, China

Hong Kong University Press is honoured that Xu Bing, whose art explores the complex themes of language across cultures, has written the Press's name in his Square Word Calligraphy. This signals our commitment to cross-cultural thinking and the distinctive nature of our English-language books published in China.

"At first glance, Square Word Calligraphy appears to be nothing more unusual than Chinese characters, but in fact it is a new way of rendering English words in the format of a square so they resemble Chinese characters. Chinese viewers expect to be able to read Square Word Calligraphy but cannot. Western viewers, however are surprised to find they can read it. Delight erupts when meaning is unexpectedly revealed."

— Britta Erickson, *The Art of Xu Bing*

Contents

Foreword

Travelling around Asia, I frequently encounter enthusiastic expressions of Singapore as a 'desired' future. Discussions range from 'how did Singapore alone manage to avoid the culture of corruption that is everywhere in Asia', to 'can we borrow your political leaders, particularly Lee Kuan Yew, for a few years to get us off the ground', and this often only partly in jest, to finally and ultimately, 'Singapore as model'. Indeed, none less than the late Deng Xiaoping, the instigator of market economy for communist People's Republic of China, had suggested that its people 'learn from Singapore'. The irony should not be lost here: the largest nation in Asia is to learn from one of the smallest.

The reason for such enthusiasm is, of course, Singapore's rapid rise in global capitalism. The People's Action Party (PAP) government, which has governed without interruption for close to five decades by now, is extremely liberal towards the market economy; although one should recognize this as more a necessity for Singapore than a virtue of the government. Foreign investments are assured of labour peace and welcomed with favourable tax regimes, making Singapore a very profitable location for multinational corporations. The economy has been growing phenomenally since the early 1960s, with only a couple of brief recessions. Within a short two decades, Singapore began to cast off low-wage, labour intensive industries and move up the technological ladder to knowledge-intensive and capital-intensive industrialization, such as bio-medical and pharmaceutical industries. Decades of sustained double digit national economic growth has transformed Singapore into a capital exporting economy, as foreign investment continues to flow into the domestic market. At the everyday life level, economic success has translated into massive improvement in material life for ordinary citizens. 'Success' has become an element of national pride, national value and national identity.

The suggestion of 'Singapore as model' for developing Asia is undoubtedly engendered by this capitalist success. This is obviously not a suggestion for the 'cloning' of Singapore; the different historical and political conditions of each location make the 'reproduction' of Singapore anywhere an absurd idea. Rather, 'Singapore as model' points to the idea that 'if' Singapore, an island without any natural resources, is able to make it, so should 'we'. Singapore is thus a 'model' in that it provides a sense of 'can do' and an 'imaginable future' among its admirers in developing Asia.

Logically, as a Singaporean, one may be excused for deriving some pride in this 'iconic' status of Singapore. Yet, most progressive Singaporeans would find it difficult to recommend without reservation, let alone wish, the Singapore 'system' on others. Reservations come from the nature of the one-party dominant political system that has appropriated the legitimising character of an electoral system and yoke it with many anti-democratic, if not outright authoritarian, features. The end result is a society that is all too self-conscious of the absence of freedom in many areas of social life. Life in Singapore is thus marked by criss-crossing contradictions that can best be explained from the inside.

Wee Wan-ling is an insider. His text maps the ideological underpinnings of the trajectory of development of Singapore over the forty years since independence in 1965. At each stage of this trajectory, there is a tension between the need to embrace capitalist economic modernization modelled after the West and an ideological desire to avoid the aggressive liberal democracy of the West. The tension drives PAP ideologues, including Lee Kuan Yew, into constant search for things 'Asian' which will enable the rationalization of economic openness with political conservatism.

As a literary scholar, Wan-ling brings into his analysis different resource materials that are often overlooked by conventional social scientists: The modernity of the urban environment is dissected through a critique of the absence of Western self-reflexivity via the remarks of the globe-trotting architect, Rem Koolhaas; in contrast, Singaporean critical self-reflexivity is seen in the dark representations of the same urban environment in local movies. The cultural consequences of the obsession with capitalist growth, at both national and individual levels, is analysed through the allegories of humanity / humanism of the late Singapore playwright, Kuo Pao Kun, especially in the staging of his play, *Descendents of the Eunuch Admiral*, by the Singaporean director, Ong Keng Sen, whose own definition of 'Asian-ness' escapes the discursive confines of that of the PAP government.

Wan-ling's very nuanced analysis of the complexity of Singapore's development trajectory challenges simplistic critiques of the PAP government's evocation of things Asian as 'self-serving' rationalizations to maintain absolute political power. This is a book from which observers of social economic developments not only of Singapore but of Asia would benefit richly.

Chua Beng Huat
January 2007
Singapore

Acknowledgements

In 2000, Professor Wang Gungwu pointedly asked, 'Don't you have enough work yet for a small book on Singapore?' He then proceeded to refer me to a university press that had asked him for a book on 'Asian values', as he thought my work might fit what they had in mind. It did not, in the end; but the 'small book' in question has finally appeared, though after some effort.

This study is in many respects a companion work to an earlier book, *Culture, Empire, and the Question of Being Modern* (2003). Jointly taken, they represent an attempt to reflect upon the changing historical relationship between colonialism (and its aftermath), modernity and national culture. The cross-cultural aspect of national-identity formation has been a key concern in both studies, first between the imperial centre and its colonised periphery, and now, between the 'modernised' periphery and not only the former British imperial heartland — the original home of industrial modernity — but also the newer centres of the modern in both the advanced West and in East Asia. Singapore has been the case study for this latter reflection on culture and modernity because, first, its small territorial size and concentrated post-independence history allow a comprehensive survey on 'national' development not always possible with larger societies; and, second, because it is an indicative example for many of the issues I had in mind. Consequently, this is 'a small book on Singapore', and yet, not really .... There are both strengths and limitations to the approach taken, naturally.

The following friends and colleagues have engaged in valuable discussions with me in regard to various parts of the book over the years: Lee Weng Choy, Ray Langenbach, Shirley Geok-lin Lim, Sharon Siddique, Benjamin K. S. Wong, Tay

Kheng Soon, Mala de Alwis, Pradeep Jeganathan, Chen Kuan-Hsing, Ien Ang, William S. W. Lim, Yao Souchou, Tejaswini Niranjana, the late Paul Wheatley, Note Osamu, Janadas Devan, Nick Freeman, Barbara Watson Andaya, Cheah Boon Kheng, T. N. Harper, Chris Connery, Bob Hefner, Gyanesh Kudaisya, Medha Kudaisya, the late Kuo Pao Kun, Mok Wei Wei, Tan Kok Meng, Tan Liok Ee, Heinrich Blömeke, Aihwa Ong, Don Nonini, Victor P. H. Li, Jeannie Martin, Meaghan Morris, Mark Berger, Ong Keng Sen, Tay Tong, Arun Mahihznan, Norma Field, Hans-Dieter Evers, Ooi Giok Ling, Terence Lee, Gillian Koh, Lucy Davis, Kwa Chong Guan, Marc Askew, Leslie E. S. Teo, Yip Chun Seng, Dinesh Naidu, Charles Lim, Ashis Nandy, Audrey Wong, S. Gopinathan, Mark Seldan, Stephen Hazell, Charlene Rajendran, Bruce Robbins, Pang Tit Khuen, Pang Kim Lock and Julia Morgan-Pang.

A few persons require special mention. Chua Beng Huat has been critically engaged with many aspects of the work for a decade. Elizabeth Helsinger and Jean Comaroff, both former teachers in Chicago, have soldiered on, despite busy schedules, with my requests for their differing thoughts on 'culture'. Vicente Rafael, Philip Holden and Rob Wilson have been part of a community of ideas that have helped me complete the book. Kwok Kian Woon shared his sociological insights on culture and Singapore with me. Dipesh Chakrabarty's and Arjun Appadurai's responses to the globalisation processes in my corner of the world have always been illuminating. Ronald Inden's acerbically stated and revealing ideas on modernity, colonialism and the global modern in Chicago (and also in London) linger on and contributed to the arguments in the book. The historical-anthropological work of the late Bernard S. Cohn — another Chicago teacher — has also remained. In general, I am grateful for the work of the historical and cultural anthropologists and the historians who challenged me to think beyond the realm of literary humanism when mulling over the nuances of that complex term, 'culture'. I also thank Wang Gungwu and Anthony C. Yu for their encouragement.

The late Krishen Jit and Marion d'Cruz maintained an enlightening and ongoing discussion on Malaysian and Singapore theatre. Thanks too to Traslin Ong and Lucilla Teoh at TheatreWorks (Singapore) Ltd., and also to Wong Yen Yen of the Practice Performing Arts School for their help with various and only seemingly mundane matters.

I thank the Humanities Research Centre at the Australian National University for a visiting fellowship in 2006 that helped me complete part of the revision of the manuscript; particular thanks here go to Caroline Turner. The specific and ongoing support of Lubna Alsagoff, the head of English Language and Literature, was also important in this regard, as was staff development leave and, also, a research grant to cover the cost of the colour plates for the book, both given by the National Institute of Education, Nanyang Technological

University. Thanks, too, to colleagues and to students in Singapore who have heard and responded to parts of the argument in the book. Colin Day at the Hong Kong University Press made demands that I make much clearer the larger significance of the work on Singapore, and is to be thanked for that; Ian Lok, too, was constantly helpful in the process of preparing the manuscript. Thanks also to Phoebe Chan.

The book includes significantly revised or expanded versions of previously published articles: 'Mediating "Progress": The National Narrative of Economic Development and Liberalism in Singapore', *Communal/Plural* 9, no. 2 (October 2001): 223–242; 'Capitalism and Ethnicity: Creating "Local" Culture in Singapore', *Inter-Asia Cultural Studies* 1, no. 1 (April 2000): 129–43; 'Staging the Asian Modern: Cultural Fragments, the Singaporean Eunuch, and the Asian Lear', *Critical Inquiry* 30, no. 4 (Summer 2004): 771–799; 'The End of Disciplinary Modernisation? The Asian Economic Crisis and the Ongoing Re-Invention of Singapore', *Third World Quarterly* 22, no. 6 (October 2001): 987–1002; 'Contending with Primordialism: The "Modern" Construction of Postcolonial Singapore', *positions: east asia cultures critique* 1, no. 3 (Winter 1993): 715–44, Special Issue on 'The Nationalisms Question'; and '"Asian Values", Singapore and the Third Way: Re-Working Individualism and Collectivism', *SOJOURN: Journal of Social Issues in Southeast Asia* 14, no. 2 (October 1999): 332–58, Special Issue on 'Asian Ways: Asian Values Revisited', guest ed. Raul Pertierra.

C. J. W.-L. Wee
February 2007
Singapore

Credo in unum Deum, Patrem omnipotentem….

Introduction

What does the Asian modern of a 'globalising East Asia' — a phrase now both clichéd and yet still resonant — look like? In the discourses that have emerged over the past two decades, East Asia has become increasingly viewed as industrial, capitalist and urban — and committed to frenetic development. All the three elements mentioned contribute to what is almost a mantra to be intoned by those who wish to represent East Asian cultural dimensions. In 1999, the Paris-based, mainland Chinese curator Hou Hanru co-curated with Hans-Ulrich Obrist the touring arts-exhibition extravaganza that started in London's Hayward Gallery called 'Cities on the Move: Urban Chaos and Global Change — East Asian Art, Architecture and Films Now'. They proclaimed that:

> A kind of mixture of liberal Capitalist [*sic*] market economy and Asian, post-totalitarian social control is being established as a new social order [in industrial-capitalist East Asia]. Culture, in such a context, is by nature hybrid, impure and contradictory. Accordingly, the new architectures and urban environment [*sic*] are being renovated and transformed into a sort of 'Theme Park' oriented cityscape. ... [T]his [urban modernity] incarnates perfectly the image of the post-colonial and post-totalitarian modernization in the region: the impulsive and almost fanatical pursuit of economic and monetary power becomes the ultimate goal of development.[1]

This type of breathless prose, proclaiming the latest version of the new — now available in East Asia — with a vocabulary drawn from postcolonial theory of the 1980s and postmodern and globalisation cultural theory of the 1990s, along with a hint of Asian one-upsmanship, though, is not always well received, or is received ambivalently. The revival of aspects of postwar 'modernisation', a term that seemed superseded but is now updated to include the information industry and the warm reception of the globalised free market in former Third World regions, surprises cultural critic Fredric Jameson: '[Modernity] is in fact back in business all over the world, and virtually inescapable in political discussion from Latin America to China, not to mention the former Second World itself.'[2]

The 'developmental' city-state of Singapore[3] in many respects has contributed towards the now-established image of an Asian modern urban formation in which, it has become almost predictable to say, East meets West, and in which centre and periphery, old and new, are conjoined. Looking at one representative critical response to Singapore allows us to ponder why the East Asian modern could be perceived as an inauthentic modernity, or perhaps as a distorted form of modernity.

The year 1993 is a good place to start, for it was the year the World Bank released its report on the Little Tigers' economic development, *The East Asian Miracle*.[4] It was thus a year when Asian triumphalism seemed at least implicitly validated by that major international organisation. A *Time* article of that year on Singapore captures the image of success the People's Action Party (PAP), which has ruled the city-state since 1959, wants for the country. The writer, though, suggests that Singapore's Asian modern is a trifle sterile, that it is an inauthentic capitalist society. It begins by quoting Francis Fukuyama: 'the "soft authoritarianism" of countries like Singapore "is the one potential competitor to Western liberal democracy, and its strength and legitimacy is growing daily"'.[5] Significant (if backhanded) praise from the 1990s high-profile champion of the teleology of progress and liberty based on European Enlightenment thought — an intellectual heritage, as we will see, which the first-generation PAP leaders adapted for their own use. Singapore's 'legitimacy', it is suggested, come from its technicist, narrow and therefore distorted understanding of modernisation: 'Singapore Inc.' is 'the world's busiest container port, the third largest oil-refining center, the major exporter of computer disk drives', and 'has attracted some 3,000 foreign companies with generous tax breaks, ultramodern telecommunications, an efficient airport, and tame labor unions' (36–37). Despite such achievements, full universal progress and a complete modernity have not arrived in the city-state.[6]

The photograph which straddles two pages of the article is apt, embodying as it does the writer's physical description of Singapore as an inorganically evolved and thus incoherent urban space: 'With low pollution, lush tropical greenery, a mix of modern skyscrapers and colonial-era buildings, the city resembles a clean and efficient theme park ...' (36). The *Padang* — the city green with its playing fields — occupies the foreground of the photo and the Singapore Cricket Club the centre. On the right of the *Padang* (from back to front) are the well-maintained Parliament, Supreme Court and City Hall buildings,[7] present reminders of a former resplendent imperial authority now passed on to local people. Behind Parliament House and the Victoria Concert Hall (until 1979 the Victoria Memorial Hall) — in front of which stands a statue of Sir Thomas Stamford Raffles, harbinger of colonial modernity, advocate of free trade and the official English founder of Asian Singapore — lies the Singapore River, another reminder of the imperial commercial past: Singapore as entrepôt.

At the back of the photo is the central business district, with its skyscrapers — one of which is designed by the modernist, Chinese-American architect, I. M. Pei. It has been argued that out of an older, English-inspired commercial modernity has risen 'the rebirth of the sort of interstitial centres characteristic of world trade in the Middle Ages. City states like Hong Kong and Singapore revive, extraterritorial "industrial zones" multiply inside technically sovereign nation-states like Hanseatic Steelyards ...'.[8]

Time's critical transnational picture of modernity is in certain respects actually, though naturally more positively, enshrined in official representations of Singapore's identity. The Ministry of Culture's[9] *Singapore 1984* yearbook is a good example of such representations. As 'authentic' Asian identities (apparently) have not dissipated (despite steady, post-independence socio-cultural engineering by the state), there is a cosmopolitanism to Singapore national identity: 'the people have gradually acquired a distinct identity as Singaporeans while retaining their traditional cultures and lifestyles'. The religious incarnations of the people are even more complex: Chinese (either vernacular-, Mandarin- or English-speaking) who are Buddhist, Taoist or Christian, Hindus, Sikhs, Jains and Zoroastrians, not to mention Malay-Muslims, 'exist side by side under the protection of the Constitution of the Republic'.[10] Singapore is no India; but the vertical, ethnic and linguistic divisions are confusing enough for an island of some four millions.

The multi-ethnic citizenry are a key reason for the PAP's deracinated and deculturated version of modernity: this multicultural reality made it difficult to erect a clear-cut national culture. Being unable to adopt the more common 'assumed isomorphism of space, place, and culture',[11] which often results in problems for those who may inhabit the borders of national boundaries, the PAP decided to make Singapore *all* 'border', as it were. It is true, as cultural anthropologist Akhil Gupta suggests, that: 'The [postcolonial-nationalist] recognition that different ethnic groups, ... communities and religions each have their own role to play in the national project undermines their difference at the same time that it homogenizes and incorporates them.'[12] However, in Singapore, this homogenising by the state is complicated by the fact that 'ethnicity' is a category which is harder to impose in a place composed of people each with their 'own' country — for example, Chinese, China; various Indians, India, Sri Lanka. The endgame of marshalling and defusing national differences is the creation of a globally oriented community which will be able to *transcend* the purely national even while the modern nation-state category is complicatedly sustained for the purpose of developing the island as a whole.

The technicist orientation of Singapore hails from it history; it is a smaller-scale, Asianised version of the British Whigs' 'Our Island Story', as the opening paragraph of the section marked 'History' in the yearbook infers:

> The story of Singapore as a commercial centre began with its founding in 1819. It grew increasingly important from the 1860s with the coming of the steamship and the opening of the Suez Canal in 1869. Singapore became the entrepôt centre of the region, a role enhanced by the development of the tin and rubber industries in the states of the Malay Peninsula (19).

The imperial past is not necessarily debasing, for it has led to the present export-oriented, industrial-capitalist developments.[13] As for pre-colonial history and origins, on the whole '[l]ittle is known of the early history of Singapore' (19).

The most space is devoted to Singapore's struggle for self-rule (gained in 1959), the triumph over communism, the merger with Malaysia (1963) and the subsequent separation (1965). Details are given of the setting up of the powerful Economic Development Board and the first industrial estate in 1959, and of the inter-ethnic riots between Malays and Chinese in 1964. The history concludes with the 1970s, when 'the thrust in economic strategy was to attract industries needing higher skills and to develop Singapore as a financial centre and as a regional centre for brain services' (28). While there is validity to the claim that colonial history is essential to understanding the present urban-modern condition, the city-state is probably distinct among postcolonial societies in its valorisation of the colonial past as part of the *telos* of progress and freedom that results in the not-quite-democratic and sterile cultural inauthenticity ascribed to the island. Emancipation arrived — but not quite in a full-fledged manner.[14]

Development therefore has resulted in a modern Anglo-Asian city-state that doesn't seem quite part of Southeast Asia, though it certainly is not part of the advanced part of the West its political leadership admires. During the Cold War, Singapore was — and still remains — the most pro-West entity in the region. Benedict Anderson has acerbically described the city-state's Southeast Asian status thus: 'There was … the anomaly of the municipality of Singapore: formally multi-ethnic or multi-racial, but in effect a third Chinese national possibility, under the interminable regime of Lee Kuan-yew [*sic*] and his henchmen.' Anderson's annoyance centres on the political regime of the first prime minister, Lee Kuan Yew: 'Lee first became Chief Minister in 1957, thanks to the support of the then powerful organized Left[, who were then later suppressed].'[15]

This sort of ambivalence towards the PAP government's not-really-democratic and not-quite-authentic Asian modern by both the left and liberals in the West occurs with some regularity and actually *reveals* the complex if subordinate role that the city-state has played in the advancement of capitalism in Southeast Asia. Ultimately, it is a response to the strategies undertaken to become thoroughly modern, strategies in which socio-cultural engineering and selected parts of the West are used to create a 'pragmatic' Asian modern. Using Singapore as an indicative instance, this book concerns itself with the Asian modern's relation to the advanced West and the links between them that are simultaneously affirmed, denied, sublimated and (mis-)recognised.

A 'Revealing Distortion'

> *... the notion of an authentic culture as an autonomous internally coherent universe is no longer sustainable [in either the First or the Third Worlds,] except perhaps as a 'useful fiction' or as a revealing distortion.*
>
> Renato Rosaldo, *Culture and Truth* (1989)[16]

The earlier economic development of Singapore had been a later part of the beginning of the postcolonial age on midnight, 14 August 1947, during which postcoloniality led to supposedly sovereign states under the industrial-capitalist world order. The PAP's early vision of the modern and commitment to modernisation were part and parcel of a larger experience of decolonisation. The Second World modernity of the communist bloc did not appeal to Lee Kuan Yew and his co-leaders, but the call of First World modernity did.

The city-state specifically comes into its own during the 'second epoch' in the genealogy of postcolonial states, as the anthropologists Jean and John Comaroff describe it, from perhaps the 1980s onwards. This epoch has a more fluid, market-driven world coming about, one in which the state was held to be somewhat in crisis against supranational forces, and in which 'liberty' came to mean the right to assert 'culture' in the form of identities, subjectivities, ethnic differences and even localities.[17] The city-state moved on from a Nehruvian commitment to industrial and technological modernity to the 1980s discourse on a New Asianism and Asian modernity inspired by the 'unique Japan' hypothesis on modernisation, and thus by the enormous success of 'Japan as Number One'.[18] Singapore's 'Asian values' period of state formation, marked by a culturalist orientation that was a clear departure from the technicist 1960s–70s, was part of this second epoch of the post-Second World War 'life' of capital. Singapore thus participates in the 1980s–90s story of a burgeoning East Asian capitalism, which will then be the central period the book examines. These two decades also set the stage for the re-emergence of the People's Republic of China onto the regional and world stages.

The island, in effect, is a national project taking place in an offshore economy, and a particular formation integral to the free-trade regime. While small, it displays the tensions within and the cultural (il)logic(ality) of the present globalising modernity. Its smallness in fact offers a 'test-tube' intensity by which to consider the problematic of presumed non-Western or alternative modernities.

What bothers a progressive critic like Benedict Anderson, one suspects, is the sort of quasi-authoritarian, petit-bourgeois and sometimes smug and priggish modernity that smoothed the path to economic success. The city-state stands for a very ordered, capitalist society that seems to have been rewarded, despite its repressive impulses. From this viewpoint, Singapore seems a *distortion* of the models of socio-economic development that it inherited from its British rulers, regardless of whether one prefers the social-democratic or the liberal variety. The 'new' model has come to stand for a dynamic and even iconic, if bland, multicultural utopianism adapted from and yet still dependent upon the West, but one in which both democratic impulses and cultural difference and historico-racialist 'irrationalities' were suppressed, homogenised or sanitised in the name of industrial-capitalist modernity's pure truths.

In 1963, the anthropologist Clifford Geertz noted that 'peoples of the new states are simultaneously animated by two powerful, thoroughly interdependent, yet distinct and often actually opposed motives — ... a search for an identity ... [and] a demand for progress'.[19] Singapore's statist Asian modern by and large excluded — or suppressed — primordial sentiments and popular culture (folklore, ethnic cultures and traditions) from the nation-building process, and instead focused on making industrial-capitalist modernity the metanarrative that would frame Singapore's national identity.[20]

For some observers, the city-state's modernity seems obvious: it represents a form of capitalism that, because it has landed on Asian soil, has run amok. Singapore is a *whole* society subjugated to the needs of capital. What happened to the other aspects of modern life such as literature, music and the visual arts, the achievements that we need to be *cultured* in the modern world, in fact of what we need to be deeply modern? Why did the PAP regime not value the high symbolic and aesthetic goods that represented one major part of the spectrum of human autonomy? (In 1968 Lee Kuan Yew, while addressing an audience at the then-University of Singapore, famously remarked: 'Poetry is a luxury we cannot afford.'[21]) The modernisation process does not diminish or suppress the role of the symbolic market beyond a degree (take, for instance, the romantic revolt against a narrow socio-economic modernisation in the very homeland of the Industrial Revolution[22]).

The aesthetic home of the PAP state's utopian impulses was not painting or literature — which cannot feed mouths — but building, the art we live in and do business in.[23] Architecture in the form of extensive modernist public housing and a revamped downtown that reached towards the sky was the social art form that nobody could escape, and was needed if the new citizens of the city-state were to live well, materially. It was the people's ethnic and traditional cultures that needed watching over — and the art of architecture was useful in the wish to rationally homogenise the nation.

If, as Néstor García Canclini has argued, that 'the most-reiterated hypothesis in the literature on Latin American modernity … [is that they] have had an exuberant modernism with a deficient modernization',[24] then Singapore represents the near-opposite case, an exuberant socio-economic modernisation with a deficient cultural modernism[25] — with, in fact, a deficient idea of 'culture', taken broadly.[26] 'Cultural policy' in the island did not refer to aesthetic or high-cultural policies until 1980 or so.

Despite the apparent distortions of Western modernity, some would say the city-state still follows the simple determinations of capital. If so, would Singapore's modernity then be a sort of twisted or discrepant extension, or an attempt at mimesis gone awry? Or perhaps — if one is take the claims seriously of both detractors and supporters of this position in *both* East Asia and the advanced industrial West — this distortion is the result of local / regional (that is, *inherently Asian* rather than indigenised or Asian*ised*) capitalisms being shaped by 'Asian' cultures. In the process, supposedly *alternative* modernities — if not *completely* Other to Western modernities then significantly different from them — based on indigenous value systems, could be conceived as starting to challenge Western capitalism and worldwide US cultural hegemony, at least before the 1997 Asian economic crisis was triggered by the devaluation of the Thai baht.

In general, such views as discussed above on Singapore's Asian modern suggesting that the city-state, along with the other Tiger and emerging Southeast Asian economies in the 1980s–90s asserting their own supposed brand of Asian modernities, whether claimed to be Confucian or Islamic, represent a *distorted* modernity in effect are a 'useful fiction' (to use Renato Rosaldo's words from this section's epigraph) that covers up or disavows the fact that capitalism is *one* phenomenon. At the same time, we also must also recognise that this 'one-ness' does not imply that capitalist modernity will be the same everywhere: it is neither monolithic nor unified.

We know capitalism is not quite the same even to itself in this (impossibly hypostasised) entity which we call *the* West. Given this, Singapore's apparently distorted reflection of the selected parts of the Anglo-American West 'inside' it, then can be seen as a '*revealing distortion*', to quote Rosaldo again, that only iterates the fact that the hegemonic and metropolitan Euro-American powers can always define for the non-Western 'Them' what is supposed to be incoherent. Such differences, though, between 'Western' and 'Asian' capitalisms cannot be characterised as predominantly 'ideological', as something more than and different from the disagreements of stronger and weaker economic areas insisting on the importance of their disagreements. In the post-Cold War world of the 1980s–90s, the question that separated the established economic zones from the emergent economies was the question of attitudes towards cultural difference in the construction of capitalist practices: the established powers wanted to eliminate difference, and some emerging Asian economies thought it to their advantage to insist on it. The 'conflict' of those two decades, then, was at best a conflict over whether Asian capitalist societies could rise up in the hierarchy of capitalist societies. This is a conflict continued by China in the new century, as its politico-economic presence grows in East Asia.

Culture and the Asian Modern

I will argue that it is the *mixed attitudes* towards Singapore by those outside it, and, even more significantly, also the attitudes of those *within* the city-state towards the oftentimes hidden or unrecognised presence of the Anglo-American West, that are more telling of the Singapore's developmental strategies. Its modernity contains complicated levels of assertion, recognition and misrecognition regarding the island-state's relation to the West and to the immediate region and East Asia. This offshore hub of transnational cultural-capitalist flows is fashioned by the city-state's leaders and yet is *already* fashioned by the capitalist powers.

The book's first hypothesis is that during the 1960s, a period of political, ethnic and economic instability within and without the city-state, the PAP regime 'used' parts of the British (and later the American) West — taken as a neutral or indeed universal culture, even as culture was downplayed on the island — as the source of its postcolonial identity and state formation.

The second hypothesis follows from the first. This version of the West was used to *deterritorialise* — to further the loss of culture in relation to social and geographical territory — the various immigrant and local cultures as the means to create a society ready for the jump to export-oriented industrialisation. Such deterritorialisation was facilitated by the fact that the Chinese and Indian sections of the population, being immigrant stock, were already partially deterritorialised. An inconsistency in the construction of Western nationalism, connected as it was with the essentialising function of history in relation to primordial or historical identities for national identity, was a flaw in the Western politico-cultural legacy that the PAP thought avoidable.

However, capitalism itself *is* a cultural form, and for it to be embedded in ways amenable to multinational companies, more proletarians had to be formed out of farmers in the *kampongs* (Malay: villages), consumerism encouraged, and so forth. The enforced rationalising modernity was in keeping with the 1960s universalist teleological thinking, and the cultural logic of capital that underlay modernisation theory. One key policy initiative was a tremendous emphasis on the teaching of the English language — taught as a sort of technical language to make it culturally neutral — so as to link the new nation with the international economy. 'Culture', under the PAP, was (and is) conceived of as a *residual* category to be revamped instrumentally as part of the radical reconstruction of subjectivity itself for the economy. This policy perspective, not unexpectedly, entailed the assumption that the economy is *not* cultural.

As the city-state gained in confidence and came into a more market-driven period of international capitalist development, there was an actual (if also simultaneously cynical) attempt at *reterritorialising* the city-state; this was the 'Asian' and 'Confucian' values period of the city-state's cultural and state formation from the 1980s to the mid-1990s. The problem here was the supposedly 'natural' relation of Singapore to a vague, pan-Asian 'territory', or, just as problematically, the non-physical and symbolic relation of Southeast Asian Singapore (even if primarily Sinic) to a Confucian identity. The idea of a Greater or a Cultural China, shored up by the then extremely influential work of philosopher Tu Wei-ming, floated around in the 1980s to the early 1990s.[27] The linking of city-state to this imagined and inflated cultural entity did nothing to make non-Chinese Singaporeans feel comfortable. This phase represented an *ongoing collusion* with global capital that was also a *resistance*: it was yet another 'space-making' device that allowed the city-state to function more ably within the Euro-American hegemonic confines of global capitalism.[28]

Singapore in the 1980s importantly illustrates that the opportunities for national economies to participate in the emerging global economy may lead to the need to focus on alternative identity and political legitimacy in which the earlier commitment to cultural homogenisation as an inevitable concomitant of modernisation or industrialisation may be questioned. The 1980s–90s occupies the core of the book as it is when the conceptualisation of alternative Asian modernities becomes possible in Singapore and elsewhere in East Asia.

While 'culture' had returned in an odd official way, earlier rationalising imperatives had not disappeared. However, culture was now seen to be able to *support* economic development, unlike the 1960–70s, when ethnic or traditional cultures seemed retrograde. The re-ethnicising of the city-state and its insertion into the region 'Asia' through the Asian values discourse in reality *reinforced* a presumption of capitalism's universal status by allowing the national state greater individual space to manoeuvre. Singapore's Asian modern thus was fashioned as much by the Anglo-American West, even as it attempted to manipulate that West for its own survival process. The oppositional quality of the discourse gave Singapore and all who used it an agenda to protect the more contentious practices (e.g., a less-democratic polity; suppressed trade union activities) that helped maintain their position within global capitalism.[29] New opportunities in China from 1978 — as Deng Xiaoping instituted economic reforms — was another key reason for the PAP to stress the 'Sinic' qualities of New Asia's capitalist identity; this was the romance of 'network' (*guanxi*) capitalism. Even high aesthetic culture was incorporated (admittedly slowly) as part of the state's development agenda formally from 1989. While an Asian modernity was asserted, the state simultaneously supported a universal form of free-tradist and neo-liberal economics that became dominant after the USSR's collapse. The point when Singapore transcended its Third World status in the 1980s was also when cultural distinctiveness was marshalled to sustain competitiveness.

However, in re-imag(in)ing Singapore, there also was an unexpected and significant authorisation of the arts (primarily in the theatre, but also in the visual arts and in film). The cultural production that resulted used this very authorisation to resist the government's heavy-handed cultural planning. The results represent at least partial artistic relocalisations of life in the city (through a re-envisioning of daily life in the vast socialist-style public-housing estates) and in the older forms of culture (through the rethinking of the island's multi-ethnic past), along with symbolic productions that were intercultural reterritorialisation of an 'East Asia', productions that countered the state's version of East Asia.[30] The contradictions in the formation of Singapore's Asian modern, ironically yet fittingly, are expressed in the domains of aesthetic culture and its intersection with politics. The burst of high-cultural development in the face of a statist, petit-bourgeois philistinism indicates the point at which the culture of economy has turned upon itself and started to hollow out the plural cultural 'reality' that once was 'Singapore'. This is the reason why the book examines both the culture of the state and the state of cultural production it helped foster, albeit accidentally, in return.

The artistic responses to remember and re-imagine 'Asian' identity in the face of the deliberate loss of cultural autochthony by the state is significant as they offer instances of what transpires when the attempt is made to make a small island-territory the *tabula rasa* upon which a 'purer' modernity could be erected. Political scientist Partha Chatterjee argues that the task for postcolonial societies is to trace in their mutually conditioned historicities the specific forms that have appeared in the domain defined by the hegemonic project of nationalist modernity and in the numerous fragmented resistances to that normalising project.[31] But what if such non-nationally dominated cultural spaces are heavily weakened?

My final hypothesis is that Singapore is a case study of original authenticity being given up and of various versions of both the 'West' and 'Asia' being used to reterritorialise cultural space. It is clear that an authentic culture as an autonomous and internally coherent universe is no longer sustainable in either the advanced *or* the less-advanced worlds — except, perhaps, as a simple yardstick as to what possessing a modern culture truly means, with the implication that non-Western societies will never attain that standard.

The book is in two sections. The first looks at the deterritorialisation of local cultures, and how some artistic production attempted the 'relocalisation' of daily life in the city-state in the 1990s. The second section examines the attempt to reterritorialise Singapore in the name of 'Asian values', and the opportunities this offered for the artistic counter-reterritorialising of the country within the larger idea of East Asia. Both instances of non-statist cultural production do not function in the void: a symbiotic relationship to the state's national-culturalist activity, one also in relation to the reality of the dominance of Western capital, is always present.

The first chapter examines some of the key terms and contextual concerns within East Asia that frame the book. The second and third chapters analyse the immediate postcolonial creation of a state that was not-quite-a-nation. The narrative that finally became dominant was a Whiggish *telos* of economic development.

The third chapter also considers what, retrospectively, might be thought of as the prelude to the 1980s discursive construction of 'Asian values'. We should not take at face value the differentiation between 'East' and 'West'; it would be better to think through the values raised in the discourse, such as freedom, individualism and collectivism. How can a state have an idea of collectivism, given the neo-liberal emphasis on the free market? The Asian values discourse was a proleptic attempt to reflect upon the relationship between polity, ongoing state formation and economic growth that would later surface in Tony Blair's and Anthony Giddens's Third Way discourse, which proclaimed that the re-fashioning of social democracy by market-driven means was possible. In reassessing its earlier commitment to a homogenising modernity, the logic for the PAP management of ethnicity became revamped, resulting in the 're-ethnicising'/'re-Asianising' and thus the reterritorialising of the city-state.

The fourth chapter examines both the state's extensive modernist housing programme and decontextualised urbanism as a major component of its socio-cultural engineering and the reaction it produced in the arts and, more specifically, in 1990s independent film. Film made an embryonic re-entry as art form after its demise as an industry in the 1960s. Eric Khoo's *Twelve Storeys* (1997), for instance, depicts the social dysfunctionality of the city-state's less-'globalised' citizens living in public housing slabs. Such films examined the problematic and bizarre aspects of non-élite life and deployed the use of both Mandarin-Chinese and the officially suppressed Hokkien-Chinese. These films are attempts to re-assert and, indeed, reinvent 'locality' amid a state-projected, deterritorialised and happy-clappy modernity.

The fifth chapter examines the modifications in how ethnicity was managed from the 1980s. The earlier general, if deterritorialising, commitment to the West as universal civilisation was replaced by an identititarian and reterritorialising discourse on Asian values and modernity. These changes indicate that states are capable of managing culture as an instrument to maintain economic competitiveness; such culturalist reterritorialisation stood for an actual change in local cultural values.

The next chapter studies how theatre has dealt with the gap between the older utopia of autonomous creation that cultural and artistic modernism stood for and the reality of the suppression of the symbolic realm in the city-state. Theatre was the most dynamic contemporary art form that burgeoned in the 1980s. Against the virtual impossibility of constructing a different order, the late playwright and public intellectual Kuo Pao Kun and intercultural director Ong Ken Sen worked to extend cultural memory in the face of a culturally fragmenting economic development by envisioning a fractured Singapore-Asian humanism that countered the state's version of 'Asia'.

Finally, the epilogue thinks through how the end of the Cold War and the 1997 economic crisis has problematised the existing disciplinary modernisation that had delivered economic success. The Singapore government has hastened economic deregulation and now desires more autonomy and 'creativity' from its citizenry, manifesting a contradictory wish for what has been called in the city-state as 'managed change'. The actual experience of modernity in the city-state seems to have exceeded and is starting to dislocate the policies of its earlier modernisation. This is an 'epilogue' rather than a conclusion as the casting about for new directions implies that the end of the Cold War has not resulted in a post-historical world. Watch this space as the first decade of the twenty-first century comes to an end.

Singapore remains a humourless morality lesson as an economic success story, as a paternalistic-pragmatic modernity, and as a managed and generally benign multicultural society (even if now complicated by the events of 9 September 2001[32]) that created a measure of respect for ethnic and religious differences. It notably increased equity in socio-economic opportunities. As a consequence of the elevation of petit-bourgeois values, it also became a 'cultural desert' known abroad as a land of shopping centres. Historical amnesia — the inevitable by-product of modernisation — is prominent and surpasses, one suspects, the level of dehistoricisation in developed Euro-American societies. In many ways, this radical experiment in modernising a small Asian locality into a sort of hyper-petit-bourgeois modernity is unique. As with Japan, beneath the assertions of the 'unique Japan' hypothesis of modernisation, parts of the West have become parts of Singapore's 'Asian-ness'.

The deployment of the 'modern' should be contextualised within the once-commanding dream of what the modern world should undergo: endless renovation. It is now hard to think that anyone could believe that the slate could be wiped cleaned. While critics consider the PAP state 'conservative' or even 'reactionary' for its illiberal capitalism, the way the 'modern' was adapted might be better described as 'radical'. And so — contradictorily, in strict ideological terms — there developed a city-state that strongly supported the free market outside its borders while planning and the consistent interference in the realm of the private became hallmarks of PAP rule. The state effectively married social democracy's penchant for planning with the belief in the free market.

Singapore is indicative, if not representative, of identity concerns at the city-state level trying to function as a nation-state when placed under pressure to survive and then flourish under the conditions of a burgeoning global economy, and to develop a national culture able to mobilise society towards the developmental goal of becoming a First-World society. The very *lack of representativeness* — its small population and lack of territory — helped rather than hindered this objective, and Singapore can be seen as a contained laboratory test-case of one postcolonial Asian struggle to be modern and economically successful as the Euro-American West is thought to be modern.

1

The Asian Modern

Before the analysis of Singapore's experiment with an Asian modern commences in detail, it is important to reiterate the point that the People's Action Party (PAP) government's imagining of a local and indeed regional modernity that it was part of was not something quirky: it was one part of the ongoing East and Southeast Asian responses to the colonial legacy of Western modernity.[1] This chapter attempts a limited genealogy of the 'nativisations' of modernity, and sees such nativisations as problematic if they are to be conceptualised as alternative sets of modernities that have achieved an Otherness to their Western colonial origins.

As I have suggested in the introduction, the recognition and misrecognition of Singapore's relation to the West both inside and outside the island are revealing; a similar recognition and misrecognition of the East Asian modernities that developed from the 1980s and their relation to the advanced industrial West also exists. Returning to the visions of the modern from the postwar era of decolonisation of the European empires would help one to see the transformations and adaptations of the parts of colonial modernity that have been involved in the 'rise' of the New Asia.

Alternative Modernities and the New Asia

To begin with, though, is the general question of 'alternative modernities'. This is an issue that has become pronounced in some academic analyses of non-Western cultures from the 1990s to the present. Dilip Parameshwar Gaonkar's view on alternative modernities is representative of this vein of what might be described as transnational culturalist thinking:

> To think in terms of 'alternative modernities' is to admit that modernity is inescapable .... Born in and of the West some centuries ago under specific sociohistorical conditions, modernity is now everywhere. ... And it continues to 'arrive and emerge', as always in opportunistic fragments accompanied by utopic rhetorics, but no longer from the West alone, although the West remains the major clearinghouse of global modernity.[2]

As a consequence of such 'opportunistic' fragmentation,

> alternative modernities produce combinations and recombinations that are endlessly surprising. The [book Gaonkar introduces] ... submit the following tentative conclusions: *everywhere, at every national/cultural site, modernity is not one but many; modernity is not new but old and familiar; modernity is incomplete and necessarily so*. (23, emphases original)

Gaonkar's position, in many respects, seems a sensible one.

My concern here is more in the adjective 'alternative' that qualifies the term 'modernity'. It still seems to suggest an emancipated zone of modern life, free from the dictates of Euro-American economic hegemony, since the other modernities could resist the 'one' that was '[b]orn in ... the West ... under specific sociohistorical conditions'. Gaonkar emphasises the possibility of a 'creative adaptation' (20) to the modern: 'Non-Western people, the latecomers to modernity, have been engaged in these [creative-adaptive] maneuvers now for nearly a century' (22).

One response to the Gaonkar stance would be Fredric Jameson's; he acerbically comments on what he calls the alternative modernities 'formula':

> there can be a modernity for everybody which is different from the ... hegemonic Anglo-Saxon model. Whatever you disliked about the latter, including the subaltern position it leaves you in, can be effaced by the reassuring and 'cultural' notion that you can fashion your own modernity differently .... But this is to overlook the other fundamental meaning [of modernity] which is that of a worldwide capitalism itself.[3]

The difference in perspective comes from Jameson being able to see that proclamations of the new can come from 'top-down' locations such as states and political elites occupy, rather than from a more generic entity called 'Non-Western people'. Such proclamations of the new and the alternative tend to be party political broadcasts, especially when the semantic complexities of 'modernity' generally have been narrowed down to refer mainly to capitalism.

Gaonkar's position actually echoes a sentiment already expressed by Marshall Berman in the 1980s: 'Now it would be stupid to deny that modernization can proceed along a number of different roads. (Indeed, the whole point of modernization theory is to chart these roads.)'[4] But with Berman, we see a pertinent point not raised by Gaonkar. Modernisation theory from the 1960s already contains, *within* its conceptual framework, the possibility of *socio-cultural difference* and thus creative adaptation in the modernising process. Modernisation as a process was not singular in the West, and as others modernise, the lack of singularity and incompletion continues. Therefore, the modernities one may see 'elsewhere' are not the 'fragments' of some coherent whole — though they can be 'opportunistic' and 'utopic' formations — but are part of what might be said to be the modernising 'condition' itself. The question that arises is: what difference does it make that non-Western players in the modernisation stakes proceed 'along a number of different roads' that remain very much part of the modernisation or development process?

A series of questions previously raised by Rob Wilson and Arif Dirlik also function as an important qualifying supplement to Gaonkar's position on alternative modernities:

> To put it bluntly, do social and cultural differences finally make any difference in the transnational formation of postmodern markets whose aim is to generate the same fantasies, localize the same products, and infiltrate a mythic banality of social progress and shared prosperity, even if the agent of domination and fascination [in parts of East Asia] … is not America but postmodern Japan? How can we continue to discuss these transcultural complications of global/local relations and national identities 'in a world where Japan, South Korea, Hong Kong, Taiwan, Singapore, or Indonesia simply don't exist, certainly not as *forces* in emergent structure of world power'?, as [cultural critic] Meaghan Morris challenged the Eurocentric and trans-Atlantic speculations of post-Birmingham 'cultural studies'.

Does the 'creative adaptation' of modernity — whether in its older or 'postmodern' senses — mean that there is a challenge to the existing capitalist system? Wilson and Dirlik go on to ask, will 'Little Tiger' societies such as Singapore or Taiwan decentre or help entrench the emergent idea of a wealthy 'East Asia' now apparently different from their colonial or quasi-colonial pasts, or will they 'perpetuate hegemonic relationships, since they themselves are shaped by the capitalist world-system?'[5]

With the weakening of the Tiger economies and Japan since the end of the 1990s, it will be China that will become the latest 'alternative' modernity in East Asia, with its repressive post-communist/authoritarian-capitalist modernity increasingly able to challenge the one superpower left in the world, the USA. Do we like the creatively adapted challenge of this latest Asian modern, one in geopolitical terms that may be much more destabilising than the Tiger economies' supposed 'East-Asian' challenge of Euro-American economic hegemony?

What also needs to be directly addressed — given the book's central concerns with the recognition and misrecognition of the Asian relationship with the Anglo-American West, and that 'new' modernities manifest themselves in 'old and familiar' ways — is what 'the West' is in relation to East Asia. Coming to grips with that will require a broader statement about what I call the 'global West'.

Perry Anderson has written: 'For the Third World generally, a kind of shadow configuration of what once prevailed in the First World does exist today.'[6] While Anderson's essay was published in 1984 and refers more to Latin America, the idea of Third-World development as shadowy repetition still has purchase. If this book rejects that idea, it also does not accept the argument that the once much-vaunted 'coming Asian Century'[7] would firmly entrench alternative and more communitarian modernities that would put the individualistic West in its place. The case of Singapore will indicate that the various parts of the Anglo-American West, along with the modernity that was wrought within its local boundaries, can no longer simply be called the enemy, intimate or otherwise,[8] though obviously this does not mean that the economic domination of Asian economies by the Euro-American transnational institutions of a now-globalised West somehow vanishes or that, alternatively, we will become a happy global village. The ability to think through our relation to the 'West within', as it were, may help us better come to terms with the cultural and other violence it took to become modern Asian societies and, one hopes, enhanced capacities to deal with the so-called Washington consensus of market liberalisation and privatisation.

Anthropologist Fernando Coronil has observed that economic and political power has shifted away from a geographical location called the 'West' to a less identifiable position in the 'globe'. Capitalism's evolution in the 'imperial present' has led to the West's 'invisible reterritorialization in the elusive figure of the globe [, and this] ... conceals [the] diffuse[d] transnational financial and political networks that integrate metropolitan and peripheral dominant social sectors'.[9] The upshot is that 'the image of a unified globe dispenses with the notion of an outside. It displaces the locus of cultural difference from highly Orientalized others located outside the metropolitan centers to diffuse populations dispersed across the globe' (TCG, 368). Further, the 'differences between [Western] centers and [non-Western] margins' are effaced, with non-Western subjection appearing 'as a market effect, rather than as the consequence of a Western political project' (TCG, 369).

There is a risk, though, Coronil notes, that in the process of 'referring to capitalism by a single word (and in the singular) and attributing to it features that may give the impression that it is a bounded or self-willed entity, rather than as complex, contradictory, and heterogeneous process mobilized by the actions of innumerable social agents' (TCG, 353).

While Coronil's image of a West now dispersed into the globe is a cogent one important for this book, indicating that we must qualify how we speak of 'the West' and 'the non-West', we must not allow this formulation to be so general that it loses its analytical usefulness. Not to inflect how various parts of the world relate to and connect with capitalism now is indeed to make capitalism look like a 'self-willed entity' and possibly even fails to let us see how 'innumerable social agents' respond to capitalist modernity as a complex phenomenon. Late capitalism may be propelling the world 'toward ever more ever more immaterial domains' under 'ever more abstract forms of control', but the processes he writes about are not as 'abstract' as he makes it out to be[10] — and neither do developing societies see their subjection as 'merely' a market effect, with their sense of (postcolonial) marginality or being semi-peripheral (for the more economically advanced) effaced. The reterritorialised West has become part of its Others, like it or not; but of course this does not mean that the Others actually can exert direct ownership of this West. The now not-quite-Other in question possesses it enough to rework it — but even such 'resistance' entails some potential collusion with the global West.

From the publication of Edward Said's *Orientalism* in 1978, we have seen analyses of how Euro-American colonialism, travel and exploration have produced 'the rest of the world' for the West. It is now time to ask how this 'rest of the world' produced and still produces itself out of the very same colonial experiences, and time to understand how the (post)colonised 'Them' unevenly and very problematically are *both* owned by *and* (even if in a limited way), in turn, own parts of the West — and not only when 'They' are immigrants in the great Western metropolitan centres of London, New York or Paris, often the subject of postcolonial and other culturalist criticism in the Anglo-American academy, but even when 'They' actually live in Asia.

Mapping Modernity onto the Postcolony

It follows from the above that one cannot assume that capitalist modernity, while a single if not singular phenomenon, is mapped or 'writes' itself on the postcolony in a necessarily predictable manner. The issue clearly is no longer whether we are all modern or not; as historian Dipesh Chakrabarty has commented, 'We are all, one way or another, products of world capitalism and the institutions, practices, and ideas that have accompanied it.'[11] The issue is more how the particular society one is looking at has reacted to or what it *has made* of its modern colonial 'inheritance', whether wanted or not.

Modernity and becoming modern were concerns for postcolonial societies, and continue to be so in the present context of a dominant neo-liberalism (even if in the post 9/11 world that dominance is qualified): they have to deal with the old shadow of their (presumed still more) modern, former colonial masters. Colonialism itself was part of the invention and experimentation in social forms — of the diverse construction of norms and forms to regulate what comes to be known as 'modern society'.[12] Postcolonial Singapore's search for scientifically or rationally comprehensive means to regulate a society in the commitment to production and efficiency from the mid-1960s is the result, I suggest, of wanting to be even *more consistently modern* than the former colonial masters were.[13] Such desire meant that becoming modern remains a process riven with tensions and ambiguities, and a process in which agency can be simultaneously reactive and pro-active in relation to the presence of Western capitalism after independence.

One way of investigating the heterogeneous forms of postcolonial reactions to the spread of capitalism would be to reflect comparatively upon the different trajectories taken by three countries that were committed to a post-independence modernising imperative — India, Malaysia and Singapore. All are culturally diverse societies. Both the latter two countries were once one country (1963–65) and remain in some key cultural ways close to each other. Significant differences and similarities will emerge even from a cursory comparison of the three entities as to how unpredictable the mapping of modernity onto the postcolony may be — and yet, despite these differences, they all remain within the ecumenical sphere of the modern.[14]

It is clear that part of the legacy of empire is the intellectual and institutionalised presence of the European Enlightenment. India, is this regard, is especially important and a useful starting point for the significant postcolonial Nehruvian legacy of a progressive and secularist state commitment to the economic sphere.[15] His commitment to science, industry and the inventive capacity of the modern state was linked to the idea of the realisation of community. In a nation divided by various religions, including Hinduism and Islam, religiosity needed to be tempered by modernisation.[16] These issues that Jawaharlal Nehru struggled with are discussed in his book, *The Discovery of India* (1946).

Partha Chatterjee notes Nehru's secular (here meaning also modernising) goals,

> What [for Nehru] is necessary [for a post-independence India] is to create a new framework of institutions which can embody the spirit of progress or, a synonym, modernity. Progress ..., according to the terms of the 20th century, means giving primacy to the sphere of the economic, because it is only by a thorough reorganization of the systems of economic production and distribution that enough wealth can be created to ensure social justice for all.[17]

The moment of the Indian colonial encounter, Nehru thought, had occurred at a point when Western culture was virile and Indian culture stultified. Even the Mughal emperor Akbar, with his attempt 'to interpret religion in a rational spirit', made no long-range 'basic difference to that [static] social context of India'.[18] So, at a time when Europe saw revolutionary technological changes, Nehru felt that 'Asia, static and dormant, carried on in the old traditional way of relying on man's toil and labor'.[19] When the British came to India, to make things worse, all vital development was checked: 'Technical changes would undoubtedly have come and changed India ... [but t]he normal power relationships of society could not adjust themselves and find an equilibrium as all power was concentrated in an alien authority, which based itself on force.'[20] Nehru, therefore, was a critic of British modernity, even while he accepted that 'technical changes' were necessary for the modernisation process; an Indian state-led modernisation that helped the country achieve a true national and not multi-sectarian identity would be the fulfilment of what he thought to be the historical Indian toleration of minorities.

Singapore's initial attempts at nation-building under the PAP not only followed the Nehruvian diktat for industrial and technological modernity but, distinctly, went *further* than Nehru and tried to forsake *any* primordial past. The decision was linked with the attendant dangers of what the British called 'communalism' (or 'racialism'). Subjectivity and ethnic identity — 'culture' writ large — significantly came under the gun. This instrumental attitude towards culture and the dominance of the economic dimension since the 1970s meant that the city-state deliberately forsook cultural autochthony in many aspects of its overall development — to its detriment. The PAP used the reforming impulse within the cultural-intellectual inheritance of the postwar European welfare state (in its English Fabian version) of active state intervention not only in the economic cycle but also in what philosopher Jürgen Habermas calls the 'life-worlds' of its citizens. While life-worlds have always been colonised by market forces and administrative systems, it is the *extent* to which the PAP state is committed to the instrumentalising notion of modernity as a tool for its nation-building that is notable. More than anywhere else in Southeast Asia, in Singapore, to use Fredric Jameson's words, the 'reification and commodification [of economic forms] ... have become so universalized as to seem well-nigh natural and organic entities'.[21]

The immediate post-independence Alliance government in Malaysia (now the National Front government, or the *Barisan Nasional*), too, if more slowly, took the path to state-led modernisation. In contrast to Singapore, though, despite a similarly plural society, the Alliance government wanted the elevation of Malay identity and rights first, and only then would it follow with non-communalism. Both responses, though, were linked to a common British colonial regime that had seen them as one country until Singapore was carved out as a separate colonial unit upon colonial Malaya's independence in 1957.[22]

The 1980s started to see distinctive changes to earlier post-independence ideas of modernity, certainly for Malaysia and Singapore. In India, some notable intellectuals started reassessing Enlightenment rationalism, a reassessment that the Indian Left has seen as a quixotic rejection of materialist values.[23] Other Indian critiques of modernity also have come about, which draw upon developments in cultural theory and poststructuralist thinking.[24] The Babri Masjid incident in Ayodyha of 6 December 1992, in which a Muslim mosque was systematically torn apart by Hindu extremists,[25] 'has now caused an understandable backlash against these critiques of "modernity"'[26] such that an unfortunate polarisation between 'liberalism' (a secular outlook) and 'fascism' (an anti-modern, irrational and fundamentalist outlook) has emerged. The Bharatiya Janata Party's rise, at the expense of the Congress Party, perhaps indicates that the older Nehruvian rationality has its limitations. The dichotomy in the Indian context is not a surprising one, as it follows from a progressive orientation.

From the 1980s up until the 1997 Asian economic crisis, in parts of East and Southeast Asia, the desire for modernity in both national and regional contexts manifested itself in a general discourse on 'Asian values' and an East Asian modernity (oftentimes implicitly or explicitly read as a 'Confucian modernity'), in which tradition and modernity were unexpectedly combined. Singaporean and Malaysian leaders — though from different national positionalities — were among the leading champions of this discourse. What is extraordinary about the question of an East Asian or Sinic modernity is that Confucianism, of whatever variety, could even be considered at all as a source for generating capitalism and modernity. It was only in the 1960s that most sociologists, historians and philosophers in the West (*pace* the Weberian high-modernist version of development) believed that Confucianism was static and thus incompatible with rapid modernisation. A key example of this opinion is Joseph Levenson's major work, *Confucian China and its Modern Fate*.[27] The sometimes deliberately obscured complexities of tradition and modernity in 'Asian modernities' need to be uncovered and understood as part of and as a reaction to the legacy of European imperialism and as different responses to contemporary global capitalism.

Such developments, I suggest, were the consequence of the attempt among many postcolonial élites to manage the apparent antinomies in their cultural makeup that were themselves the result of the colonial retooling of local cultures. In the colonial era, aspects of 'native' life were made over to become more like 'Us', though any real belonging to the master race obviously remained impossible. How were newly independent societies to escape from the larger homogenising philosophico-cultural logic of European modernity? Lee Kuan

Yew and some of his generation of post-independence political leaders, during the 1980s–1990s 'rise' of the wealthier countries of East and Southeast Asia, tried to challenge the West on cultural terms not predicated upon the cultural homogenising logic that was dominant in the 1960s.

The similar yet contrasting responses to the question of tradition and modernity between India and some parts of Southeast Asia indicate how unexpected the formations of Asian modernities may be, and the importance of different or changing politico-cultural contexts: the Singapore state in the 1980s attempted what might be called — contradictorily — a *neo-traditional modernity* that (supposedly) would bridge the familiar modern/traditional dichotomy. The cultural formation of semi-peripheral but not marginal states in relation to the various social agents sustaining a globalised capitalism tells us the modernisation process is a contradictory set of processes that functions within the global West.

As Tani Barlow observes, 'Asian modernities perform their own recodings of the discourses of modernity within a hegemonic capitalist world … [and] were undertaken in multiple, overlapping colonial dominations, ... participat[ing] in the shaping of global forces under numerous local exigencies that it behooves us to fully understand.'[28] The result, in Singapore and Malaysia, was a complicated 'anti-neocolonialism' strangely at ease with 1980s global capitalism: it is as if parts of the Non-Aligned Movement have reinvented themselves into the World Trade Organisation. This, as a matter of fact, is literally the case. Surviving in the post-Cold War economic world of transnational capitalism can mean a simultaneous collusion with, and resistance to, the global West.

Witness the intensive, possibly obsessive, building of virile skylines. The twin towers of former Malaysian prime minister Dr. Mahathir Mohamad's Petronas Centre in Kuala Lumpur[29] — with its architectural gestures towards Islamic sources, the world's tallest building until 2004 — make a statement about being successful counterplayers in a post-Kiplingesque Great Game of global capitalism: now, you can no longer look down on us as Third World countries, as simple recipients of World Bank aid. We can play up, and play the game![30]

That the Islamic and the modern seem ideologically compatible in the Petronas Centre should not say to us that the difficulty of being modern is resolved in either Malaysia or Singapore, despite pronouncements by major the spokesmen for a Southeast Asian Islamic modern such as Dr. Mahathir during the 1980s and the 1990s[31] and his former deputy prime minister, Anwar Ibrahim, who was seen in the 1990s as the brilliant new face of Islam — modern but still pious.[32] And the fact that Islamic and Confucian modernities can *both* take shelter under the umbrella of an Asian values and modernity discourse should remind us that the 'postcolonial' is now an extensively heterogeneous category.

Japan and the New Asianism — and Also China

What were the larger circumstances that may have contributed to the change in Singapore's and Malaysia's nation-building approaches in the 1980s, when the national indexing of what constituted acceptable modern standards were changed from British to putative pan-East Asian standards? What contributed towards the very authorisation of a broad New Asia discourse within East and Southeast Asia?

This section addresses the regional changes that led to differences in the way the colonial inheritance of modernity was approached. Such changes confirm that even as 'the image of a unified globe [that] dispenses with the notion of an outside' (TCG, 368), social agents within that 'inside' remain 'complex, contradictory, and heterogeneous' (TCG, 353). It then returns to Malaysia and Singapore as two versions of the changes. Malaysia's cultural closeness to the city-state means that the former's cultural-political strategies actually throw light upon the latter's strategies, as they have a similar cultural logic — and even if the actual content of Islamic modernity and Confucian modernity seem to contrast starkly.

Japan and Asian Modernity

The answer begins with Japan's importance in the world in the 1980s and then proceeds to the re-emergence of China. Perhaps unsurprisingly, we once again need to return to the relationship between tradition and modernity. As is known, Japan's stupendous economic growth in the 1960s and 1970s threw a spanner in the works of modernisation theory; as some commentators note,

> where the Japanese tradition till then had been seen as an obstacle in the path of rationalization/modernization, to be gradually transcended as Westernization advanced, now the Japanese tradition was redeemed and proclaimed a uniquely suited vessel for modernization by a new school that developed around the 'unique Japan' hypothesis.[33]

Japan, significantly, was now a model for modernisation — maybe, some argued, a new, not-entirely-Western modernity itself. Consequently, Harvard University political scientist Ezra Vogel published his influential 1979 book, *Japan as Number One*. In December 1981, Dr. Mahathir announced his 'Look East' policy, in the midst of notable local and expatriate opposition, which sought to introduce within Malaysia the Japanese work ethic and managerial systems.[34] There was a 'Learn from Japan' drive in Singapore, most notably from the early to the mid-1980s, though unlike Malaysia's 'Look East' policy, 'Singapore's efforts to learn from Japan — although receiving a clear endorsement from the [political] leadership — have never been declared a policy *per se*'.[35] Thus, the possibility of envisioning a Japanese modernity was brought about, and with that, countries could now choose to 'Japanise' rather than 'Westernise' in their modernisation trajectories. (Ogura Kazuo, for instance, confidently stated that: 'The "Asian" elements that have supported Japan's economic development [though there is the question of how accurately these can be defined] have come to serve as a model for the world ....')[36] The stage was set for the possible imagining of other Asian modernities.

The success of a Japanese-style modernity surely has at least partially contributed to the development of what Saito Seiichiro has called 'the new Asianism' in Japan:[37] various Japanese, by the late 1980s, and of course before the impact of the deflating bubble economy was apparent, were casting their gaze upon East Asia (here taken to include Southeast Asia). Nakanishi Terumasa has suggested a number of reasons for this gaze: one would be Japan's attempt to redefine its international identity in the post-Cold War world; another is, having completed the industrial catch-up with the West, 're-Asianisation' offered a new perspective on the Japanese place in the global scene; and last, but not least, was the then-economic vigour and attraction of the Little Tigers, as well of the newer Newly Industrialising Economies (NIEs) such as Indonesia and Malaysia, which promised new vistas for economic activity.[38] The following quotation from an article by Kobayashi Yotaro, president of Fuji Xerox, has been cited to indicate that 'Japan's return to Asia disguises its economic orientation with a nostalgic justification':[39] 'Just as Gorbachev once declared that Russia's home was in Europe, so it is natural for us to say that Japan's home is in Asia, not in the United Stated or Europe.'[40] At the rhetorical level, this suggests a shift in Japan of a long-time cultural orientation towards the advanced West. There is also the Liberal Democratic Party's Ishihara Shintaro's view in the mid-1990s that Japanese militarism was the result of a mindless mimicry of Euro-American colonialism; with that in the past, Japan can return to a supposed earlier belief that 'its transformation into an industrial and military power was based on the doctrine that prosperity for the Asian region should be achieved with Japan as its nucleus'.[41] This sounded like a call for Japanese hegemony if not renewed domination over East Asia.

What does the Japanese interest for increased influence in Southeast Asia in the 1980s and early 1990s say of Japan's standing among, say, Singapore's political elites at a point when their discourse on East Asian modernity manifested their willingness to increasingly resist some of the suppositions (individualism and individual rights) in liberal democracies? 'Japan' as an idea does play a role in the discourse — Japan is, after all, the first Asian nation to achieve a triumphant modernity. But, in the end, it is not seen as possessing the foundational culture of an Asian modernity — that privilege goes to China. Japan is seen as possessing neither the essence of a neo-Confucian modernity nor the cultural attraction of the advanced West. Nonetheless, Japan's success counts for much in authorising a New Asia discourse and, more specifically, an idea of 'East Asia' that now contains entities such as Malaysia and Singapore that cartographically had been imagined earlier — certainly during the Cold War — as being part of 'Southern Asia'.

Obviously, it should not be assumed (though it is, clearly, by some) that a fundamental civilisational entity called 'Asia' exists, possessing a possibly marketable, possibly culture-based strategy for economic development.[42] Governments in Singapore and Malaysia used this newly minted version of Asia strategically for their own internal and external agendas. After all, no less an academic personage than Harvard University's Ezra Vogel was arguing that while specific 'situational factors' account for East Asian industrialisation, 'this achievement cannot be separated from the institutional practices and underlying attitudes ... that [East Asians] ... absorbed in growing up in their culture'.[43] The once reprehensible thing called 'Asian tradition' now had been rehabilitated and validated by political and academic actors without — but also within — East Asia; the Japanese story has been importantly instrumental in this process and a major reference point in the discourse.

What is noticeable is that in most references, 'East Asia' invokes a broad Sinic quality but only a limited Japanese quality. (India did not warrant attention in this period, though of course since the late 1990s, its economic potential has slowly returned it to the main stage of world attention.) Vogel, for example, writes of an 'industrial neo-Confucianism'. Certainly, he says one of the situational (but not foundational) factors to be taken into account when examining the Little Tigers is 'The Japanese Model': 'After World War II, only the governments of South Korea and Singapore consciously studied the Japanese experience in detail ... [but all four Tigers] saw the crucial role of government in guiding [economic] changes. Having the Japanese model provided both the confidence that they too could succeed and a perspective on how to succeed.'[44] Thus, while Japan, as earlier stated, was a trailblazer, its specific contribution to Asian modernity Vogel takes to be *a* but not *the* factor involved. He then proceeds to identify four Confucian 'clusters of institutions and traditional attitudes' common to the Little Tigers and — though adapted — to Japan itself: first, a meritocratic elite; second, an entrance examination for bureaucrats; third, the importance of the group; and finally, self-cultivation.[45] The originary moment of Asian industrial modernity belongs to China's and not Japan's deep socio-cultural past.

Thus, within the political deployment of East Asian discourse, even if Japan is not the originary foundational culture of Asian modernity, it became a component part of an oppositional Asian values discourse for which Singaporean and Malaysian leaders became the chief spokesmen of within Southeast Asia — ironically probably because the extent to which English is spoken in both places gave them an access to the Western press out of proportion to their (and certainly Singapore's minuscule) size. Indeed, the discourse on Asian modernity that Malaysia and Singapore appropriated in the 1980s and the 1990s served the purpose of trying to territorialise that vacant cultural space, 'Asia'.

Malaysia and Asia

In Malaysia, Japan by and large seemed not-much mentioned in their 1980s–90s deployment of the discourse on Asian modernity, despite the 1981 'Look East' campaign, inaugurated after a government-issued 'Buy British Last' directive.[46] At least part of the reason for the omission may have come from the fact that Dr. Mahathir and others were disappointed that the expected technology transfer from Mitsubishi for the national car company on which so much federal government prestige has been staked, PROTON,[47] did not occur in the 1990s. Still, in the 'Look East' campaign, Japan became for a while the paramount non- and also post-Western role model for development. In the end, however, the overall desire seemed to be to imbricate Malaysia within a larger conception of Asia than Japan offered.

As early as 1982, Mahathir addressed a Malaysian and Japanese business meeting and argued that Malaysia was actually within 'the Pacific community', whatever people may think of that proposition; the reason for this assertion seemed clear enough to him, and he strove to make it clear to his audience: 'This vast area is predicted to be the growth area of the world, replacing the Atlantic shores.' And Malaysia, when Mahathir was at its helm, was going to be a part of the Pacific Rim — and had a *right* to be, despite its differences from other Pacific Rim cultures; at this point, given all the qualifications that Mahathir had to make, it reasonably could be said that his speech started to strain: 'Although we differ in terms of ethnicity, language, history, tradition and culture, there is sufficient commonality in terms of political philosophy and economic thrust that co-operation would be easy to achieve.'[48] If, as historian Gyan Prakash has said, anti-colonial nationalism had to invoke difference to produce 'a national essence opposed to that of the colonizers',[49] then Mahathir's invocation of Asia-Pacific unity is no less such an invocation of difference — but on *what* a scale.

A decade later, in October 1993, then-finance minister Anwar Ibrahim addressed the Asian Forum of Parliamentarians on a similarly large-scale view of Asia and Malaysia's role in it: 'Western capitalism attempts to displace traditions, while we in East Asia integrate the positive values of modern technology and commercial practice.'[50] Now East Asia also contains not only Southeast Asian Chinese but also Islamic cultures — and this coming from a former Muslim youth radical, who showed a decided intellectual flair as a political leader. This new East Asia has learnt that modernity can be (multi-)ethnicised.

All in, however, in Mahathir's and Anwar's general politico-cultural rhetoric, 'Asian values' had a generic rather than Sinic suggestion to it (not unexpectedly, given the various ethnic groups in Malaysia, of which the majority are Malays, and the Chinese the largest of the minority groups), though they both asserted that Malaysia stands for a balanced Islamic modernity. Nonetheless, the possibly Sinic underpinning of Asian modernity was paid tribute to in a stunning and daring academic conference held in March 1995 near Kuala Lumpur, the federal capital, sponsored by Anwar himself: the International Seminar on 'Islam and Confucianism: A Civilisational Dialogue'. The seminar burnished the idea of a Malaysian multiculturalism for which the United Malays National Organisation (UMNO), the chief component in the ruling National Front government, stood for, despite discriminatory national policies; and doubtlessly, the prestige of the federal government was also enhanced by the dialogue in what was an election year.[51] The main speaker was no less than that champion of neo-Confucianism, Tu Wei-ming of Harvard University.[52]

Anwar was less confrontational in regard to the West than Mahathir had been, and he had previously debunked Samuel Huntington's notorious 'civilisational clash' theory.[53] He argued in his opening speech at the seminar that postcolonial Asia was now free from old uncertainties: 'We are at the threshold of a new Asian consciousness, characterised by self-confidence, … And a genuine interest in the traditions of our fellow Asians. If one can risk drawing a parallel, it is a new consciousness in the cultural sphere, as Bandung was in the political domain.'[54] If the 1955 Bandung Conference that led to the 1961 founding of the Non-Aligned Movement marked the moment when the Third World gained a voice, when it was dominated by 'a preoccupation with the West', Anwar advanced that the seminar promised the start of an Asian counter-universalism that would be a 'countervailing force against fanaticism, chauvinism and ethnocentrism', while at the same time not being an 'un-Asian', Western liberalism redux. Modernity can be progressively traditional: an Asian universalism is capable of balance and impartially — it does not at all fit into the old, imperial stereotypes of the East.[55] The New Asia, to Anwar, can be as 'responsible' as the West. After all, 'the economic rise of East Asia has effectively debunked … [Max Weber's] sweeping generalization' of a retrogressive Confucian-Chinese culture. As in the case of Singaporean rhetoric, Japan occupies — here implicitly — the place of the first Asian nation-state which has attained culturally empowered Asian confidence, but no more than that. Orientalist notions of the East are challenged, re-inscribed, and then re-used for Anwar's own purposes.

Singapore and Asia

Singapore's construction of a Sinicised East Asia, in relation to the management of its multi-ethnic population and its ideological shoring up of its development success story, will be addressed in chapter 5. This part of the chapter will consider how Japan has been highlighted in various outlines of the successful Asian way by politicos and a senior civil servant.

Lee Kuan Yew, by the 1980s ensconced as the Founding Father of the city-state, contended in a 1995 Chinese New Year address that cultural 'trappings' such as US-style fast food are the 'outer trappings of inner strength, a strength acknowledged by the world': 'The Japanese were the first non-white race to match the West. In certain sectors, they have excelled, producing superior, zero defect goods [and also] new products like the Walkman, [and the] Discman. Japan's success has encouraged South Korea, Taiwan, Hong Kong and Singapore.'[56] The rest of Asia must follow and in toto develop the cultural power to be influential that the USA has at the moment, for this will indicate a similar 'inner strength'. This is to say, really, that cultural 'trappings' are much more than merely decorative. However, Lee does not show in his speech an interest in a mass-cultural solidarity led by Japan.

Not all cultural-economic discourse in Singapore was so stridently oppositional — much of that actually had disappeared by the mid-1990s, before the Asian economic crisis — and Japan was also used to suggest a model of how a 'fusion' of East and West is possible. In an address to the International Institute for Strategic Studies in Vancouver, Kishore Mahbubani — the former permanent secretary in Singapore's foreign affairs ministry (1993 to 1998) and a 1990s outspoken advocate of Asian values who took the advantage of fora from Harvard to Davos, Switzerland to be 'the scourge of the West' (as *The Economist* satirically called him[57]) — said the Japan 'remains the most powerful "Westernized" rational bureaucracy in the world'.[58] Again, while Japan offers a model of an ethnicised but still hyper-rational modernity, Japanisation is not advocated. Mahbhubani proceeds to the question, 'Who is number one [in East Asia]?', and significantly remarks that 'it was immensely significant that the Japanese emperor, the most hallowed figure in Japan, chose to visit China in 1992 at a time when China was still relatively internationally isolated'.

Singapore's bias towards China, given the intense economic interest that the PAP government has shown in that country since the late 1970s, is not surprising; the encouraging of a supposedly diasporic Chinese cultural identity — one the PAP state had vehemently rejected in the 1960s–1970s, and once again repudiates in the post-Asian crisis period — was based upon that numerous asset in Singapore, Chinese people. The sort of unabashed Chineseness displayed in the 1980s 'Asian values' phase of state formation would have been denounced just a decade earlier as ethnically chauvinistic behaviour by the very same English-speaking Chinese and other PAP élites.

At the foundational base of that entity Asia for some major Singapore political elites was a progressively traditional, neo-Confucian culture. Japan becomes the first to make that heritage show its modernising potential. In the aftermath of the Asian economic crisis, though, as I have already noted, with Southeast Asia in a weakened economic position, the city-state abandoned the notion of a regional Asian modern and went back to a more direct affirmation of global capitalism as universal truth, a position similar to its immediate post-independence stance. Such vicissitudes in the regional imagining of Asian modernity should lead us to realise that we perhaps have yet to fully comprehend how what was once called 'modernisation' (and later, 'globalisation') were mapped onto the literal and also quasi-postcolonies of Southeast and East Asia.

Multilateral Construction of East Asia

A final observation needs to be made — one thus far only made indirectly — and that is that the construction of this alternative Asian modern was a joint construction by key actors in the Euro-American West and East Asia. The mass media, too, not unexpectedly, participated in this project of thinking the new lineaments of a traditional-modern East Asia into existence. The diversity of the newsmagazines and papers in the 1980s–1990s, Asian and Western, that seemed to agree on the role of traditional, community-oriented Asian values in the Asian 'miracle' was amazing. The mass media's role in the ongoing construction of East Asia still calls out for serious investigation. It would shed light on the complex adversarial collusion between the 'Occident' and the 'Orient' in the reformulation of Oriental cultural identity within the Great Game of global capitalism.[59]

In 1993, *Asiaweek*, published from Hong Kong, for example, offered the USA Asian values for its salvation: 'Americans' own [best] values [are] found nowadays across the Pacific in family-centered Asian cultures which prize respect for elders, upright morals, discipline and hard work.'[60] China, *Le Monde* reported to its readers in 1994, 'is fascinated by the two models of Asian economic success represented by Singapore and South Korea'.[61] Asians could now be the modern role models for other Asians.

The hegemonic Euro-American West, reterritorialised into a varied yet consistent vision of the Asian modern, could then be recycled back to that West: a unified globe may not truly allow a notion of an outside — but the misrecognition and sublimation of the cultural and intellectual traffic between (and within) the 'East' and the 'West' allows the civilisational essentialisation of Asia to continue, no matter how nuanced now to let in the modern.

PART 1

Deterritorialisation

2

The 'Modern' Construction of Postcolonial Singapore

Modernization consists in continually exiting from an obscure age that mingled the needs of society with scientific truth, in order to enter into a new age that will finally distinguish clearly what belongs to atemporal nature and what comes from humans, what depends on things and what belongs to signs. … The present is outlined by a series of radical breaks, revolutions, which constitute so many irreversible ratchets that prevent us from ever going backward. In itself, this line is as empty as the scansion of a metronome.

– Bruno Latour, *We Have Never Been Modern* (1991 [1993])[1]

E. J. Hobsbawm, in an address to the American Anthropological Association, remarks that, 'Nations without a past are contradictory in terms. What makes a nation is the past, what justifies one nation against another is the past, and historians are the people who produce it.'[2] The past is thus 'what we are', immutably and essentially, and each state has a nation and national culture with deep, primordial roots. The essentialising functions of history and its connection with the discursive construction of nationalism of course have been much criticised,[3] not least by Hobsbawm himself; nevertheless, as cultural anthropologist Akhil Gupta has written, 'National identity appears to be firmly spatialized [in everyday life] ..., becoming almost a "natural" marker of cultural and social difference .... It is difficult to imagine what a state that is not a nation would look like and how it would operate in the contemporary world.'[4]

My argument in this chapter will be that Singapore functions as a type of transnational formation using the organisational form of the nation-state, a formation that draws its intellectual and cultural inspiration from parts of the British West and Anglo-American ideas about being modern. In the process, we get a Singapore that is *precisely* that 'state that is not a nation' which Gupta has difficulty imagining.

What happens when a postcolonial state's recourse to primordial national identity is hamstrung because it possesses several ethnic groups with the attendant dangers of what the British called 'communalism' (or 'racialism') within its national boundary?[5] When 90 percent of its population is comprised of immigrant and therefore deterritorialised Chinese and Indians? And when there had been a postwar communist insurgency led mainly by Chinese in a Malay-dominated region?[6] This is the position of Singapore when it was part of the Federation of Malaysia (1963–65) and later when it left the Federation (1965). Singapore, like West Malaysia, is composed primarily of peoples of various Indian (mainly Tamil) and Chinese descent, 'Eurasians' and Malays;[7] unlike West Malaysia, though, Singapore is mainly Chinese[8] and the leaders within the People's Action Party (PAP), which has ruled Singapore continuously from 1959 until today, felt obliged to create Singapore as a multicultural entity in which no racial or linguistic group[9] was seen to be privileged, and in which being modern itself would link the messy parts of each ethnic culture to the other parts, as it were. There was to be no state-supported history of the 'nation' stretching back into a distant origin, as might be expected from a newly-formed nation-state.[10] The Alliance Government in Malaysia, in contrast, wanted inter-racial harmony first through the elevation of Malay rights, and only then would it follow with non-communalism. The Malay in Malaysia is considered to be *bumiputera*, a son or prince of the soil.

The aim of the PAP under Lee Kuan Yew, the forceful first prime minister of independent Singapore, was to try to *reject* the primordialism so entrenched in the Western European model of nationalism[11] and, also, primordialism's possibly violent consequences, and to effect another strategy for Singapore's survival, despite it being Asia's smallest state with no natural resources and, in the 1960s, being surrounded by hostile neighbours and threatened by communists. The modern European, mainly British, model of the nation-state was to be *rearticulated* for the PAP's own purposes. Since there was no one racial identity, and thus no single 'nation', upon which to safely erect a national identity, Lee and his colleagues aimed to make *industrial and capitalist modernity* the metanarrative which would frame Singapore's national identity, and to create a 'Global City' which because of its trading links would escape the restraints placed upon it by history and geography. The 'national' as a category was not to be jettisoned but instead to be renovated so that Singapore's racial and cultural difference could be contained and, if possible, to some extent homogenised and therefore deterritorialised for the leap into modernity. It was to be a 'West' purged of what was 'unsuitable' that was to be used to socio-culturally engineer the new Singapore. This process eventually was executed in a manner that effectively denied that the new industrial society to be formed had any cultural dimension to it: post-independence Singapore was simply to be part of the unfolding, rational process of development itself. Its people would have to adapt their way of life to this process.

Singapore is thus one instance which complicates Benedict Anderson's influential 'modular' characterisation of how Western versions of the national state become Third World norms for nation-building:

> Nationalist leaders are thus in a position consciously to deploy civil and military educational systems modelled on official [Western] nationalism's; elections, party organizations, and cultural celebrations modelled on the popular nationalisms of 19th century Europe; and the citizen-republican idea brought into the world by the Americas.[12]

As Partha Chatterjee notes, 'Anderson seals up his theme with a sociological determinism' rather than pursue 'the varied, and often contradictory, *political* possibilities inherent'in the process of creating the national state.[13] This is not to say that there is no derivative quality in the Singaporean nation-state formation, but that postcolonial state formation is not an inevitable, clear-cut extension of the European model, even while it was still framed by that model.

The chapter examines the discourse Lee and two of his key cabinet colleagues, Dr. Goh Keng Swee, alternatively finance, national development and defence minister, and S. Rajaratnam, the culture and later foreign affairs minister, maintained in the formative period 1959 to the early 1970s to construct a modern Singapore.

On Not Being 'a Wet': Lee Kuan Yew's Masculine Modernity

Common to the discourses of the three men I proceed to look at is the logic of an empirically based 'reasonable thought', tempered by political 'realism'. Lee, however, seems the most ambivalent towards the concept of primordial ethnic sentiments as the irreducible core of identity — with the retrospective view that the present affords us, we can see that an embryonic Sinicised, Asian-modern thinking was already present in an incipient manner in the 1960s. However, this by no means suggests that he would directly condone what in Singapore used to be called 'Chinese chauvinism'; Lee is a more complex figure than that, as commentators, sympathetic or otherwise, have observed.[14] Goh Keng Swee, on the whole, seems the most 'scientific' in his pronouncements. Both S. Rajaratnam and he possess more consistent attitudes towards modernity as a universal force, though both also argue that it needs to be Asianised.[15] These similarities and differences will surface in the discussion following.

Lee Kuan Yew is known to be an articulate and deadly serious man, who thinks himself more than a match for any white interlocutor (this is often borne out in various face-to-face confrontations with Western or Australian journalists); he is forceful and is quick in debate, though usually without much humour. 'Modernity' to Lee at one level seems to mean the capacity to measure up to or exceed the white man, to be a serious counter-player in the politico-economic game. He is not, as the English say, 'a wet'.

Lee's general orientation towards nation-building, or 'winning the hearts and the minds of the people', as it is sometimes called in Singapore, can be glossed from the homage he pays to Jawaharlal Nehru (a man he not surprisingly admired) in a mass meeting in Singapore on 30 May 1964, three days after Nehru's death. Lee says:

> A Brahmin from an elite family, he set out to build a modern India, secular in its approach, socialist in its structure. It was a task not to be finished in his lifetime. But when, in the years ahead, India emerges as a modern industrial nation free from the bonds of caste and privilege, it will all have been because he laid the foundations of modern India ....[16]

Even given that Lee uses certain Orientalist (in Edward Said's sense) and ahistorical ideas of India in speaking of its caste identity, his tribute to Nehru functions in a context more troubling now, since the trouble at the Babri Masjid at Ayodhya in 1992, than it was then. Lee's implicit stand on national life is clear: the privileged must act responsibly in the direction of rational progress so that an industrialised nation can emerge. In a way, it is the paternal voice of the English administrator which speaks, though it is a voice which has become Lee's in an intimate manner;[17] and this voice is confident that the chains of Asian 'traditions' can be broken.

But how is one to attain this modern society? In Singapore, especially, there is even no pre-figured nation to mobilise. Lee struggled to define what 'Malayan' identity might be from the start of his ministry. Mrs. Indira Gandhi recognised this dilemma in nation-building during his official visit to India in September 1966. She speaks of India's antiquity and how it gave a certain positive outlook for the future even while it could be a burden for present development; Mrs. Gandhi then adds, 'In that sense, you [Lee] are fortunate. You start with nothing to hold you back. You only have a bright future to beckon you forward.'[18]

On 1 July 1961, two years after gaining self-rule,[19] Lee spoke to the Socialist Club of the then-University of Malaya in Singapore.[20] The people of Malaya and Singapore — he saw the current boundaries drawn up after Malaya's independence in 1957, when Singapore was reconfigured into a separate Crown Colony, as arbitrary — did not have a common race, 'descent, language, history and political institutions': 'Independence has preceded the creation of these attributes required for nationhood ...' (151). 'Malaya' to Lee is thus an artificial nation-state, the problem being with the hyphen and the singular term 'nation' in that expression. Can this non-cohesiveness be turned to advantage? The university students he addresses in 1961 'are the group nearest to the norm of what a Malayan should be ... [f]or in no other educational group has there developed more homogeneity of attitudes, of values and social cohesion, cutting across racial and cultural lines' (151). They, the English-educated, and thus the best lot to imbibe at Western modernity's springs, have 'the feeling of oneness which results from a common experience' (153).[21] 'Malayan' here seems to be an adjective with little content, save that of having a 'common experience', details of which are not specified. The 'lack' of history for elites in Singapore can be turned into a positive factor for national development.

In the National Day celebrations of the same year, 1961, on 3 June,[22] Lee fills out what a 'common experience' may be: it is, crudely put, managing ethnic difference as a necessary step in the creation of an indigenous, country-wide consumer culture as a mark of success:

> We are hoping to build a modern society in which everybody will have a better life because we will have factories to make more and more of the things which make life easier .... Recitation of poetry and writing of essays are important things in a civilized society. But important also is the turning of screws and lathes. They make our modern world hum. (172, 173)

In its own way, it is a visionary passage. An industrial-modern and consumerist society is what lies beyond ethnicity or race, the more prevalent term and concept in the city-state. Lee nearly becomes lyrical in this Futurist vision of the world — it is 'screws and lathes' that will provide the music for the new Singapore; 'poetry and [the] writing of essays' may be 'civilized', but they seem to recede into a genteel datedness. He goes on to add that older Malayans 'were brought up in a different world', in 'a backward community' of small-holding farmers, rubber tappers and tin miners; in this world there was no 'tolerance and respect for each other' (172). That time, like the time for a pure, high humanistic culture, for airy-fairy poetry, is over: the Machine Age had to be brought to Singapore. The poetry to come will be in the 'factories' creating the things 'which make life easier', which will 'make our modern world hum'. Modernisation, as it manifests itself in social policy and economic development, must overtake art, culture and — it seems — even sensibility. We have laid out before us here what will develop into a technicist, rationalist and hard-headed modernity.

Racial or cultural difference, in fact, must be somehow *harnessed* to effect a new civilisation. The charged atmosphere brought about by Chinese-Malay riots in July 1964 seemed to Lee to insist on such a development. Such direct inter-ethnic clashes exacerbated the problem of communism in Malaya and Singapore — especially since most Malayan Communist Party (MCP) members were Chinese-speaking Chinese, a fact obviously not lost on the Malay population. Lee makes one of his most emotional and impassioned appeals for a new society on 6 June 1965, at the height of the events leading to Separation from Malaysia. The setting was the Malaysian Solidarity Convention in Singapore, a mostly Chinese gathering with representatives from Malaya, Singapore, Sabah and Sarawak. The meeting is described by Lee as the 'beginning of a new tide in the affairs of the people of Malaysia'; the 'snarling, guttural notes on which they [the Malay communalists, or "ultras"] sent out their signals to their followers' (392) lead to the conclusion that the still-new Federation of Malaysia of 1963 will not belong to all Malaysians. Lee proposes instead cultural hybridity or cultural miscegenation as the way to bring forth the new identity. He simultaneously declaims and makes an implicit appeal for his nationally framed transnational alternative — this is possibly whistling in the dark: 'We are in no hurry .... We can go slowly .... And this will be a nation that will survive for hundreds of years as a separate identity in Southeast Asia, a multiracial community — a confluence of four of Asia's major cultures and civilizations, superimposed with a streak of British civilization ...' (392).

Lee has no problem in incorporating English or British elements in his new society, as long as Asians do not pretend to be Englishmen. After all, he tells the United Kingdom Manufacturers Association and the Confederation of British Industries in Singapore on 7 February 1967, Raffles made possible his family's success in Singapore:

> my great grandfather came here with nothing .... My tragedy started when he left his son behind [after returning to China] who was my grandfather; and here I am. I inherited what you [in the process of decolonisation] have left me. In a way, it was not all created by you because my great grandfather did play a subsidiary role and so did my father and so did I myself. So we have left [the statue of] Stamford Raffles standing on his pinnacle outside the Victoria Memorial Hall. But for him, Singapore would still be a mudflat. (538)

And thus, the derivative source of Singaporean modernity is oddly acknowledged — oddly because there is a simultaneous disdain and admiration of English actions shown. In the early 1980s, a replica of the Raffles statue was erected on the spot by the Singapore River where he first landed. The modern society that Lee proposed did not require a strong qualifier such as 'Asian' in the 1960s.

On 24 August 1966, a year after Separation, Lee introduced a significant American-style daily pledge for school children written by S. Rajaratnam, which stresses the role of Enlightenment modernity in the country:

> We, the citizens of Singapore, pledge ourselves as one united people, regardless of race, language or religion, to build a democratic society, based on justice and equality, so as to achieve happiness, prosperity and equality for our nation.[23]

Behind the increasingly relentless search for the new and the culturally hybrid is, among other things, a deep and abiding fear of a supposed ancient darkness and irrationality in racial identity. The deployment of animal imagery — snarling, guttural-sounding Malay extremists — in Lee's declamation to the Malaysian Solidarity Convention indicates this. Lee, to some extent like Nehru, seems genuinely mystified by the attraction of racial politics — 'communal mumbo-jumbo' (313) as he calls it — even while *simultaneously* being deeply proud of his 'possessing' an ancient Chinese culture which more than matched the might of British imperialism. This comes out in an interview with British and Australian journalists on 30 August 1965. Lee suggests to the journalists why Viscount Head, the British High Commissioner in Kuala Lumpur, was so tactful the day the news came out about Separation: 'he never showed the mailed fist, not once, except for this flag [on his limousine] .... Who is he to fly that flag? We kept quiet .... He has got 400 years of empire, and my ancestors have got 4,000 years of written, recorded history ...' (417).[24] Despite his commitment to the homogenising force of a universal industrial spirit, and his efforts in trying to create a cosmopolitan, enlightened Singapore identity, the fear of cultural deracination — or perhaps emasculation, given the English-style, late-Victorian manliness of much of his discourse[25] — never disappears. In fact, 'true' Chinese can be very dangerous. In a blunt rejoinder to Syed Jaafar Albar, the Secretary-General of the United Malays' National Organisation (UMNO), the central party within what was then called the Alliance Party, now the National Front (or *Barisan Nasional*),[26] in one sitting of the Malaysian Parliament on 30 May 1965, Lee warns against his call for Malays to unite:

> He hasn't spent his time calculating the significance of what he is doing. The Chinese will never unite under the MCA [Malayan Chinese Association, the Chinese component of the Alliance Party] because they are political eunuchs .... [B]ut supposing we real, virile Chinese stood up and shouted 'Chinese, unite!' there would be real trouble in five or ten years .... (390)

If Jaafar Albar wanted to play the primordial nationalism card, well, Lee could too, and he would do it better.[27]

In 1966, Lee warns the students of the Mandarin Chinese-speaking Nanyang University that 'the survival of our society' may be threatened 'if we are going to produce anaemic, up-rooted floating citizens [who are neither truly "Western" or "Chinese" and thus] without the social cohesiveness and the cultural impetus that gives the drive and the will to succeed as a group' (517). The question, once again, is what identity source produces the dynamism of a modern society — only this time, his answer is different from his 1961 National Day speech where he declared: 'Only the English-educated are completely Malayanized in their political outlook, but they are not in the majority ...' (256).[28] A mixed socio-cultural policy statement was being made in the middle of a university nurturing the best students from Chinese high schools, though the reality was that if your English was not competent, one could not get a civil service job.

This tension, or perhaps ambivalence, which marks Lee's attitude towards the English language and the Anglo-Asian culture which can bring 'progress' is, I believe, never resolved, though he has a strong sense of Englishness on his part, and this tension continues in contemporary Singapore. This undercurrent of Chinese race consciousness was to surface in a more pronounced way in the Asian values / modernity discourse of the 1980s.[29]

However, in Lee's attempts to achieve a 'Malaysian Malaysia' rather than a 'Malay Malaysia' in the 1960s,[30] he manages to be entirely consistent in denouncing any hint of primordialism or racial exclusivity. In the first sitting on the new all-Malaysian Parliament on 21 May 1964, Lee says that at a point in history when the Chinese, Indian and Malay 'cultural and linguistic heritage are ... undergoing a renaissance, and are stimulating ... chauvinism in the respective communities ..., we have to pull our various communities together, away from their origins'; after all, Malaysia commands 'the material loyalties of her people' — but '[h]ow long we shall occupy this pre-eminent position in Asia no one can tell ...' (301). The inability to maintain material progress will lead to the imperilling of the multicultural national project, inasmuch as the imperilling of the multicultural project will likewise lead to the end of an industrialising, increasingly wealthy society.

A Belated but Utopian Modernity: S. Rajaratnam

Sinnathamby Rajaratnam, like Lee Kuan Yew, also stridently denounced what is taken to be racial primevalism disguising itself as nationalism — a nationalism invalidated by its lack of a notion of 'progress'. The tenor of his talks and exhortations is polemical, like Lee's, but he has a more consistent commitment to modernity as a universal, homogenising force capable of great good. Rajaratnam is also more literary and philosophical than Lee, as befits a former journalist of the now-defunct *Singapore Standard* and still-existent *Straits Times*. Lee, in contrast, speaks in the pragmatic-empiricist imperial tones of the governor-general. Reflecting (in an understated manner) on his role in the PAP in 1990, Rajaratnam said, 'I am among the few who articulate and emphasise the PAP's stand when attacked. In that sense you can call me a public relations man or the chap who projects the PAP image.'[31]

Rajaratnam read law at King's College, London, and therefore, like the Cambridge-educated Lee, saw Western modernity at first hand. Further, since he was in London from 1936 to 1947, he also saw the devastating aspects of European nationalist competitiveness at first hand. That experience seems to have helped create a sensitivity to transnational connections, political or otherwise, and possibly explains his role as a sort of PAP visionary in conceiving of Singapore as aiming to gain what can described as a 'belated modernity', purged of nationalism's irrationalities, and later as a 'Global City'.[32]

In a speech to the Eighth Congress of the International Union of Socialist Youth in Vienna on 2 June 1966, Rajaratnam highlights the process of social, economic and cultural modernisation as the end goal of the 'Asian Revolution' against colonial rule. He concedes that 'innovation' in 'traditional' Asian societies is disorienting; but, 'On the other hand, a society dedicated to conservation will stagnate and decay.'[33] After two decades of independence, most of Asia has 'steadily fallen back' (243) with the exception of Japan. The Cold War has made modernisation more complicated as it leads US and USSR aid to be used for arms and armies, 'very often draining national resources which should have been spent on economic and social development' (245).

The 'prevailing mood of disenchantment' with modernisation, which has contributed to compensatory national primordialisms, however, must be resisted. Here is the fear of a primitive or not-entirely-modernised nationalism that exerts a supposedly undefilable national self:

> Other disappointed leaders have turned their backs on the Asian Revolution by offering what I will call political archaeology. Instead of pressing forward with modernisation, they glorify and revive the archaic elements in Asian life. Ancient political, social and cultural institutions and the ideas associated with them are restored to life — or rather given the semblance of life. I do not believe that there can be no harmonious blending of tradition and modernisation or that modernisation means Asia becoming a carbon copy of the West. (246–47)

Traditional and modern, Asian and Western — these can be blended into something new and possibly unprecedented in world history, though it is patently obvious that Rajaratnam's emphasis is really on 'pressing forward with modernisation'. Recovering an unsullied national history and culture is impossible and should not be tried. Like Lee, Rajaratnam thinks that a manly attitude must be adopted and people told to soldier on: 'The trouble is that no one has dared to tell the people frankly that modernisation demands its price' — 'hard work, sacrifice and discipline' (247). To stop now would be to end the promise of the anti-colonial revolution: nationalism must look to the future, not to the past.

Forcefully — and possibly unexpectedly, given that 'irrational' nationalism is usually said to be the intrinsic problem of Asian and African countries which unsuccessfully derive their nationalism from the orthodox, liberal Western models[34] — Rajaratnam argues that primitive nationalism is an infectious *European* disease:

> In Asia we see a repetition of the conflicts sparked off by the pathological nationalisms of Europe in their infancy and which culminated in two world wars. What is worse is that in Asia nationalism has now reached a phase where it is being fragmented by the emergence of new kinds of competing religious, racial and tribal nationalisms. (249)

Modern nationalism, even in Europe, is already a problematic, self-absorbed phenomenon which does not need revived or reinvented Asian primordialisms to highlight its inherent imperfections. It is Western Europe that fails to gain the full promise of modern life. As such, becoming 'a carbon copy of the West' is not on — Asia must *exceed* the limits of Western nationalism; the late modernity coming to Asia actually must be made *more* rational than the original version. The stand is: by all means, we *must* and indeed *need* to draw upon one's inherited Euro-colonial politico-cultural heritage in nation-building, but we must learn from the mistakes that were made. The 'Asian' revolution needs a purification of the irrationalities in the West's present version of modernity, as Rajaratnam sees it.

What Rajaratnam seems to hold as his standard for 'good' nationalism is a version of the liberal nationalism of the nineteenth century in which the nation exists as one unit, larger than historically earlier units of people such as the family or the village, that can be potentially part of an even larger unit of people — ultimately a world community of some sort.[35] (However, it is unlikely that Rajaratnam believes that the nation-state ought to be entirely given up.) Thus, as early as 1966, Rajaratnam was arguing for the increasing difficulty of envisioning the 'national' as a purely autonomous sphere, either culturally, socially or economically: 'The fact is that our world has entered a genuine era of world politics and world economics which constitute the iron framework within which our national affairs must be conducted' (251). The developing world *must* come to terms (as Singapore has) with modern, transnational cultural and economic flows, or else come to grief: 'The old, purely nationalist ideologies can no longer provide the ideas and policies which the second phase of the Asian Revolution needs so badly' (252).

In Singapore's case, Rajaratnam (as with Lee) thinks that there must be a common Malayan culture if Malaya or Singapore are to survive in the brave, new postwar world: Singapore must not have a national culture which would inhibit the full Asian Revolution. As Singapore's first minister of culture, he was quick to attack the poet-academician D. J. Enright's 1960 critique on the PAP government's activities to create 'culture', which Enright delivered in his inaugural lecture as the Johore Professor of English at the then-University of Malaya in Singapore. Such government activities were obviously not in accord with Enright's concepts, probably drawn from the work of English cultural critic F. R. Leavis, of how culture and society organically develop through time.[36] One of Rajaratnam's rejoinders appears in two September 1960 issues of *Petir*, the PAP magazine. He announces, 'We do not regard culture as the opium of the intellectuals or as something to tickle the fancies of gentlemen or gentlewomen. For us the creation of a Malayan culture is a matter of practical politics ... [and] nation-building' (119). More than Lee, Rajaratnam stresses the less-material side of building national community — and in fact, unlike Lee Kuan Yew, he recognises that becoming a modern economy and society is a deeply *cultural* process: 'My contention is that communalism cannot be eradicated solely by destroying its economic and political roots. This must be reinforced by a cultural solution as well' (121). Rajaratnam was giving notice — as early as 1960 — that socio-cultural engineering would be deployed to makeover the former colonial entrepôt into a nation-state.

Unlike Enright's 'high' usage of 'culture', Rajaratnam contends that he is more interested in, as he thinks of it, an anthropological or sociological basis to 'culture' — that is to say, culture as a general way of life. If culture is a man-made way of life, it can be *re-made*, socially and culturally engineered. Chinese culture, for instance, is not an immutable object and it is, in any case, a very porous object: 'except in the case of isolated cultural groups, many Malayans live under the influence of two and very often three cultures .... Communal cultures transform their character through interaction with and assimilation from other cultures' (126). Rajaratnam is willing to dispense with cultural organicism and use the various tools of the modern state, such as the creation of a national education system, to constitute a hybridised Anglo-Asian identity:

> Malays, Chinese and Indians live under common [political and] economic institutions and respond to the pressure of 20th century economic practices and beliefs. The introduction of modern technological innovations — the radio, cinema, motor cars, electricity and so on — has made for greater uniformity of attitudes and behaviour .... We not only eat and appreciate one another's food but many kinds of foods are commonly shared — rice, coffee, butter, tinned food-stuffs, beer, spirits and so on. (127)

The PAP Government will continue to make sure that Malay culture is not the basis for a Malayan culture and it will encourage a consciousness of 'the cultural beliefs and practices we share in common' (128). In such a manner, already deterritorialised Chinese, Indians and, even more complicatedly, Eurasians can be *further deterritorialised* and merged with the indigenous Malays into a future-oriented society. Modern 'technological innovations', after all, have already led to 'greater uniformity of attitudes and behaviour'. That is to say, the hybrid identity to be created is tilted in favour of the modern that will further weaken the hold of existing local cultures. It is a breathtakingly and startling audacious claim, and in many and varied ways, the PAP state has used socio-cultural engineering to systematically make the city-state progress economically from the 1960s to the present.

On 6 February 1972, Rajaratnam gave an address to the Singapore Press Club that contained a retrospective of Singapore's successes in the 1960s and, we can now say, a prescient attempt to outline the strategy for future survival.

How did Singapore escape annihilation? As an independent city-state, it was stripped of the hinterland that was West Malaysia before Separation. Rajaratnam acknowledges that the PAP harboured this fear of being annihilated. The unexpected complete withdrawal of British troops in 1971, originally scheduled for the mid-1970s, rekindled fears of economic collapse. However, these 'gloomy predictions', relished by those gleefully awaiting Singapore's demise, were based on the understanding that 'an independent Singapore would be a self-contained city-state; that it would, at the most, be a regional city and therefore its fate and fortunes would depend wholly on the economic climate in the region' (227). While Singapore's past role as entrepôt is not to be derogated, 'times are changing' and so, the party's future-oriented policies have paid off:

> Singapore is transforming itself into a new kind of city — a Global City. It is a new form of human organisation and settlement that has, as the historian Arnold Toynbee says, no precedent in mankind's past history. People have become aware if this type of city only very recently. They have found a name for this distinctive type of city. They call it Ecumenopolis — the world embracing city. (225)

Further, the city Singapore is becoming is not like the 'World City from the cities of the past ... [that] were isolated centres of local civilisations and regional empires'; instead, Singapore 'is the city that electronic communications, supersonic 'planes, giant tankers and modern economic and industrial organisation have made inevitable.[37] Whether the Global City will be a happier place than the megalopolis out of whose crumbling ruins it is emerging will depend on how wisely and boldly we shape its direction and growth' (225–26).

It can be inferred from the above that the nationally disciplined constitution of a new Malayan and later Singaporean culture or identity has played its part in helping Singapore's becoming 'linked intimately' (226) with a system of Global Cities — perhaps 'not a major component [of the system] but a growingly important one' (227). Now the world is the city-state's hinterland: shipping trebled from 1959 to 1970, as has the number of scheduled airline landings. Rajaratnam tells his audience that it would be best to visualise Singapore's openness to global capital flows 'by tracing on a map the daily movements of aircraft and ships, the contacts made by telephone, cable, external trade and money transactions .... Each technological breakthrough in communications and media annihilates distance and brings us closer to other Global Cities' (228). Singapore's deliberate 'linking up with international and multinational corporations' has also 'offered a short cut to catch up or at least keep pace with the most advanced industrial and technological societies' (229). It would seem that a city-state of deterritorialised people seized the opportunity to pull in an increasingly deterritorialised money and finance casting about the world for suitable spots for investment: 'We have been aware for a long time that consumption is no longer wholly a national matter. Economic nationalism has not prevented people from buying and consuming goods from all parts of the world' (229). Singapore becomes the emblem of a new transnational potential for mankind — Rajaratnam thus speaks of the 'transnational flows of capital' in a 'globalised world' before such jargon existed.

Rajaratnam's address displays an acute understanding of how existing centre-periphery models of the global cultural and economic order were already becoming inadequate in the 1960s, even if 'the Americans are [currently] in the vanguard' of '[i]nternationalised production' (229). The address also indicates the boldness of the PAP's moves and highlights the unusual nation-building that transpired in Singapore with the attempt to localise modernity by using the parts of it that they thought most economically and otherwise rational: free trade does not mean a free-wheeling society, for that may undermine the discipline it took to create the new society. Rajaratnam concludes: 'So it is up to us to equip our people intellectually and spiritually to make the Global City into the Heavenly City that prophets and seers have dreamt about since time immemorial' (231).

In 1994, Rajaratnam was diagnosed with dementia, and by 2001 he was unable to move or speak. He passed away on 22 February 2006 of heart failure. It seems unlikely that he would have liked the bluntly materialistic society that the city-state had become at the moment of his demise.

Victorian Values and a Detached Rationality: Dr. Goh Keng Swee

If Rajaratnam is one of the PAP's visionaries, the generally acknowledged economic architect of Singapore, Inc., is Goh Keng Swee, who gained his Ph.D. from the London School of Economics after the war. Of all the figures discussed, Goh's voice is the most rational and detached — almost ruthlessly so; he is the voice of the scientific analyst and the advocate of Victorian thrift — in other words, of the (now assimilated) values of free-trade imperialism itself. His discourse, like Lee's and Rajaratnam's, stresses the need to harness Western modernity for Singapore's own purposes.[38]

On 24 July 1966, in a speech to the Malayan Economic Society, Dr. Goh — as he is usually addressed in Singapore — takes apart the Decade of Development which was 'so confidently launched'[39] by the United Nations in 1960. Like Rajaratnam, what disturbs him is the 'serious retrogression' (32) of the economies of the Afro-Asian world: 'Indeed, the position in many places threatens ominously to be like that of medieval Europe in its darkest age after the collapse of the Roman empire' (32). Medieval darkness now threatens the former colonial and Conradian dark places of the earth.

Part of the problem, as Goh diagnoses it, is the inability of many of Singapore's fellow developing societies — the 'poor and the backward', as he unsentimentally, almost offensively, puts it, deliberately eschewing the euphemistic terms 'underdeveloped' and 'developing' (32) — to Asianise or Africanise the unsuitable aspects of modernity and the postwar European (really British) state:

> Modern ideas of liberalism, egalitarian ideals, welfare state concepts — all these are appropriate in an affluent society but are largely irrelevant to a nation struggling to escape age-old poverty. These concepts encourage a propensity to laziness and inaction, inculcate a belief that society owes every man a comfortable living, and proliferate trade unions whose main purpose is to get more pay for less work. (35)

Once the exploiting colonial power is cast out, 'there unfortunately have been very few instances where the [local] political leadership has acquired a complete grasp of the facts of economic growth' (34). It was hard to anticipate the harshness of the first stage of industrialisation and only a really resilient political structure can drag a country through that — and politicking which does not take this into account will come to 'a cropper' (34). Liberal egalitarianism grows *out of* a strong economy and not vice versa: 'it is worthy of note that Western Europe, the Soviet Union and Japan, during the time they achieved their economic breakthrough, did not have universal franchise. [The f]ranchise was severely restricted in Western Europe. As for the Soviet Union and Japan, the political leadership remained under the tight control of the ruling elite' (35). The facts of history speak for themselves. Rationality speaks for itself. The first generation of PAP leaders liked to think they called a spade a spade.

Still, having made the above analysis, Goh is not certain that either Malaysia or Singapore offer a perfect democratic-industrial model for other Afro-Asian nations: as with Lee, Goh believes that the imperialists brought the starting stages of modernity to the Malay archipelago, with the result that Singapore and Malaysia 'have [already] gone through the initial birth pangs of economic development': 'That part of our common economic history was no more attractive in its social aspect than British social conditions as depicted in the novels of Dickens' (36). We should note that Dr. Goh was not speaking in the halcyon days to come in the 1980s, when the PAP could comfortably advertise that an Asian modern linked to Asian values and culture was on offer, but in the challenging years after Separation.

Goh ends by reiterating the need for postcolonial states to contextualise the liberal-egalitarian political institutions they have inherited, and the same applies to 'the economic ideas of modern countries' (40). His advice is 'to throw away all the books published on economic growth since World War II' and instead to read Samuel Smiles (author of *Self-Help* [1859]) on 'thrift, industry, ambition, honesty, perseverance' (40). Though to a generation happy with the Beatles, Smiles may seem an 'odious Victorian character', 'sanctimonious' (40) as he sometimes is, yet he may be relevant to today's needs, given the failure of the economic planners.

Goh gives more advice regarding the need for modernisation at the inauguration of the World Assembly of Youth Asian regional seminar on 'Urbanisation' on 16 April 1967. This talk seems something of a precursor to Rajaratnam's on Singapore as a Global City as Goh argues for the role of cities in Asia as the nexus by which a country can modernise. So far, the cities of Asia — the centres where the modern reigns — have been leading 'by and large a self-contained and isolated existence': 'there has been no serious attempt to get the countryside into the grip of a dynamic modernization process' (28). Again, the need for strong leadership is pressed: how else will one be able to 'upset the strongly held sensitivities of a traditional society. And, of course, without upsetting these sensitivities, you cannot hope to transform a traditional society ...' (29). When the central activity of a government is to gather enough votes for the next general election, the government *cannot* be suitably muscular. Obviously, primordial identity has no place in this thrust to erect the modern, developmental nation-state.

Rapid modernisation, Goh tells an audience in Canberra in a 1967 talk entitled 'The Nature and Appeals of Communism in Non-Communist Asian Countries', will result in a transitional stage 'from traditional forms to those consistent with the twentieth century' (233), and this leads to another problem: that of a communism which will be quick to take advantage of the 'economic friction and dislocation' of 'the traditional order' (233). Goh and the other PAP leaders were of course acutely conscious that the 1960s were a precarious moment not only for Singapore and Southeast Asia, for the official ending of the Malayan Emergency in 1960 had not meant regional stability, but also for a world at the height of the Cold War. Strong government was essential if modernity and modernisation were to be acquired and national stability to be achieved.

While Goh is conscious that Singapore's circumstances as entrepôt and city-state make it different from other Asian situations, there is no doubt in his mind that it has been the strength of the state and the efficacy of its approaches that has developed Singapore. Pre-university students — 17- and 18-year-olds — were told this in a national seminar organised for them by the Ministry of Education in 1971: 'In a democratic system such as ours, political stability in the short term can be produced by strong, effective and efficient government. At the risk of sounding immodest, I suggest that this is the situation in Singapore' (186). For the future, however, what will be needed 'is an influential and cohesive social class that will ensure a high standard of performance among [all] political parties contending for support among the electorate' (186). But this, he makes clear, is *not* for 1971 Singapore, the still immature scion of Western modernity. The students are also warned against people who 'regard political ideas' to be 'topics for idle discussion' without connection to a still fragile Singapore: 'contemporary ideas fashionable in the universities of the West ... [may have] little meaning or relevance' (187). As in his speech to the World Assembly of Youth, Goh's demand is that Western liberal ideas be radically contextualised: take the modernising and free trade bits of it for these seem universal (the imperialists were, 'though doubtless quite unintentionally, the standard-bearers of modernisation' [21]), but be careful of liberal egalitarianism. The culture of the advanced Euro-American West is globally important — but not all of it.

It can be seen that the 'modern' plays a key and multifaceted role in the nation-building discourse of Lee, Rajaratnam and Goh in the foundational decade of the 1960s. Through modernisation, racialism or communalism can be tamed, for modernity offers the carrot of an urbanised and more prosperous society. What the PAP leaders also do is to take advantage of the non-cohesiveness of Singapore's many diasporic communal groups, each possibly a nation in the making, and suggest to the entire country that a new society with a complicated blend of Western and Asian elements can be created, a new society that *because* of its small size can participate in to increasingly transnational and interactive economic movements. However, a sort of updated manly Victorian government is needed to bring to existence this nation-state, which is not really a nation in the accepted sense of that term. Any section of its population that clings to traditional cultures will, ultimately, be left behind.

A 'Pragmatic' and Hegemonic Discourse of Modernity

To conclude this chapter, it must be stressed that while the PAP clearly dominates Singapore, these circumstances did not evolve only through the continual display of strength on the part of Lee and his colleagues, though there was that: the discourse of modernity (along with its applied practice of cultural deterritorialisation) also had hegemonic status. The PAP leadership manoeuvred their way through the 1960s with care but also with determination, alternatively cajoling and using force. If all primordial pasts were to be put away, the extent of Lee and his cabinet members' determination is evidenced in their willingness to be 'pragmatic' about even the recent past, regardless of the emotional difficulties: they would bring in Japanese capital to Singapore in spite of the memory of the Japanese invasion. This pragmatism thus was a form of 'commonsensical' and economically oriented rationality in keeping with the impulse towards cultural deterritorialisation.

The city-state needed Japanese capital for its programme of industrialisation; by the 1960s, the Japanese were involved in oil refining and the PAP was keen on getting their trade and technical knowledge. A stiff upper lip was required for the leap to being competitively modern — and if that most successfully modern of Asian countries could be brought in to help with development, whatever the domestic sensitivities, let us carry on.

In April 1963, soon after the start of industrialisation, a thorny circumstance arose. There was a discovery of another cache of human bones — an additional instance of the massacre of Chinese brought to light. Lee promised the public on 21 April that while he would deal with the Japanese, their role in Singapore must be maintained. But the blood debt issue would not disappear: the Singapore Chinese Chamber of Commerce helped keep the issue alive. Lee finally decided that the government had to take some anti-Japan measures and addressed on 25 August 1963 what British journalist Alex Josey describes as 'the largest crowd ever assembled in Singapore' (262), gathered on the *Padang*. Josey adds, 'Elaborate security precautions had been taken [because of the pro-communist elements' interest in using the issue to de-rail Singapore's entry into Malaysia]: Lee himself had a revolver in his pocket ...' (262).

Lee reminded the crowd of the PAP's policy to 'heighten the tempo of industrialization' (262). The Japanese offered the 'cheapest technical and managerial skills that can come to Southeast Asia' (263). However, given recent events, Lee said that the government has decided against issuing any new visas to the Japanese to come for fresh industrial or commercial projects until 'a fair and just solution has been found' (263). He then gave his tough line: 'Japan must come to terms with us in Malaysia, or else lose the Malaysian market — at present and in the future one of the wealthiest in this part of the world' (263). He went on to say that he himself had only just escaped execution by the Japanese and that Goh Keng Swee's brother-in-law had been shot by them; the Chinese tragedy was their tragedy. Degradation at the hands of Europeans was bad enough, but 'at the hands of a conquering Asian nation' (264) ... it was insufferable.

The crowd seemed to accept what Lee had to say. Josey tells us: 'In 1966, the Japanese offer of [Singapore] $25 million and the loan of another $25 million on very liberal terms was accepted ....'[40] In due course, Japan and the USA became the two largest investors in Singapore, and there is a wax recreation of the surrender of Singapore to the Japanese by the British in 1942 — ironically recreated by the famous Madame Tussaud's in London — on a resort island (later turned into a sort of theme park) called Sentosa. This is the success of the PAP's pragmatism.

This pragmatism, of course, was hardly as culturally neutral as it is made out to be: the logical-positivist outlook on the world it embodies depends on a notion of universals drawn from an English cultural-intellectual background. Not only did it draw upon inherited colonial understandings of an imperial past of progress, it also drew upon the idea of what development meant in postwar US social-sciences paradigms, dependent as they were in turn upon evolutionary perspectives.[41] 'The global scenario [of that era], which included newly independent states', as the late historical anthropologist Bernard Cohn observed, 'had now to be understood within a *telos* of "modernity", where national development was graded against a model of Western development.'[42] In Singapore's case, this model of development was used systematically to further 'deracinate' and socially evolve an already quasi-modern multi-ethnic society so as to receive the 'full' culture of modernity, though purged of the 'irrelevant', overly democratic and inconsistent primordial bits. Even if the various local peoples were not inertly traditional, being already partially deterritorialised, that was still *not* enough to be thoroughly modern.

The discourse of a universal modernity dominating over various Asian identities engendered by PAP pragmatism, however, was dramatically reconfigured in the 1980s. The new discourse appeared even more complex than the one it replaced. It speaks of a generalised Asian identity which allows scope for distinct Southeast and South Asian identities (Malay and various Indian identities) while yet elevating a pan-East Asian and Confucian identity as the basis for an apparently inherently Asian (vs. an indigenised Western) logic of modernity that underwrote (if not exactly caused) the success not only of Singapore but of the other Pacific Rim 'Little Tigers'. Singapore, in the terms of this new discourse, gained a new cartographic identity as a member (or at least as a subset) of 'East Asia'. Rajaratnam, in retirement from politics by 1990, not surprisingly, was critical of the new directions taken by the PAP leadership. In the same year, he wrote a public letter making a call for a return to a 'Singaporean Singapore', echoing the 1960s call for a 'Malaysian Malaysia': 'At this rate, there will be a long ethnic queue of Singapore citizens proclaiming Sikh identity, Jewish identity, Ceylon Tamil identity, Cantonese[-Chinese] identity, Hokkien[-Chinese] identity — and goodbye Singapore identity.'[43] Prime Minister Lee Kuan Yew did not take well this public intervention by 'Raja', as he is known in the city-state.

It would be reductive, I think, to say that the newer discourse was mainly or only a 'resurgence' of the primordialism that was present as an undercurrent in Lee Kuan Yew's nationalist discourse of the 1960s. The causes and consequences of the newer discourse are diverse and even contradictory. I will come to this major issue in chapter 5, but first there is a need to examine at a little more length the national narrative that was not quite a national narrative that emerged for Singapore.

3

Economic Development and the National Narrative

Of all Southeast Asian postcolonial societies, Singapore is distinct in the way the People's Action Party (PAP) government has recreated the city-state for the central purpose of economic development. The now-standard(ised) historical narrative of commercial and industrial emergence reflects this purpose, and a key result is that the usual divisions between pre-colonial, colonial and postcolonial are weakened. What also becomes foregrounded is the ruling party's paramount role in effecting the achievement of 'happiness, prosperity and progress for our nation', as stated in the 1966 Singapore National Pledge. This historical position of the party has become entrenched as the economy 'took off', to use Walt W. Rostow's influential term of the 1960s.[1] While Singapore's national narrative is certainly as linear in its historical emplotment as one centred on the story of a pre-colonial past destroyed by the colonialists, and, like some other national narratives, also legitimises the present government, this nevertheless does not detract from its distinctiveness.

This narrative of capitalist emergence is the corollary to the attempt to construct a 'modern' nation initially using selected cultural components largely taken from the British West, as examined in the previous chapter. Such a narrative of commercial-industrial arrival in effect complements and then completes the impulse towards cultural deterritorialisation. The primordial and the particular of various cultures that, if left unchecked, could lead to communalism, are replaced with that which appears more neutral: the technicist, universal narrative of progress, freedom from present limitations and for development. This narrative of progress was also part of the intellectual-cultural inheritance gained from the British, though eventually fused with the assumptions and dictates of American modernisation theory. However, what progress and freedom might mean eventually was modified by the PAP government. National independence was both a type of freedom and progress. Thereafter, the emphasis came increasing to be on material notions of progress, one that was best gained, it was argued and then practised, by maintaining a paternalistic discipline within the city-state and supporting a free trade regime outside the confines of the island. This paternalism strikingly resembled aspects of a colonial-era paternalism. Eventually, the inherited patterns of colonial (quasi-)authoritarianism were submerged, reformulated, and then re-emerged in the 1980s as the quasi-authoritarianism of an alternative Asian-Confucian modernity that favoured what was called economic rights over individual rights. Increasingly, as the immediate post-independence years recede into the past, Singaporeans themselves no longer recognise the various 'Wests' in the city-state that were essential parts of their paternalistic Asian-Singaporean cultural formation.

This chapter seeks, first, to set out the inherited elements of 'progress' and 'freedom' and to examine how the PAP renegotiated and, really, made these elements its own in the narrative of an emerging modern Asian country; and second, to contend that the appearance of the state's Asian modernity discourse represents the moment when the West that is already 'inside' the city-state gets hidden. This misrecognition of Singapore's relation to the West — whether deliberate or an entailment in the process of asserting the autonomy of the postcolonial 'self' is of no direct consequence — becomes part and parcel of the larger misrecognition of the relationship of a regional oppositional discourse on Asian values and modernity, a discourse empowered by the region's economic successes, to global capitalism.

However, before we can begin, it needs to be recognised that two inter-related narratives were possible at one time. The first, which became hegemonic and is the subject of this chapter, has to do with a Whiggish *telos* of economic development, progress, modernity and modernisation since 1819, when a '[t]rading station was established by Sir Stamford Raffles under an agreement between the British East India Company and the Sultan of Johore and Lingga, and the Malay Governor of the Island', signifying the beginning of modern Singapore.[2] The second has to do with the communist-, leftist- and communalist-inflected 1950s, from which the Lee Kuan Yew-led faction in the PAP emerged the victor in 1959, to play the leading role in establishing a self-ruling State of Singapore. This chapter examines the first of the two inter-related narratives as the second is dominated and sometimes displaced by it. But it is important to recognise that, as with many other postcolonial societies, there are alternative narratives of the nation that could be articulated. The submergence of this other narrative possibility is of consequence as it helped define the conception of the freedom and progress that were to become hegemonic.

The second narrative more narrowly pertains to a liberal- or neo-nationalist historiography which foregrounds élite personalities, institutions and ideas, and often sees the making of the nation-state as an idealist venture in which the indigenous bourgeoisie lead the people from subjugation to freedom. The PAP was formed as a sort of pact between the bourgeois English-speaking faction led by Lee and the Chinese-speaking faction which was brimming with revolutionary zeal and powerfully connected with the unions. It certainly is true that, in Singapore, the militant leftist-led initiatives were finally unable to develop a full-fledged nationalist liberation. And it is also true that the economic thrust of the moderates in the PAP, situationally created and planned, triumphed, reducing the historiographic immediacy of many of the earlier socio-cultural and political difficulties.

Having said this, Lee and the moderates' relationship with the influential and charismatic leader Lim Chin Siong and the PAP's militant leftists in the 1950s up until the party fractured in 1961[3] should pluralise the moments of socio-political change as the postcolonial state was being formed, so that we can see these historical moments as *confrontations* between the moderates, the leftists, the communists and the 'Chinese-speaking world' — itself not homogeneous in political opinion[4] — and not as a *transition* from a colonial society to a modern, capitalist one.[5] A pluralistic perspective suggests that the agency of political change was not located entirely in the moderates' hands, as it is generally made out to be, and that the national-political narrative of emergence did not start in 1959 with the PAP's first major election victory. We need not accept a progressivist or evolutionary set of presuppositions to measure the failure or success of Singapore as an independent city-state.[6]

The more important issue for this chapter in the confrontation between the leftists and the moderate socialists is the clash of two related modes of left-oriented progress and the cultural logic of what it means to stage modernity. The idea of liberty, and liberation as autonomy, is fundamental to the project of modernity: both factions in the PAP subscribed to a common project possessing an overall sense of history's direction within which discourses on liberation from British colonial control emerged.

The moderates' triumph, though, led to the embedding of their version of the story of political freedom, a story that remained *within* the overarching colonialist story of Singapore's emergence as the most modern, albeit colonial, society in the region. It was clear by the late 1950s that the PAP moderates were pro-independence but not anti-British. There was not a deep antipathy towards the benefits of colonial modernity. As was mentioned in the Introduction, during the Cold War, the English-educated PAP faction chose the First World's capitalism and version of modernity. After 1965 and the loss of a possible Malaysian common market, the city-state industrialised by letting in multinational corporations (MNCs). This seemed a natural extension of allowing the world into Singapore, as it had done during the colonial period when being an entrepôt secured prosperity for the island. Industrial development was not seen as collusion with neo-colonialist forces, as other postcolonial leaders in the Afro-Asian world might have seen it.

What happens to the discourse and narrative of political liberation with the ascendance of the PAP moderates? The colonial state had maintained a *laissez-faire* orientation narrowly concerned with economic freedom. This clashed ideologically with the early Fabianism espoused by Lee's faction. In the end, however, they created an interventionist state that emphasised the more material aspects of 'progress'. This progress, it was argued, is best maintained by encouraging a liberal, international economic order rather than an individual freedom or *laissez-faire* bias within the city-state. A critical counterpart — a discourse on disciplinisation — resulted. The paternalistic discipline resembled colonial paternalism; indeed, this could already be found in the Fabian variety of Socialism, which, by the earlier part of the last century, had been willing to do away with parts of traditional Liberalism and its commitment to individual freedom for the sake of social efficiency.[7] There is more continuity with the colonial past of Singapore than might be expected.

The PAP leadership has inherited certain intellectual frameworks in which there was a conflict between individualism and collectivism. The colonial legacy helped determine the PAP's world-view and some generalities about Singapore's place in the world. What reinforced aspects of this world-view was the change in the global economy away from the economic formation of the immediate postwar world into something that resembled more the *laissez-faire* world under *Pax Britannica*. These intellectual and historical considerations, I shall argue, form the context from which the narrative of Singapore's economic emergence arises: it then gives us the cultural logic that undergirds the city-state's commitment to maintain its position within post-1989 global capitalism.

Becoming Modern: 'Our Island Story'

Among all the newly independent states that emerged in the 1950s and the 1960s, Singapore must stand out in having an official history in which a white man, and an official of the colonialist East India Company at that, is its official 'founder'. What accounts for this historical representation of Singapore identity, and how does it relate to the struggle for independence?

But first, a note on historiography and some methodological matters. It is now an orthodoxy that needs little additional justification that the analysis of narrative historiography entails attention to the intellectual context of past historical works.[8] What I am interested in here, however, is less the personal visions of various scholars and more the *subscribed public visions* in relation to the political élites who have helped formulate the Singapore Story. Given how relatively short our past is — if we accept that modern Singapore indeed did commence in 1819, even more so if dated from independence in 1965 — this seems to be a more suitable and less grandiose scheme for analysis than studying individual authors on Malayan and Singapore history in depth. In any case, thinking through the recently written nationalist histories of postcolonial societies is scarcely the same thing as sorting out, as intellectual historian John Burrow has done, the question of 'Victorian Historians and the English Past'.[9] Further, I am less concerned with the 'facticity' — though that is an important question — of who did what, and the cause of this or that, but more the cultural logic that drives an economic vision of 'who we are'.

In terms of the immediate past of anti-colonial nationalist liberation — that bit of 'freedom' from Victorian Liberalism that must occupy centre-stage in any account of any struggle for independence, be it Tunku Abdul Rahman's Malaysia, or Jomo Kenyatta's Kenya — the question is: who has set the historical agenda in Singapore? Historian Hong Lysa's answer here is simple: it is the first-generation PAP politicians. We therefore start first with them before proceeding to the academic historians.

In a study of S. Rajaratnam, Hong cites his signed account of internal party history — 'PAP's First Ten Years' — that appeared in the *PAP Tenth Anniversary Souvenir 1964*. Among the watershed events in this account are the 1961 defection of the party leftists and that faction's internally conflicted stand against Merger with Malaysia that was shown-up as weak, as Rajaratnam would think, in the 1962 referendum that elicited a 71 percent majority for the moderates' pro-Merger position. Another threatening party was the mainland United Malays National Organisation (UMNO). The 'ultras' — as Lee Kuan Yew described whom he thought to be the more extremist members of UMNO — were, he charged, inciting communalism. Rajaratnam's call then was to 'instill in our people the conviction that they and their children have more to gain by way of peace, prosperity and happiness by being Malaysians than by remaining Malays, Chinese and Indian'.[10] With the 1965 Separation, the term 'Singaporeans' is used in place of 'Malaysians', but the national-collectivist logic of working through an Enlightenment-derived idea of 'equality' is the same.

Hong draws the following trenchant conclusion about Rajaratnam's 'template of Singapore history':

> More than 30 years after it was written, the understanding of the period has not moved one iota from Rajaratnam's rendition of it. Studies of the period — whether by John Drysdale or Dennis Bloodworth, the two authors who were given privileged access to documents of the

> period and to the political leaders themselves — have only confirmed the story. ... The plotting of the PAP story as Singapore's history has not been seriously challenged by professional historians or by former political actors, who were [thus] doubly defeated.[11]

Part of the reason for 'fixing' history is that, unsurprisingly, to the victor goes the ability to entrench their account of the past. But there is more at hand. As Hong goes on to note,

> Rajaratnam's greatest fear for Singapore was the exploitation of racial cleavages — hence he stamps the coming of Raffles ... as [Singapore's] genesis. This unprecedented homage to the colonial heritage ... was a 'proper use of history', because [quoting Rajaratnam] 'the price of a more impressive genealogical table would be to turn Singapore into a bloody battleground for endless racial and communal conflicts and interventionist politics by the more powerful ... nations from which Singaporeans had emigrated'.[12]

The issue of communalism and communism led PAP leadership back to colonial elements in their imagining of a modern Singapore. Lee Kuan Yew himself, before he started championing Confucian values in the 1980s, had no problem in incorporating English or British elements in the history that led to a new society. The derived source of Singapore's modernity was clearly acknowledged in the city-state.

Hong notes that in recent years, the PAP leaders have tried, if indirectly, to extend the history of Singapore, as it were, to before 1819 via the state's 'Asian values' programme, from the 1980s until its cessation in the mid-1990s. By the early 1980s, there was also an emphasis on the 'hyphenated' Singaporean — Malay-Singaporean, Chinese-Singaporean — which was to fly in the face of the National Pledge's sentiment, 'regardless of race, language or religion'. For both cases, the question seemed to be how we could develop an *Asian* rather than *Asianised* modernity without being 'Western' in some way,[13] though such 'Westernisation' was explicit in the 1960s acceptance of the Rafflesian version of modern Singapore's birth.[14] While in the earlier years the PAP leadership seemed to accept the notion of 'modernisation' as a universal process, there was, by the late 1970s, fear among sections of the public, and also the government, that 'Western decadence', if not checked, could actually jeopardise the modernisation process. Still, the criticism from many quarters of 'Asian values' as nothing more than collusion, corruption and nepotism that arose during the 1997 Asian economic crisis seemed only to confirm the wisdom in dropping the Asian values rhetoric before the crisis exploded.

What underlies such questionings over the national self, and its plural or singular, Western or non-Western historical genesis is the issue of what it means to be a modern, economically developed society. In postwar Singapore, communism and communalism were depicted as impeding effective development. Eventually, this dash to become modern significantly defined all major discussions of Singapore's identity and cultural development; this by and large meant that racial and cultural differences must be contained and at least to some extent homogenised for the leap into modernity.[15] The 'Asian values' debate and the 'Asianising' of Singapore identity[16] arose because, in the late 1970s, the notion of a universal cultural homogenisation as an *inherent* part of modernisation had become perceived (by some) to be an obstacle to economistic nation-building. The underlying desire to be thoroughly modern, though, has remained consistent from before Singapore's independence from Malaysia.

The above may be taken to represent experiments in how a distinctively Singaporean 'progressiveness' may be grounded. The British industrial bourgeoisie had in the Victorian era proudly spoken of 'growth' and 'improvement', and these became pertinent issues for the new leaders of the new nation-state, and remain so.[17] The inherited idea of progress was seen, broadly, as industrialisation together with the associated political and socio-educational institutions of a 'developed' and 'free' society. The telos of the English Whigs' 'Our Island Story',[18] with its promise of representative government directed by a spirit of liberty — in the anti-colonial, democratic-socialist version of it that the PAP made their political platform — increasingly seemed uninvigorating to some of the PAP leadership in the face of communal and leftist challenges. As Peter Osborne remarks, 'Indeed, one might say that in its perpetual anxiety to transcend the present, modernity is everywhere haunted by the idea of decline.'[19] In Singapore's case, while the anxieties of what Singapore 'is' and how its economic success can be sustained are hardly resolved, this need for progress has meant, generally, using the colonial past and the modernity the British brought to the island colony as its foundational national history. This updated colonial modernity authorised the blocking of both 'irrational' cultural identities and an alternative, more-leftist, modernity as possible elements in a national narrative that could help build a nation able to 'match-up' economically to the former colonial master. In the midst of such nation-building, internal freedom became less of an issue. Thus, we arrive at the cultural logic driving the Singapore historical narrative, a historical narrative based on the very imperative of being modern itself.

We can now proceed to look at some of the actual narratives that have been generated by the acceptance of the first-generation PAP's historical agenda, an agenda that has a continuity with the accepted colonial history of Singapore's success as an entrepôt, later to become a modern city-state useful to global capitalism's development beyond what its small size would indicate. In noting this continuity, one needs to say that these largely accepted narratives in

Singapore do not represent some sort of conspiracy between historians and the PAP historical agenda, but more the way a certain vein of historical thinking has been naturalised.

Raffles, Free Trade and Economic Development

This section looks at what I take to be *representative* narrative texts. I do not make an attempt to cover comprehensively all recent historical writings. The objective is to examine the way economic development is made a key part of what is now called 'The Singapore Story'. Specifically, I will look at the national narrative as it is navigated from the economic *laissez-faire* ethos of the colonial period into the post-independence period, with a no-longer minimal interventionist state that nevertheless supports the maintenance of a liberal and open international order necessary to the post-independence Export-Oriented Industry (EOI) strategy.

First, it will be instructive to look at some of the potted histories we encounter in the official publication, *Singapore: Facts and Figures* (later *Facts and Pictures*), put out by the Ministry of Culture and its successor incarnations. While it is important not to take the 'state' to be a unitary entity, the several versions of this publication can be taken to be an acceptable expression of the 'official' Mind. Despite changes from edition to edition, there is a pattern to the way their brief histories are assembled. What initially can be noted is that despite the 1980s–1990s Asian values discourse, the chronology of Singapore's genesis invariably begins in 1819.

The 1964 edition, issued the year before Separation, does not offer a short history but only historical dates. Not surprisingly, the bulk of the dates focus on the events leading up to moments of self-rule in 1959 and the 1963 Merger.[20] Looking at the dates from the colonial period, we find a number that recur in all the editions I looked at. They are:

- 1819: Trading station established by Sir Stamford Raffles under an agreement between the British East India Company and the Sultan of Johore and Lingga, and the Malay Governor of the island.
- 1824: Singapore ceded in full sovereignty by the Sultan to the East India Company. Population already over 10,000.
- 1826: Incorporated, with Malacca and Penang, as the Straits Settlements.
- 1830: Straits Settlements brought under the Presidency of Bengal of the East India Company.
- 1851: Transferred to the direct control of the Governor-General of India.
- 1867: Control transferred to the United Kingdom Colonial Office.

We can surmise from the above dates, obviously inherited from a colonial historiographical structure, that some notion of the history of governance is being offered, significant in indicating both the importance of the island to the British — the bringers of order and commerce — and a colonial administrative structure that paradoxically made possible, in the end, a separate independent state.

The 1967 edition, published two years after independence from Malaysia, offers a brief history rather than a chronology composed of dates, and we can start to enquire if what is emphasised represents some of the aspirations of the newly independent city-state. While a 'prosperous commercial centre flourished at Singapore in the 13th and 14th centuries', '[m]odern Singapore was born in 1819'.[21] Further, '[h]er strategic position in the centre of an area rich in tropical produce, coupled with a free port policy, soon attracted traders and settlers to her shores. The first 40 years of her existence saw the most rapid increase in her trade and growth' (3). By the turn of the century, 'Singapore was to inaugurate the modern Malaya of tin and rubber. Finance, promotion and organisation were provided from Singapore ...' (4). The core of the colonial island's identity, we may note, was trade and commerce, rather than anything specifically 'cultural' provided by the diverse immigrants or native people.

By the 1976 edition, the economy has evidently taken off, and the brief history now indicates that the colonial Rafflesian project has not faltered in the anxiety-causing post-Malaysian years but, indeed, has found fruition. The Suez Canal's opening in 1869 is explicitly mentioned, for it 'shortened the trade route between Europe and Asia and freight charges decreased; as a result, Singapore's prosperity and progress gained momentum'.[22] After the Second World War, 'With peace restored and the pace of commerce resumed, Singaporeans [though such nomenclature is anachronistic] began to agitate in earnest for greater involvement in government' (27). The history concludes:

> With political and labour stability, Singapore continues to grow in strength and dimension. It has consolidated its pre-eminence in commerce, finance and communications, while its manufactured goods have made impressive inroads into sophisticated world markets. As envisaged by Sir Stamford Raffles in 1823, Singapore has become 'the emporium and pride of the East'. (28)

The founder has been truly visionary, and post-independence national identity apparently lies in Singapore being 'the emporium and pride of the East'.

The 1986 edition has a narrative that stresses how well the PAP has functioned at the polls, underlining how the party is intrinsically part of Singapore's postwar history. Apart from that, the other major innovation is a list of 'Heads of Government', which starts off with 'Col. William Farquhar (Resident and Commandant)' (1819–1823); moves on to a period marked as 'Internal Self-Government', which has Sir William Goode (1957–59), and then David Marshall and Lim Yew Hock as the only two chief ministers; there follows three entries for Lee Kuan Yew, first as prime minister in the last stretch of the period of internal self-rule (1959–63), then during the Malaysian period and thereafter.[23] If the publications previously had indicated continuity in the economic project, we now see a sort of continuity in the form of governance in Singapore.

The 1998 version no longer has the Heads of Government list and restores a brief, three-paragraph discussion of the pre-1819 history of the island. However, it may not be useful to read too much into this as the early history of Singapore exists as a vague or semi-mythic narrative to do with Sang Nila Utama, a prince of Palembang in Sumatra who, according to the *Sejarah Melayu* (Malay Annals; c. 1612) ruled the island, then called Temasek, from 1299 to 1347. The chronology retains the key colonial dates of the 1964 edition, and the PAP's electoral victories are listed.[24]

How do the more scholarly histories compare with the official representations of the city-state's history? I begin with two narratives dealing with economic growth. The first is the late, distinguished historian Wong Lin Ken's 'Commercial Growth Before the Second World War'.[25] Wong begins almost immediately by emphasising Raffles's vision as, in a sense, a salvific one: 'Raffles'[s] initiative and foresight in the choice of Singapore and the enterprise of Asian and Western merchants had rescued Singapore from obscurity in history, turning it into the most successful Western enclave in South-East Asia developed almost wholly by untramelled private enterprise' (41). His essay reminds us that 'globalisation' is scarcely a recent phenomenon, for the liberal markets that Liberal Imperial Britain supported allowed the backwater of Singapore to connect with the industrialising Western world:

> Singapore's entrepôt trade was global in character, and the two sides of the entrepôt trade were complementary, manufactures being paid for by the Straits produce. Thus, Singapore thrived as the intermediary for the trade between the advanced industrial economies and countries with lower levels of achievement. ... Singapore was the example par excellence of a colonial port that had prospered on global trade because its overlord had the wisdom not to confine its trade for narrow imperial gain. (42)

Singapore, so to speak, was an early version of a hub of capitalism's global flow of goods.

Wong then traces the rise of Britain as the foremost naval and industrial power in the world, the rise of free trade and the consequent decline of mercantilism. Open Singapore 'could not have prospered in the earlier era of mercantilism' (47). The expansion of colonial rule also brought with it political order and the legal framework for private enterprise and international free trade. Private enterprise had been the engine of growth in pre-Second World War Singapore; the *laissez-faire* colonial state had mainly provided laws and infrastructure for the port. The inter-war years, unfortunately, saw a decline in free tradism, and even Great Britain resorted to imperial preference — a system Singapore actually did *not* benefit from. Wong's conclusion emphasises the externally created modernity and the freedom in trade it brought:

> Pre-war Singapore was an alien creation. ... [I]t represented what could be achieved with private enterprise unfettered by indigenous customs and institutions, or governmental interference in trade. It started as the spearhead in the region of an expanding international system based on free trade and private enterprise. (63)

This is a universal progressivism that marginalises the local — of 'indigenous customs and institutions'. Freedom in this era was the freedom of safe sea travel, and under this benevolent imperialism, the opportunities for 'postwar Singapore nationalists to face new challenges with solid historical advantages' (63) actually were *created*. This is a view of nationalism that is appreciative, at the minimum, of the supposed otherness of colonial rule.

How do the postwar years fit into the narrative of private enterprise and free trade? I now turn to another article in Ernest Chew and Edwin Lee's *A History of Singapore*, a volume that is a major effort at plotting Singapore's history. Cheng Siok Hwa's 'Economic Change and Industrialization' records that the 1940s 'closed ... with often well-founded expressions of anxiety regarding the prospects for the future development of entrepôt trade'.[26] Growing economic nationalism and the desire to regulate foreign currency in the region were part of the causes for the questionmark over entrepôt trade. Still, trade mattered and the Korean War raised primary commodity prices. Nonetheless, the new PAP government took on the equally new task of 'economic development via industrialisation based on the free-enterprise capitalist model' (187).

The Economic Development Board (EDB) was established as a state agency in 1961 to encourage industrialisation, and Singapore maintained an 'open economy' which benefited from the 'boom conditions' prevailing in the 1960s industrial West. That is to say, foreign capital was encouraged into Singapore, and the now-independent state — more so than in British times — provided strong infrastructure in the form of basic services such as power and water supplies, 'and more directly in aiding secondary industry — conducting research, upgrading industrial and vocational training' (186), and so forth. The real difference from the colonial *laissez-faire* era was that '[t]he Government also participated directly in the economy, establishing wholly owned and partly owned industrial and commercial ventures' (213). This state participation in the

1970s 'mitigated somewhat the preponderance of foreign investment *vis-à-vis* local investment in the economy' (214). Of course, external factors beyond the state's control — 'such as the state of world trade, the international monetary system, inflation' (215) — directly affect Singapore's growth.

We can see that despite the difference that the pre- and post-Second World War histories show, between the *laissez-faire*ism of the colonial state and the more interventionist post-independence state, influenced by aspects of a democratic-socialist concern for the social and thus some form of collectivism, the assumption is one of strong continuity of a commercial (later expanded to an industrial) modernity free from excessive irrational, local cultural baggage. This assumption gives us the *generating core* (or 'deep structure', if you will) of the city-state's national narrative. While a *laissez-faire* colonial modernity had its limitations, it taught nascent Singaporeans that an international order committed to liberal free trade was, and continues to be, vital for Singapore's success.

'Continuity' is a theme that is explicit in Edwin Lee's 'The Colonial Legacy'.[27] This article functions usefully as a sort of *de facto* commentary on aspects of both Wong's and Cheng's work. This is clear from the opening paragraph of Lee's article:

> From that date [1819], a new society was born at one of the nodal points in the maritime trade of the world. The British presided over every stage of its growth and development from the time of its birth to 1959, when the new creation was deemed ready to rule itself internally and to become fully independent in the 1963–65 period. (3)

And with this thought, we also can see why the 1986 edition of *Singapore: Facts and Pictures* did not seem to have a difficulty setting up a list of 'Heads of Governments' that could flow from the colonial period into the post-independence periods. Lee foregrounds very much the context of *laissez-faire* colonial rule: 'The founding ... owed a great deal to major reorganisations of the world's economic system' (3). The first was the increasing importance of the China trade, which led the British to look for a Southeast Asian base, and the second was the Industrial Revolution, which led to the demise of the mercantilist system of trade. Raffles, in spite of being an East India Company employee, 'was a firm believer in free trade' (4).[28]

Like Wong, Lee also advances the idea of the externality of Singapore's modernity, along with a certain cultural philistinism and a lack of a sense of history:

> The city was indeed a modern construction. Singapore, even in the days of British rule, lacked historical atmosphere and had few monuments erected .... Grace, elegance, and beauty were not altogether absent,

> but the emphasis was on the utilitarian and modern rather than the aesthetic or antiquarian. (40)

The insistent present of a utilitarian modernity ruled. In terms of governance, the British 'set standards of justice, efficiency, and incorruptibility which in turn generated feelings of well-being, trust and confidence in the subject peoples' (41). 'Culture' writ large, as aesthetic or high culture, was not useful.

Does all this explain why democracy is emaciated in Singapore? Or why freedom is manifest mainly in the support for international free trade? Or why collectivism is suitable as long as it remains the sole preserve of the state? Or even why colonial historiography becomes postcolonial historiography as a queer memory of the present? While Lee doesn't directly answer these questions, an answer is implied in his thinking on colonial irresponsible rule, one not accountable to an electorate, which, inversely, can be very 'responsible' in a paternal fashion. One colonial example of such irresponsible rule is Lord Alfred Milner's South African 'Kindergarten'. Milner and his associates saw themselves as 'British race patriots'[29] engaged in what was once described as 'the endless adventure of governing men'.[30] Lee writes:

> One hundred and forty years or so of British rule have etched on the Singapore consciousness certain principles and values which have become part of the national ethos. Singapore today is a country where the responsibility of government is assumed as a sacred trust, where the prime minister sets the tone of public life as the colonial governor once did, where the rule of law prevails .... It is this combination of the spiritual and tangible aspects of our colonial heritage that makes it such a power for good. (42)

Committed irresponsible rule is now an intrinsic — one may say *embedded* — part of the city-state's democratic life. The local national consciousness has become effectively reinscribed. Lee's unvarnished and indeed simply 'factual' statement indicates why, in postcolonial Singapore, it is not a problem to have an officer of the British East India Company as the founder.

Political scientist Chan Heng Chee's take on the historiography that Lee's article represents is less positive. She agrees that 'colonial values and precepts ... provided the original foundation to the [PAP] administration', and that these values 'were soon modified or jettisoned to meet the demands of a dynamic post-colonial government engaged in the rapid transformation of society and a search for effectiveness'. However, in the final analysis, '[t]his legacy favoured the development of a paternalistic authoritarian government, a style which came to characterize the PAP government, and more surely, the Singapore Government'.[31]

Chan's negative opinion on a colonialist mentality, however, only reinforces the fact that there is an overall consensus regarding a continuity from the colonial period in the progressivism entailed in the Singapore version of 'Our Island Story'. The original constitutionalist direction of the British 'Story', though, is re-cast so that it is economic development and the freedom of markets backed by the rule of law that move forward, rather than individual freedom.

Freedom and Modernity, Interventionist State and the Free Market

What accounts, above all, for the particular historiographical trajectory outlined above is the desire to catch-up with the former imperial master's modernity by using and assimilating aspects of their cultural as well as economic legacy.[32] Economic development is taken to be a 'neutral' way not only to achieve the modernising goal that avoids the stirring up of communal differences but to present a type of national identity itself. How this goal of catching-up functions to motivate the historiography has at least two intersecting or overlapping dimensions to it. The first is the transformation of inherited sets of ideas within which Singapore to some extent still functions, even if not so strongly now as in the 1950s–1970s. The second is the nature of the world economic order within which the city-state came into its own, and how that order parallels aspects of the Victorian world in which free trade was important.

First, the question of the key ideas of liberty and liberation within the inherited British view of the world, especially as they relate to PAP state formation and nation-building. The break in cultural-intellectual continuity between pre- and post-independence obviously cannot be absolute. Problematic as terms such as 'postcolonialism' or 'postcoloniality' are in defining any coherent or practical space, the term 'postcolonial' is useful in two ways that Sangeeta Ray and Henry Schwarz suggest. First, as indicating 'the strictly historical and sociological study of what happens after colonization ...'; and, second, in the way 'the term "postcolonial" can be seen not merely as the political moment of the break from the colonial past but also as the philosophico-cultural departure [or, in Singapore's case, the *lack* thereof] from the larger homogenizing logic of European modernity'.[33] The latter accounts for the irony of postcolonial Singapore as the fruition of a colonial project.

In Singapore, as discussed earlier, in place of the individual freedom of Liberal England, the PAP government offered a redefined (or narrowed) notion of freedom as *economic* freedom and a heavy-handed collectivism. This take on freedom was the result of a combination of colonial authoritarianism and the interventionist inclination of the postwar European welfare state.

The PAP was a democratic-socialist party; we need not take that commitment to a benevolent paternalism as sham, as such paternalism could exist amid the accusations made by the Dutch Labour Party against the PAP in 1976 of repression and the suppression of the trade union movement and intellectual freedom. (This led to the PAP's withdrawal from Socialist International.[34]) The issue of 'freedom' is more complex. How do the exported values of democratic socialism fare in a colonial society that retained marks of a Victorian *laissez faire* heritage, in the midst of the Cold War in Southeast Asia? The national narrative that later resulted is a local negotiation of the 'freedom' concept so important to Liberalism and the conflict between Individualism and Collectivism,[35] which emerges from earlier British debates over state intervention. The result of this negotiation or transformation is a Singapore that has become an internally interventionist and paternalistic collectivism that is the strongest champion of the international neo-liberal economic order in Southeast Asia. This is an ideologically conflicted position to take, though it has held together through the 1980s and until the 1997 Asian economic crisis. The 'pragmatic' economic position the state generally takes ('it works') in large measure has offset the need for a rigorous sorting out of the situation's ideological complexities.

It must be emphasised that the PAP's pragmatic scrambling of British political-economic thinking is not unique, either in past or present contexts. One need only think of the complex history of mid-Victorian Liberalism *itself* as it threads its tortured way into the twentieth century. By the time it reaches Margaret Thatcher in the 1980s, Liberalism's economistic free-market aspects are absorbed into something called the 'New Right' of the Tory Party, becoming an odd admixture of authoritarianism, nostalgic and nationalistic imperial adventurism, privatisation and support for the free market. That is to say, the British West is not the same to itself — so why should it be any less complex when it enters other societies?

The collapse of the right in Western Europe — which included the Tory government of Thatcher's successor, John Major — saw the re-emergence of social-democratic parties which might have countered the economic neo-liberalism of previous regimes, but this did not happen. Tony Blair's and Gerhard Schröder's victories in Britain and Germany instead became, respectively, a 'Third Way' and a '*Neue Mitte*' (new centre), which are, in Blair's own words at the Labour Party's 1998 Blackpool conference, 'pro-business and pro-enterprise'.[36] What is now left, in both senses of the word, is a need for that popular buzz word, 'governance' — meaning depoliticised systems of regulation — rather than now 'old-fashioned' interventionist government. Despite this, the Blairite catchphrase, 'no rights without responsibilities', would work well in politically contrasting 'authoritarian' Singapore.

The confusion of the combined parts of Liberalism with some dissipating socialist-democratic elements in Blair's Third Way and Singapore's 'pragmatic' developmental discourses can be reduced if we recall the debates that revolved around the limits of state intervention as it related to the conflict between individualism, as connected to economic thinking, and collectivism in the decades before the First World War. Concepts or values such as 'individualism' shift in meaning; the contexts and arguments that framed them mutate, even while their polemical force suggest that the variety of meanings were not infinite.

There is often a conflictual relationship between economic and social thinking. A recapitulation of the vicissitudes of liberal and collectivist values will remind us, first, that Liberalism and Socialism have had a checkered (co-) existence; and, second, that the contradictory economistic, communitarian and also historiographical navigation of the ideological terrain of free-marketeerism is not without its precedents.

The economic argument, then as now, was the strongest force against state intervention in the nineteenth century. The *laissez-faire* economy in colonial Singapore, we can recall, was very much an issue in the various Singapore narratives. While classical economists variously had recognised the need for some state functions, the clear presumption was that the economy was a system that regulated itself better than through forms of direct control. Alfred Marshall (1842–1924) thought it obvious that 'those tendencies of Socialism that are towards increased bureaucracy'[37] must be fought against. Also supporting the economic argument is an implicit theory of social justice in which there were *no* grounds to deprive the successful individual of any part of his wealth to give benefits to others. The moral importance of 'character' also figured in such arguments against state intervention, as 'self-reliance' became 'self-development'; this is in John Stuart Mill's *On Liberty* (1859), as it is in Herbert Spencer's *The Principles of Ethics*, Volume 2 (1893).

It should be noted that collectivism and socialism were not interchangeable terms in this period. The theorists of social reform did not necessarily espouse 'Socialism', though this charge could always be laid at their door by their detractors, given that Socialism could refer to either the ideal of the collective pursuit of the common good or, pejoratively, a radical conception of society that abolished property, marriage, religion, the family, etc.

By the 1900s, though, it had become possible to apply moral arguments to the term Socialism, and to speak of 'moral Socialists'. The Socialist Revival of the 1880s had brought a new set of socialist arguments into public view, and New Liberal political theory of the 1900s was a compromise between traditional Liberalism and Socialism. Some consequently claimed that Liberalism had transcended itself, and those who came to be called New Liberals dissociated themselves from Socialism and argued that they were only extending Liberalism's principles. What was common to both traditional and New Liberalism, however, was the commitment to the principle of liberty, whether it was freedom from tariffs, or for the individual to pursue his interests. However, just what social 'reform' meant started to differ.

L. T. Hobhouse (1864–1929), the first professor of sociology at London University, argued in *Liberalism* (1911) that his version of New Liberalism entailed the idea of the common good, which justified the state's intervention with existing individual or private property rights. 'The outcome of this exercise,' Stefan Collini observes, 'is a theory of redistributive justice in the economic sphere which would certainly be recognized as "Social-Democratic" ....'[38] Hobhouse also had a relationship with Fabian Socialism. While he approved of the Fabian recognition that the state was 'simply the people organized for all purposes of self-help to which such collective action can be made adaptable',[39] he came to be annoyed with the way Beatrice and Sidney Webb and George Bernard Shaw considered liberal values as outmoded sentimentality standing in the way of bureaucratic administration by the specialist in the name of social efficiency. The Webbs were to gain the reputation of being imperialists who looked to a national and militarist state to implement their moderate collectivism.

The above truncated history gives a sense of the desire for 'freedom' as it related to issues of individualism and collectivism, even as they were being re-worked by different political actors. Thereafter, there was a breach between the Liberal and the Labour Parties, with the latter gaining dominance. Lee and his faction in the early PAP were influenced by the Fabian version of social democracy, which had been picked up when a number of them had studied in England. In the immediate post-independence period, the PAP argued that liberty seemed less important than social efficiency through bureaucratic rule if they were to steer Singapore away from being in any sense a Third-World society. Elements of Fabian bureaucratic 'technocracy' were thus in place, but 'freedom' and 'liberty' were not allowed to stand, given the PAP's 'realist' attitudes to the world, with consequences for the national narrative. The nature of the global economy during which the PAP aggressively pursued an Export-oriented Industry strategy, too, reinforced the cultural logic of the economistic national narrative. With this, we now come to the second point: the nature of the world economic order as Singapore industrialised.

There was the collapse of the Bretton Woods semi-fixed exchange rate regime and the OPEC oil crisis, both of which produced volatility in the major economies. The USA's involvement in the Vietnam War also created global and domestic instability. Manufacturers and financial institutions compensated for domestic instability by seeking wider outlets during the inflationary 1970s, leading to large bank loans to the Third World. An acceleration in the internationalisation of the financial markets took place via market deregulation in the late 1970s, though other volatile currency markets were reigned in by the Louvre and Plaza Accords in the 1980s. There was Anglo-American 'de-industrialisation' and long-term unemployment in Western Europe, leading to the weakening of the welfare state that had promised security for all, and had been (as a concept at least) a model for a number of postcolonial leaders. Japan began to compete with the West.

Finally, a 'flexible' regime of accumulation developed, versus the more nationally rooted, standardised (or 'Fordist-Keynesian') mass production of the oligopolistic corporation, predicated upon a certain combination of labour practices, consumption habits and technological innovation. A more complex world of MNCs evolved, along with smaller, more agile firms, and with them, the so-called New International Division of Labour (NIDL). Increasingly, offshore finance mattered too. Companies set up factories outside their home country, often in developing ones with cheaper labour. In more recent years, this has become known as 'outsourcing'. If the advanced economies exported more to the rest of the world, significantly, 'the Third World [also] began to export manufactures to the developed industrial countries on a substantial scale'.[40]

The security of the postwar period, predicated upon national control, seemed weakened in the trend towards increased internationalisation, though the General Agreement on Trade and Tariffs (GATT) helped keep the world trading system open and with at least some calculable rules. Still, the postwar multilateral order is no longer with us. We return, in a way, to a renewed dominance of the economic argument, and the weakening of social democracy's collectivist orientation. As it has been succinctly put, '"Globalization" is a myth suitable for a world without illusions.'[41] Singapore was a beneficiary of these changes. Its full 'take-off' occurred when the advanced economies became more uncertain of themselves, and when transport and communications growth allowed small units like Hong Kong and Singapore to become viable hubs in the new flows of capital.

The result is a city-state which functions as an aggressive 'individual', as it were, in the global free market, but which functions as a paternalistic, interventionist state supported by a bureaucratic technocracy within its national boundaries. The PAP state displays some aspects of collectivist behaviour such as in the extensive provision of subsidised public housing, but that is done on the basis that it maximises the country's ability *to compete* regionally and globally. And so, in practical ways, the re-assessment of the social and intellectual legacies of British Liberalism and Socialism transpired in Singapore, as it seemed to be functioning in an international economic environment that had a resemblance to the Victorian free-trade era development of international manufacturing.[42] What the economistic national narrative becomes, in the end, is less a history of our past, but more a past that iconoclastically hurtles Singapore's citizenry forwards into a utopian future.

The 'Demise' of Democratic Socialism

I have contended that the national narrative of city-state's emergence is one based on the teleology of a progressive economic modernity, but with a limited scope for individual freedom. The narrative itself draws from an older colonial narrative of Singapore's development from a trading station, a 'factory' in older parlance, to the premier entrepôt in British Southeast Asia.

The overwhelming presence of the Singapore Story and the claims that successive PAP governments make about their role in this story of arrival to some extent explain why there are no 'subaltern' histories written in the nation.[43] The 'masses' — the immigrants who came to the island — are represented in the history, but usually as hardworking peasants who contributed to the larger success of the trading centre, or as the self-help, individual success story.[44] They are easily co-opted into the economic national narrative. Non-Singaporean scholars ask why Singaporean scholars — indeed Singaporeans — are obsessed by the state. The dominance of the Story and the annexation of the past for the future go to some extent towards answering that question.

It can be argued that Singapore's national economic narrative is indicative of some of the pathologies involved in postcolonial state formation. The historical fever of the nineteenth century in Western Europe 'invented', as Eric Hobsbawm terms it, national traditions to legitimate the imperial nation-state and give coherence to societies conflicted by the developments of the Industrial Revolution.[45] Many postcolonial societies followed the same path of historical invention in their national cultural formation. The PAP, however, chose another route: they saw national invention as dated and instead were more attracted by the frenzied modernisation that had marked the late-Victorian *fin de siècle*. The Singapore that resulted functioned within the zone of what Walter Benjamin has described as the homogeneous empty time of the capitalist present; the embrace of colonial modernity was thus the embrace of capitalist reification. In a way, this modernisation followed the path that the Japanese had earlier trod[46] — and, it would be a path that other Southeast Asian societies, who later wanted Asian Tiger status, would try to follow in the 1980s. The 1997 Asian economic crisis, though, has forced the city-state to liberalise its economy faster than it has wanted, with the government saying that it is less able to protect its citizens from global capitalism's ferocity. The vision of a high-tech present-future Singaporeans have lived with for a generation may possibly become a dystopian vision, as it has been for locations less in tune with the global economy.

This chapter will conclude by examining a little more closely what seems the significant moment of change, when the social-democratic justification for collectivism within the city-state disappears. Eventually, an Asian-communitarian justification took its place for the same collectivism, and the versions of the British West that the PAP publicly had acknowledged to be part of post-independence Singapore became, to a notable extent, sublated. Arguably, the transformation of this vocabulary choice in the city-state was proleptic, or at least indicative, of what was to come in the form of the New Right or Third Way ideologies or discourses in the UK. To address this issue, I return to the PAP's resignation from the Socialist International in May 1976.

'Democratic socialism' was a prominent part of the PAP's identity until the 1970s. Like many other colonials educated in the imperial centre, as earlier mentioned, PAP leaders had been exposed to socialism in the form of Labourite thinking. Lee had seen the Fabian version of it at Cambridge, and Goh Keng Swee gained his Ph.D. from the London School of Economics (where Lee also studied, but only for one term) when Harold Laski was prominent — and when F. A. Hayek, author of *The Road to Serfdom* (1944), which warned of the incompatibility of what he called 'social planning' with democracy, had fled the LSE for more accommodating intellectual climes in the USA.

By 1982, the term 'democratic socialism' had disappeared from public usage and a Confucian values debate took off locally, and was transmuted by the late 1980s into the more general Asian values debate.[47] That debate itself ceased in the mid-1990s, and Singapore seemed the state most strongly committed in Southeast Asia to what was called under the Clinton presidency 'the Washington consensus'. And yet, despite these multi-faceted identity changes, there remains a consistency to the way the state has deployed specific collectivist measures to legitimise itself at home while supporting the free circulation of capital internationally. It therefore also has used its support for the latter to create local acceptance for the former. Thus, while evidence of continuity with democratic-socialist tendencies exist, there is now no longer any direct need to index Singapore against the British colonial legacy, given the successful Story.

In 1976, the Dutch Labour Party submitted a memorandum that recommended the expulsion of the PAP from Socialist International. The terms by which the Dutch Labour Party framed their arguments and the ferocity of the PAP's response indubitably indicate the importance of the term 'social democracy' to the PAP. Singapore indeed may be a 'post-liberal' state, as some allege; but we do not need to resort to any essentialist conception of 'Asian values' or 'Asian-ness' to understand this phenomenon.

In the very introductory section of the memorandum, the Dutch Labour Party used Singapore's evident success to question its democratic socialist credentials: 'Singapore's "wonder economy" (a description recently used by

Sir Keith Joseph who attributed Singapore's success to its untramelled free-enterprise policies), however, has been established by totalitarian policies and methods which have very little affinity with the principles of social democracy.'[48] The charges are familiar — one-party repression; detention without trial; the suppression of the trade union movement, student movement, and intellectual freedom; and control of the press. The PAP, instead of being democratic, 'presides over something which resembles a corporate state'; further, 'Premier Lee Kuan Yew's élitist ideology is completely alien to the principles of social democracy', as he has argued that the city-state must spend its 'slender resources [on the country's "top layer"] in order that they will ensure that Singapore shall maintain its pre-eminent place in the societies that exist in South and Southeast Asia'.[49]

The citing of approbation of the PAP's development agenda by Keith Joseph, in retrospect, is extremely revealing. He was then a member of Mrs. Thatcher's shadow cabinet, with general responsibility for policy and research. Joseph had cooperated with Thatcher in 1974 to set up the Centre for Policy Studies that would contribute towards the intellectual repudiation of Edward Heath's One Nation Conservatism, as it had not challenged the postwar welfare-state consensus. Joseph had become interested in Milton Friedman's theory of monetarism, and later, as secretary of state for industry in Thatcher's government, started to turn the clock back on nationalised industries by bringing private sector managers into them. The PAP's economic policies were part of the worldwide tide turning against the welfare state and social democracy. It is unlikely in 1976 that the Dutch Labour Party could fully grasp the significance of the PAP being praised by Sir Keith Joseph.

Trade union leader C. V. Devan Nair's riposte, strikingly, castigates not the Dutch Labour Party but the British Labour Party, who, though they had not sent in a memorandum asking for the PAP's ejection, had submitted two articles on Lee and the media. The 'Crux of the Problem in Southeast Asia' is communist armed insurrection and the emergency laws that were used in retaliation. There were communist detainees in 1966: 'The British Labour Party and Government knew our situation in 1966 when we were invited to join the Socialist International.'[50] Devan Nair is less concerned with the Dutch Labour Party, for 'it has never mattered very much to us', but with 'the British Labour Party, which *does* matter'.[51] He continues: 'Our question to our erstwhile benefactors is posed more in sorrow than in anger: "Who are you helping in Southeast Asia, Gentlemen?"'[52] There are naturally rhetorical and polemical elements in Nair's pronouncements — S. Rajaratnam and he were the most accomplished PAP rhetoricians and ideologues. However, there is no reason to believe that there is no genuine outrage from one of the countries most committed to the 'good' civilising aspects of colonial modernity.

The response by Dr. Goh Keng Swee, the first finance minister, did not completely refute the charges, but actually took pride in some of them. If the implementation of PAP policies seemed heavy-handed, there were still the important results of such policies to weigh. In 'A Socialist Economy that Works', Goh summarises the general strategy:

> Taking an overall view of Singapore's economic policy, we can see how radically it differed from the *laissez-faire* policies of the colonial era. This had led Singapore to a dead end, with little economic growth, massive unemployment, wretched housing, and inadequate education. We had to try a more activist and interventionist approach. Democratic socialist economic policies ranged from direct participation in industry [for example, 'direct ownership and control of many industrial and commercial enterprises'[53]] to the supply of infrastructure facilities by statutory authorities, and to laying down clear guidelines to the private sector as to what they could and should do.[54]

The Singapore interventionist state thus has a clear British collectivist intellectual lineage, even if others later call it an 'Asian developmental state'.[55] Economic development via collective investment led to political legitimisation and socio-political stability. *Laissez-faire* may help the city-state if it is an *external* condition — the global free market; but within the nation, it had proved a problem, as colonial policy failure had shown.[56]

A major part of the difficulty for a number of Western social democrats — the question of state repression of its people aside — was the PAP's willingness to subscribe to what was then called 'neo-colonialism', in the form of MNCs. By letting in transnational capital, the PAP 'obviated any need to look to the Chinese-educated and China-oriented Chinese who had traditionally made up Singapore's entrepreneurs'.[57] 'Irrational' local cultures, even when they were associated with trade, could impede modernisation — and in Singapore's case, the discomfort of being 'Chinese' (even if the Chinese PAP leaders were English-speaking) in the midst of 'the Malay world' must not be forgotten. Later, of course, as the communist threat recedes, suppressed local Chinese culture becomes good *guanxi* (Mandarin Chinese: network) capitalism, as its 'localness' could be unbounded and linked back to its historical mainland-Chinese origins.

A young economist, Augustine Tan — later a government member of parliament — sees the problem that many had with MNCs to be that they 'have wrought a more interdependent world in which business cycles ... are more synchronised. This is a serious misconception. MNCs ... [are part of] a process of capitalistic organisations adapting to an interdependent world.'[58] Be pragmatic or fail in your social-democratic vision: 'what have such democratic socialist comrades *done* to make technology and know-how available to developing countries and to provide the latter with markets?'[59] The language and values of *international* brotherhood — 'comrades' — is already starting to look uncomfortable with the slowly forming vocabulary of a supposedly *transnational* world without borders.

The most biting reply comes from S. Rajaratnam, who writes a sardonic 'epistle' to the 'Synod Socialist Orthodox Church'. The New Left are slammed repeatedly: in the 1950s and the 1960s, when communist violence raged, only the British Communist Party showed any interest in detainees, not them. In fact, 'On the contrary, in the fifties and sixties the PAP and Mr. Lee Kuan Yew in particular were recipients of unsolicited praise from British progressives.'[60] He writes of the Singapore adaptation of socialist principle from 'to each according to his needs', to 'to each according to his ability'[61] — which seems to me to be a reversion, in terms of economic values, from socialism to some sort of liberal individualism, but framed by a statist context.

A key moment in Rajaratnam's text is his charge of hidden neo-colonialist racism: 'You still persist in the belief that as Europeans it is your unquestionable responsibility to whip the heathens along the path of righteousness. ... We have high regard for the achievements of Europe. *Our commitment to democratic socialism is a commitment to a European idea*' (emphasis mine).[62] His assessment is that it is not Singapore but *Western Europe* that has failed in progressive socialism, in the 'proper', orderly and collective improvement of mankind's lot following the best European traditions:

> I could enumerate the many symptoms of the sickness which today afflicts the West — drugs, sexual promiscuity, dropping out, the rash of cults of unreason, and the glorification of violence. These are manifestations associated with the New Left. The final days of the Roman Empire, as is the case now with post-imperial Europe, were tormented by crack-pot movements not unlike those of the New Left.[63]

Such claims backed by economic success can — and later will — lead to claims of alternative Asian modernities. From Rajaratnam's viewpoint, Singapore was being more true to an orderly Western concept of a collectivist modernity and modernisation than the New Left.

What transpires is that the PAP state develops what sociologist Chua Beng Huat calls a 'supply side socialism', which 'is conceptually meant to distance the economic and administrative practices in Singapore from both the socialism of communist regimes and social welfarism as a necessary safety net for the irrationalities of market-driven liberal capitalism'.[64] Through the redefined conceptualisation of socialism, Singapore manages to ride out the changes in the global economy in which a 'flexible' regime of accumulation develops, versus the more nationally rooted and standardised mass production of the oligopolistic corporation.

By the 1980s, though, this 'supply side socialism', with the success of the other Tiger economies, could be ascribed as being part of a culturally 'Asian' modernity. And so, in practical ways, the re-assessment of the intellectual legacies of British liberalism and socialism took place, resulting — via the Asian values and modernity discourse and social practices — in a statist attempt to re-'Asianise' or reterritorialise culture in the city-state. However, before we transit to examine that phenomenon, we must first take a look at the distinct urbanism that was the aesthetic expression of both the PAP state's paternalist collectivism and the attempt to homogenise the local environment, along with the 1990s culturalist resurrection and reinvention of the 'local' against state-led deterritorialisation.

4

The Homogenised Urban Environment and Locality

What emerges from the previous two chapters is that Singapore seems to be a postcolonial city-state in which both the contradictions and the complexities of becoming a modern nation-state are seemingly resolved by state-directed technocratic and technicist means. This modern-Asian city is a partial fulfilment of a modernising desire to wipe the slate clean, and to invent society from scratch. The purpose of this chapter is twofold. First, I will continue exploring the People's Action Party (PAP) state's homogenising socio-cultural engineering by looking at the bland postcolonial urbanism that is contemporary Singapore's built environment. As I have suggested in the Introduction, this urbanism is a part of a radical modernisation that seems part of a now-lost world of liberal confidence, achieved in an illiberal political environment open to a highly internationalised economy shaped and reshaped by the major Western powers, especially the USA. As with previous chapters, there is a need here to understand what it means when the West becomes part of a *self-administered* and thus not simply a neo-colonialist process of Asian modernisation, one in which cultural negotiation has effectively taken place.

Second, I want to argue that the PAP's statist modernisation is not one necessarily fully embraced by the city-state's population, even while the iconic and ubiquitous modernist public-housing estates that best epitomise the city-state's built environment houses over 80 percent of the population. Public housing — a genuinely successful housing programme in many ways, well-maintained and generally clean — is a major part of the happy face of the state's achieved modernity. In contrast, as has often been noted, the '[e]xperience with high rise, high density public housing in the Western world has been essentially negative'.[1] The other two noticeable PAP development projects are industrial estates and urban renewal in the downtown core. The Housing and Development Board (HDB) was started as the successor to the colonial Singapore Improvement Trust in 1960, and the 1960–65 development budget included S$194 million for public housing (US$1 = S$3 at that point of time). Since then, there has been no turning back, and the immediate post-independence housing shortage was effectively ended by the end of the 1960s. The problem of housing had been studied by one of the founder-members of the PAP itself, Dr. Goh Keng Swee, in the 1950s.[2] By 1968, nearly 750,000 people lived in government-built high-rise flats in a total area of just 2.2 square miles.[3] Public housing and the island's financial and shopping areas are the major aesthetic expression of the state's desired modernity, an aesthetic powered by social and economic instrumentalism and 'usefulness'.

Most Singaporeans in general have no choice but to deal with the homogenised urban environment of the PAP's Asian modern. This chapter will look at some of the unease with the city-state and its public image, despite the delivery of economic success, as expressed in recent independent film. Such film forms part of the artistic-cultural production that have arisen since the 1980s, partly in reaction to the particular PAP-created urban and socio-cultural environment, and represents recent attempts to think through and indeed *relocalise* at a non-statist level what it means to live within the projected happy-clappy if deterritorialised modernist locales of Singapore. Independent films started to appear in the 1990s and they have demanded, indirectly, both a 'Westernisation' and 'Asianisation' in order to gain what might be described as 'other experiences of the present' apart from the existing, narrow national economism. Not unnaturally, given its prominence, public housing and its denizens are often the subjects of such attempts to relocalise the built environment.

The 'local' that comes about, of course, is not a simple, bounded notion of specifically rooted culture and identities. Singapore, to begin with, is a society created with a large number of economic migrants, and the recreation and re-assertion of the local after modernisation can hardly be the simple re-assertion of what the state already, to a significant extent, has erased. The globalised 'condition', as is increasingly acknowledged, is a multi-layered one.

Creating the Modern Asian City

> *In Singapore — modernization in its pure form — the forces of modernity are enlisted against the demands of modernism. … [It] has adopted only the mechanistic, rationalistic program and developed it to an unprecedented perfection in a climate of streamlined*

> *'smoothness' generated by shedding modernism's artistic, irrational, uncontrollable, subversive ambitions — revolution without agony.*
>
> – Rem Koolhaas, 'Singapore Songlines' (1995)[4]

The above quotation represents the judgement that Dutch architect and critic Rem Koolhaas, the principal in the renowned Office of Metropolitan Architecture (OMA),[5] makes regarding the built environment that the PAP government has created. The Singapore piece is one in a series of articles on modernisation and contemporary cities — Tokyo and Lagos have also received his attention. His sprawling, subtle, yet oddly blunt and essentialising essay that attempts to assess the *entirety* of the city-state's urbanisation from the late-colonial 1950s to the mid-1990s is one of the best-circulated culturally oriented analysis of Singapore. It is simultaneously critically incisive and blind to its own insights. It is for these reasons that I engage with Koolhaas in some detail. Fundamentally, he grants that the West has become a part of postcolonial Singapore, and that this West has been 're-worked' for other purposes, as witnessed in the particular cityscape that arose, only to deny that postcolonial agency involved with transculturation when he sees he does not like the final authoritarian urbanism. The modernity Koolhaas sees, then, becomes to him an essentialised Asian modernity with no relationship to a more open Western modernity.

The post-independence city that arose, Koolhaas argues, is 'uncontaminated by surviving contextual remains' (1011) of its past, or even of its tropical location. He can only think of the city-state as a 'Potemkin metropolis'. Koolhaas's reference is to Grigory Aleksandrovich Potemkin (1739–91), who served in the court of the Empress Catherine II of Russia. Potemkin's detractors accused him of building sham villages for Catherine's tour of the Crimea in 1787, in order to give her a false picture of progress and prosperity. In Singapore's case, it is less the question of prosperity that Koolhaas questions, but more the sort of progress it has experienced, and the inauthentic and no longer internally coherent existence that is created and then reflected, he believes, by its decontextualised urbanism.

Koolhaas's positions are not easy to discern on first reading his extended essay. He asks whether a re-made society has authenticity. His basic contention is that the instrumental rationality that dominates the city-state's urbanism is a form of overly efficient progress that seems to have gone mad. He comments that Singapore is 'the apparent victim of an out-of-control process of modernization' (1013), one in which democracy has been 'suspended in return for ... development' (1015). In the end, he believes, the city-state 'is a *city without qualities* (maybe that is an ultimate form of deconstruction and even freedom)' (1077). He is thus ambivalent about Singapore's success, because in Singapore 'freedom' is the freedom of the quasi-authoritarian state to invent a decontexualised self.

In Koolhaas's synoptic view of postcolonial urban development, the HDB in the 1960s becomes what he describes as 'the major vehicle for Singapore's future overhaul' (1021). The HDB's concrete slabs, 'their only concession to tropicality [being] continuous balconies' (1021), he says, spring up as New Towns such as Queenstown and Toa Payoh. To him, they 'offered compelling arguments for the discipline of urbanism and the notion of urban renewal that have completely unraveled in the past 30 years' (1017) as these New Towns did not become the '"soulless" slums' (1034) that blighted such development in the West. With faceless public housing both in the inner but mainly at the outer zones of the city established, urban renewal in the city core proper could proceed. But despite a type of success with public housing, overall urban renewal in the city-state will be one that uncreatively 'displaces, destroys, and replaces' (1035).

For Koolhaas, the city-state seems not to have had an artistic practice and intellectual presence (that is, 'modernism' rather than 'modernisation') that, as in the case of the Euro-American city, both contested and yet in some ways also benefiting from the modernising of the cityscape. For example, Baron Haussmann's Second Empire Paris famously gave us the poet Charles Baudelaire and his poems on the relationship between *ennui* and a gritty and sometimes decadent yet incandescent sense of beauty in daily urban existence.[6] Modernist art was an art of the city.[7] Koolhaas believes that Singapore's modernity is uni-dimensional — though what this position signifies is that in many ways, he accepts the PAP's own national self-representation uncritically.[8]

Koolhaas outlines a genealogy of urban renewal that supports his position on the PAP state's cultural nullity. Urban redevelopment begins with the end of the housing crisis at the end of the 1960s. Fortified by a United Nations report, *Growth and Urban Renewal in Singapore* (1963), a programme commences which (in the words of the report) was 'not intended to be an exercise in conservation or restoration but a bold attempt to modernize and develop the city centre' (cited in 1026). The '*body of the island itself*' becomes conceived of by the 'Singapore bureaucracy … as the apotheosis of the tabula rasa: the razed plane as the basis for a genuinely new beginning' (1031), as 'raw renewal' (1035).[9] Koolhaas marshalls architectural theorist Christopher Alexander in support of his critique of Singapore's inhumane and arbitrary architecture. Alexander in 1965 had famously written that: 'The prospect that we may be turning the world into a place peopled by little glass and concrete boxes has alarmed many architects too' (cited in 1043).[10]

Koolhaas, however, does not simply want to critique Singapore's urban modernisation in itself, but to set it in the context of larger historical significance of the rise of a broader Asian urbanism. He tells us that the 1960s are also a point in architectural history when '"other" architects [such as Kenzo Tange] emerge from their "exotic" cultures' to speak back to 'male [architectural] whiteness' (1043). They will fuel the capacity for alternative or other urban-cultural modernities that Koolhaas thinks will challenge the Western view of such matters.

It is in this light that Koolhaas describes how in the mid-1960s, the Japanese architect Fumihiko Maki imagines an architectural metabolism that more spontaneously organises urban 'congestion'. Maki sees the city composed of 'buildings as *accumulations* with diffused identities' (1049) that can produce 'collective form'; this last term alone Koolhaas takes to be 'a hidden rebuke to the individualism of Western [architectural] practice' (1045).[11] Unexpectedly and ironically, in Singapore, Koolhaas continues, it is two key progressive architects critical of the present quasi-authoritarianism — they champion 'history, context, community' (1055), ideas inimical to the state's reduced and yet monolithic idea of progress, unless defined for its own purposes — who, with their firm Design Partnership, become involved with the momentous start of a radical 'metabolist' reconstruction of the city. Their People's Park Complex is built on the demolished site of popular street-bazaar stalls in the midst of the city's densely populated but low-rise, colonial-era Chinatown. Finished in 1972, Koolhaas describes the resulting 25-storey high-rise slab on a six-storey podium that has more than 300 shops, offices, restaurants, coffee houses and car parking for 633 cars as 'brutal' (1967). He concludes: 'Architecturally the complexes [the People's Park Complex and the People's Park Centre next to it] ... look like tropical versions of [artist Kasimir Severinovich] Malevich's Architectons: prismatic rectangular volumes of concrete assembled with apparent casualness.'[12] But more importantly, the two complexes are linked to each other through 'bridges extend[ed] in all directions to establish pedestrian continuity', and in the process they become, he argues, 'ideological stretches ... ready for extension and linkage in all directions' (1067), 'urban energy generators', in Maki's words (cited on 1049), of the colossal changes to come.

In this reading of Singapore, history and identity as linked to physical sites become an impossibility due to incessant urban metabolism. A central fear of Koolhaas is that this city without a 'geometry' — a city in constant transit — may turn out to be the emerging condition of the world: 'Maybe this lack of geometry is typically Asian: Tokyo is the eternal example' (1975). He feels that the decontextualised building of the city-state reflects a 'self-hatred' of the past and old cultures (see 1077).

The two high-rise Chinatown complexes become to Koolhaas both signs of the future Asia — think of Shanghai in 2005, with its wish to have the tallest building in the world — and the decontextualised and the transculturated West-in-Asia. As a consequence, the two complexes are now 'unmistakably Asian in ... [their] values' (1067). Expanding megastructures, we know, are now unsurprising in East Asia. The little city-state, Koolhaas intimates, has pioneered the structures that hold the teeming Asian crowds and are unapologetically linked with shopping, which, 'in the Asian context[, is] not a simple consumerist frenzy but an authentic essence of urban life, its equipment Asia's equivalent of the [Greek] agora' (1051). What is significant, then, for Koolhaas in regard to Maki's work is not just his theory of collective form 'but his anticipation of a regional coloring of the architectural debate, which will result, paradoxically, from its global dissemination' (1051).

With this, we return to the issue of democracy and public life. What emerges for Koolhaas is that Asians are not individuals — at the crudest level, they remain the Asian hordes of the colonial imagination: they do not have democratic commitments and certainly have no idea of the public sphere. But they do have the 'authentic essence' of a 'consumerist frenzy', the consequence of a new wealth which has bred a new 'self-awareness and confidence' (1073). Peculiarly, it seems that pastiche, postmodern and decontextualised Asian culture does have a genuine *essence* — but only that of shopping. But why should anyone care about such urban developments of a somewhat clichéd if capitalistic East? The biting final assessment of Singapore — worth quoting in its entirety — bluntly spells out the dangers of an Asian contagion of which the city-state has been a key locale for incubation. The world must learn to fear cities without geometries:

> Singapore represents the exact dosage of 'authority, instrumentality, and vision' necessary to appeal [to the re-emerging giant of China]. In numerous architectural offices in Singapore, whose names a few of have ever heard, China's future is being prepared. In these countless new cities the skyscraper is the only surviving typology. After the iconoclasm of communism there will be a second, more efficient Ludditism, helping the Chinese toward the 'desired land': market economy — but minus the decadence, the democracy, the messiness, the disorder, the cruelty of the West.
>
> Projecting outward from Singapore, an asymmetrical epicenter, there will be new Singapores across the entire mainland. Its model will be the stamp of China's modernization.
>
> Two billion people can't be wrong. (1087)

The little dot is a portent, a sign of the times. What is perspicacious of Koolhaas's essay is that even as early as 1995, before the present China fever, he could see beyond the East Asian Miracle of the four Little Tiger economies to the re-emerging core state of East Asia.

In many respects, this uncertainty over the 're-entry' of the People's Republic of China to the larger capitalist world and, also, to the region, is not unexpected; after all, despite the unitary East Asia of Koolhaas's thinking, China poses a challenge not only to the advanced West but to the way Southeast Asians and

East Asians themselves have functioned since 1949, with the fall of the Republic of China. Koolhaas, though, seems to ignore the latter knowledge. Singapore's urbanism is transferred to China, and the former then becomes an embryonic modern-cultural start of a larger regional-Asian competitor to the West, one that does not share its humanistic modernism. His extended reflection, then, even given its sophisticated vocabulary, becomes the current incarnation of an older line of geopolitical and cultural reflection on the 'East' and the 'West' that many on either side of that 'divide' have participated in. It is a geopolitical and cultural reflection that has ongoing currency. For example, according to Pankaj Mishra,

> Modernising China now poses a formidable challenge to the West. Observing a humiliated country in 1889, [Rudyard] Kipling wondered: 'What will happen when China really wakes up, runs a line from Shanghai to Lhasa, and controls her own gun factories and arsenals?' This old anxiety now has a strong basis. As an aggressive nationalistic China rises swiftly, the words once used to dismiss its potential — 'insular' and 'arrogant' — are applied to its rival, the United States, and with India waiting in the wings, the dominance of the West begins to appear [as] yet another phase in the long history of empires and civilisations.[13]

'The "Western" Is No Longer Our Exclusive Domain'

Koolhaas's argument on Singapore is a major representative analytical instance of how Euro-American modernity has produced the 'rest of the world' as a sort of bad-faith copy of the West, with Asian people destroying their authenticity in the shadow of a dominating Western modernity. For all the incisiveness of Koolhaas's views — he is correct in giving us the Anglo-American modernist intellectual and cultural lineage of the PAP's urbanism, and the question raised of the significance of the transference of the city-state's urbanism to the giant China is valid — there is also an expression of horror of Singapore as a partial fulfilment of the utopian impulses inherent within urban planning as a concept that it has appropriated from the West. His general position suggests that 'modernity' has a fixed geopolitical site, and that the West always remains the Other to even its former colonised peoples — they who seem to have no agency. The (post)colonised 'them' should not appear as only a geopolitical concept defining the Other in its negativity.

Singapore's planners, indeed, *have* to a fair extent self-reflexively worked towards fulfilling Le Corbusier's notion that all problems and contradictions of becoming a modern society can be resolved by technological or technocratic means. We might say that Singapore's cityscape is the *strongest cultural-material expression* of the statist modernity and modernisation partially accomplished with attracting multinational capital for national development. While the city that emerged after independence in 1965 is a place more 'faceless', but also more protected and ordered than the Paris that Baudelaire had walked in could be, it now, if slowly and belatedly (as possibly befits a catch-up modernity), is starting to manifest a desire for a more heterogeneous modernity and culture. But, before we get to that, this section examines the appropriated modernity as it manifests itself in the cityscape the PAP has created, for in 'modernity, ... the places of history are the cities.'[14] One can think of this cityscape as part of a negotiated modernity — as an adaptation of a modernity that was and is globally circulated. Koolhaas's essay offers us precisely such an understanding — only to take it away.

Singapore and its decontextualised cityscape indicate a radical and strongly paternalistic 'Asian' route to modernity that, while patterned on its Western origins, had either avoided or suppressed many of the pathologies and also positive ambivalences of modern existence. This neat modernity was achieved at the cost of many of the socio-cultural freedoms intrinsic to the Western liberal-democratic models of modernity. It is this particular combination of economic success with general loyalty (or, alternatively, as Koolhaas and others take it, a passive acquiescence) by the population that raises the ire of Western left-liberals and their media in relation to Singapore, for the combination questions what is still taken to be the universal liberal route to modernity. In contrast, though, it could be said that the combination perhaps represents a model of modernity and stability that would appeal to elements of the Western European Right.

'Asia' as a category becomes an unfortunate descriptor and limiting term that stops Koolhaas from a deeper understanding of the adapted Singapore modern as an instance of the global West inside the national. The world before the First World War was similar to our present globalised 'condition', in which the constitutive components of social, political and economic life were constructed less rigidly in national terms.[15] Thereafter, there was an increasing correspondence between national territory and the exclusive authority of the national state. While the state has hardly disappeared, the conditions for the modern nation-state, as sociologist Saskia Sassen suggests, are 'partly being unbundled by the processes of globalization'.[16] Out of political necessity, Singapore, as a city-state rather than a real territorial state, threw up the mechanisms of a nation-state (a national flag, a foreign-affairs ministry, etc.), and out of economic necessity (since autarchy was out of the question) began to develop itself as a link in the advanced West's economies from the late 1960s to the 1970s. The post-independence urbanscape that developed was an expression of what we might identify as the early phase of globalisation.

Singapore's deliberate self-imbrication within Western (and also Japanese) capitalism indicated some level of ownership of (and, it needs to be said, the wish to be owned by) the West. As Koolhaas himself succinctly propounds:

> The 'Western' is no longer our exclusive domain. … [I]t is a self-administered process that we do not have the right to deny — in the name of various sentimentalities — to those 'others' who have long since made it their own. At most, we are like dead parents deploring the mess our [non-Western] children have made of their inheritance … (1013)

'Our refusal', he also says, 'to read Singapore on its own terms is frivolous' (1013). In the end, however, Koolhaas does what he advises against, and *exactly* asserts that the 'West' is 'their' exclusive domain. The Singapore-Asian modern he sees cannot be anything but the corruption rather than a negotiated version of the West.

How does the West 'in' the city-state manifest itself in terms of urban development? One way we can understand this process is through the importance of a utilitarian pragmatism as a key value in post-independence Singapore. This value underwrites the development of both the modernist skyscrapers of Shenton Way and Raffles Place — the city-state's financial centre — and the seemingly contrasting, massive, socialist-style public housing slabs that mark a vast amount of the cityscape.

The PAP government discarded the British colonial master plan of 1955 — a plan that had a country-and-city divide — for the more Americanised urban renewal proposal prepared by a UN team in 1963, as discussed earlier. The result of this change was tremendous. Nevertheless, the colonial inheritance continued to have an impact on the cityscape even as the dominance of the British West was slowly replaced by the influence of the USA. The colonial master plan 'is a plan for a medium-sized town with rural hinterland, not a plan for a metropolis', Koolhaas quotes from *Growth and Urban Renewal in Singapore* (cited in 1026). His conclusion regarding the influence of the report is this:

> The language of bureaucrats is boring; the report is no exception. What gives it power is our *retrospective knowledge of its effects*. It unleashes, legitimizes, exacerbates, amplifies, encourages, extrapolates the ambitions that the regime has so far not revealed explicitly. The UN … report whispers additional radicalities .... (Twenty years later their diagram of [the 'design' of the city] is realized: around a shrunken central preserve, the entire island turned into New Town). (1029)[17]

If somewhat melodramatically, Koolhaas offers us a deep understanding of the PAP government's slowly exerted spatial will-to-power over the domestic environment, in the ongoing desire to build a modern metropolis that could take its place confidently in the world.

The HDB public estates that arose were pragmatically designed and built: 'To the extent that pragmatism has a look it is utilitarian, Anglo-Saxon: the [HDB] slabs are purely quantitative emblems — modernity stripped of ideology, like the notorious English council estates' (1021). Quite so: the urban models must come from somewhere, after all. It seems undisputed by Koolhaas that the West was part of the postcolonial city-state, even if he disapproves of a bourgeois Anglo-Saxon idea of modernity concerned with instrumental reason. The HDB blocks of flats thus are hardly a 'modernity stripped of ideology', as he contends; instead they represent the efforts at self-invention by the PAP state, drawing upon a British social-democratic model of state intervention.

The results initially traumatised the city-state's denizens:

> If the transition from the English slum to the estate was traumatic, the leap from the Chinese shophouse … to Singapore's high-rise containers is even more merciless, not only in terms of material difference — from the Asian to the Western — but because the new inhabitants, cut off from connective networks of family relationships, tradition, habits, are abruptly forced into another civilization: the slab as time machine. (1021)

The problem here is less the socio-cultural disruptions (accurately) being pointed, but the representation of multi-ethnic Singaporeans as Oriental(ised) Others whose cultures are apprehended through the now-familiar logic or strategy of binary coding: Us vs. Them; the Modern / Present vs. the Traditional / Past. This logic is opposed to what historian H. D. Harootunian has observed — that 'the here and there of modernity are coeval, even though the latter is often forgotten in the narrative of the former'.[18]

In Koolhaas's case, the modernity of the 'there' is less 'forgotten' than simply apprised as being a past different from Western modernity's present, even though colonial Singapore was a creation of a British mercantilist modernity. One may here ask if there are no commonalties between the British and later Singapore experience of modernity. While, say, Industrial Revolution-era Manchester grew more slowly than Singapore, the agriculturists forced into the factories then were no more or less forced into a 'time machine'. The general process of capitalist-industrial modernisation simply *is* disruptive, though the experience of the Asian modern is more rapid.[19]

Koolhaas's deepest analytical lapse occurs in his ascription of an *inherent* 'Confucian-ness' that supposedly underwrites an East Asian-Western modernisation, of which Singapore is one signal instance: 'To the West this [Confucianist] authoritarianism seems a temporary aberration …: but it is more likely that a new norm is being synthesized in Singapore: ... a kind of ultimate power of efficiency that will fuel Asian modernization' (1017). Koolhaas uncritically accepts the Asian values discourse prevalent in both Malaysia and Singapore in the mid-1990s, when he was writing his essay, at its face value and as a sign indicative of the West's more sensitive modernity. So, although he initially suggests that Singaporeans have *agency* and are *responsible* for their faceless if painfully wrought modernity, this modernity finally is seen as a corruption of Western modernity that now seems necessary to be seen as Confucian-Asian. He recognises but fails to see any significance in the fact that the city that underwent urban renewal did so in a period when the USA still advanced modernisation as a universal process. The PAP accepted and continues to accept this paradigm of development more or less at its face value, even if modernisation as a term has since lapsed in general usage.

Despite the clichéd depiction of 'Asian' communtarianism,[20] Koolhaas manages also to capture the unusual way the PAP has fostered the modern in Singapore. It is a 'big' or socially interventionist state (and nowhere is this 'big state' more possible than in this tiny city-state) that has turned the island into a hub that services the flows of multinational capital. The very cityscape, with its contrast between its vast tracts of public housing and the skyline of the financial district, reveals this unusualness. 'How can the republic now known for establishing the ultimate capitalist environment begin with a quasi-socialist transformation of its entire territory?' he asks (1037). This question captures the particular way the modern has been negotiated.

Singapore's urban structure was enabled by that discussed in chapter 3, an adaptation of the social-democratic interventionist state linked to the idea of social collectivity. The public housing that has replaced the rural villages and the overcrowded if architecturally distinctive shophouses of the island's Chinatown, along with the renewed downtown in which the buildings' 'exterior appears residual, ... overcharged with commercial effluence from hermetic interiors' (1075), according to Koolhaas, are the expression of a state-sponsored collective 'reality'. This urban structure was created to contain a diverse and once unstable multi-ethnic society, political leftists and general cultural behaviour inimical to industrialisation that (in the state's official historiography) marked the 1950s–60s.

In the end, Koolhaas cannot think of Singapore as a realm in which the 'Western' has become (as he himself calls it) 'a self-administered process' (1013). What horrifies is the very strident attempt to socio-culturally engineer a society for capitalism's needs. The significant subtitle of his essay is: '... Or Thirty Years of Tabula Rasa'. Koolhaas prognosticates: 'Singapore is perhaps the first semiotic state, a [Roland] Barthian state, a clean synthetic surface, a field at once active and neutralized where political themes or minimal semantic particles can be launched and withdrawn, tested like weather balloons' (1039). There is the *surface* of the modern — but it is only that. This is 'modernization in its pure form' (1041), and its inauthenticity horrifies him. But then, one is entitled to ask, is this horror any more than a revelation — indeed a sort of *revealing* distortion — of the global West's transculturated presence in Southeast Asia?

Since writing the essay on Singapore, Koolhaas has proceeded to retail design for the Prada stores in New York City (2003) and Beverly Hills, California (2004).[21] In October 2005, he returned to Singapore at the state's invitation to participate in the Ministry of Information, Communications and the Arts's (MICA) 'Crea©tive [*sic*] 2005 — Reinvent Your Future' programme, and in particular as a keynote speaker for the conference 'Beyond 2005: The Global Summit for Creative Industries', co-organised by MICA and GBF Private Limited, the organiser behind the Global Brand Forum. That is to say, Koolhaas came to assist the city-without-geometry's next phase in (post)modernist reconstruction.[22]

A Late Modernity

One way of interpreting how the PAP government has deployed the modern is to recall the once-commanding teleological dreams of what the modern world could undergo — endless renovation, the permanent revolution — at the turn of the nineteenth century to the 1960s. In the contemporary moment, it is easier to see cycles and calamity instead of progress. But the early PAP leadership of Lee Kuan Yew and his key associates did imbibe of the universal idea of the modern, an idea that was already known in colonial prewar Singapore, as examined in chapters 2 and 3. In the 1960s, 'modernisation' as a concept was taken for granted and, we should not forget, development economists and agencies tried to draw the non-aligned world into the narrative of capitalism. While many critics consider the PAP government conservative or even reactionary for its pro-capitalist but illiberal political and socio-cultural orientation, the way the 'modern' has been adapted might rightly be described as 'radical'.

In a bizarre way, the city-state's catch-up modernisation or late modernity is *truer* to the older dreams of the modern, even if aspects of its contrasting liberal and socialist versions of it were collapsed together. In exerting the effort to be like its erstwhile colonial masters, even if only in certain respects, we become something else: this modernity manifested a local difference while yet remaining part of an overall experience of modernity itself; it is neither a copy of a Western original nor an alternative modernity. As Harootunian argues, 'The problem with these conceptions of modernity is that they are based on transmuting a temporal lag into a qualitative difference (the myth of the time lag).'[23] The ideas of 'copy' and 'alternative' suggest the city-state as primarily a deluded victim, with modernisation seen as a sort of defensive or reflex action instead of the deliberate and systematic goal that it was.

It is not only Koolhaas who has described Singapore as a slate wiped clean in the interests of capitalist development. More recently, for instance, cultural critic Ziauddin Sardar, now a co-editor of the arts journal *Third Text*, visited Singapore in 2001 and was horrified at what he saw:

> Success means inculcating globalized [which seems to mean, to some extent, 'Americanised' — this adjective is not precisely defined] manners, mores and values. ... Consequently, internalizing global identity means eradicating what comes naturally [*sic*]. Singapore culture must be ersatz, like all the renovated shop houses around the downtown marina. ... Local architecture is just a quaint backdrop. When you globalize everything what you get is Singapore.[24]

While Sardar uses the term 'globalise' imprecisely and while his formulation of 'naturally' evolving or organic and possibly a primordialised notion of culture is problematic, he is at least clear that a *local agency* is involved. That is to say, the PAP leadership *chose* to do what they did, whether deluded or not in the choices made. This is important, for if not, then to 'globalise' is to make a verb requiring an agent into a noun, as happens in pronouncements such as 'Globalisation is ...'. Sardar recognises the desire for what is now is effectively taken to be universal, even if this means the 'universally problematic' — and there is no doubt that for the PAP government, capitalism is the undisputed Universal Real.[25]

I suspect that it is not only Singapore and its illiberal, faceless modernity that is at issue here, in theoretical terms of what the perception may be when people do not like the ways the 'modern' is adapted outside the West. Let me give one example, one not so far away from Koolhaas's assumption regarding the rising of the Asian Other inimical to modern, Western liberal values: 'In the emerging cities of China and southeast Asia, where profit has replaced Mao and Buddha for ideological guidance, clusters of towers akin to those in America turn out on closer inspection to be one layer thin, fascinating facsimiles and recombinations of Western architecture quickly erected and much more quickly designed.'[26] Despite the fact that the writer is a cosmopolitan architectural critic, writing in the magazine of a major international museum, the Tate Modern, there is the obvious othering of Asian modernity as simulacra. The new East and Southeast Asian tower blocks trumpeting capitalist development are only poor photocopies of the West.

The point is not to say people need to approve of the emergent Asian (re-)formations of the modern — which in China destroys huge swathes of the environment and swells urban centres — or that Singaporeans should uncritically receive and appreciate the PAP version of the decontextualised Asian modern, but only to say that if we think of the 'modern' or the 'global' as being coterminous with the term 'Western', then the West is no longer a geographical concept. The dispersal of the 'West' into the 'globe' represents a partial decentring of the West — never a unified entity to begin with — and this in turn has allowed Asian statist and non-statist cultural imaginaries to assert themselves, even if these imaginaries are themselves a part of the dispersed or global West in Asia. While Asians may not quite 'own' the West, the West nonetheless has become part of the semi-peripheral 'them' out there. The lack of 'ownership' of the West is a recognition of the real power of the Western centre *as* centre: Singapore's semi-peripheral status is acknowledged by its government, and the commitment to modernisation does not lead to a utopian assertion of equality — the unequal condition that was historical colonialism and is now, still to a considerable extent, contemporary capitalism is not forgotten.

But to move on to the second part of the chapter: how is one to imagine disagreement with the seemingly totalised socio-cultural norms of Singapore's environment? And yet, aesthetic-cultural production since the 1980s indicates that disagreement there must be, even if it is not tantamount to an ideological struggle. Another aspect of this question is: what sort of art arises from the city-state's homogenised urban environment? It is worth recalling that Singapore after the fall of communism has changed, and those who 'resist' the ruling party now, unlike those in the 1960s–70s, do not seek even its electoral defeat or otherwise, and do not reject capitalism, but instead seek more space to participate in Singapore's general life. It is 'resistance' that the government actually *needs* to sanction, as it has seen that the heavy state intervention since the 1960s has produced, ironically, a passive (and thus successfully homogenised) population that may not have the necessary cultural dynamism to propel the city-state to be a player in the supposedly more freewheeling and less-Fordist New or Creative Economy that marked the closing decade of the twentieth century.

Asserting Locality: The Arts and Film

> *Any city which has the ambition to be a city of global importance must encourage its artists and listen to them.*
>
> – Robert Palmer, General Director of Brussels 2000

It can be argued that production in the arts and related cultural fields in Singapore since the 1980s, when the economy effectively 'takes off' and the government starts to be more supportive of aesthetic-cultural activities, represent a re-assertion — or, more accurately, also a reinvention — of 'locality' in reaction at least partially but also specifically to the PAP-created homogenised urban environment, and more generally to the social and cultural costs paid by the citizenry for economic success. Such artistic responses question the nature of the deterritorialisation that the PAP state's modernisation programme entailed. There emerged a contention that there is more to the city-state's cultural cityscape — that is to say, other local differences apart from the state's own particularised capitalist modernity — than lay on the sterilised surface.

The reason why 'locality' as a term appears within inverted commas is that the aesthetic-cultural responses that came about, as in the state's modernity itself, cannot be located via the now-clichéd opposition of local vs. global. The artists draw on existent contemporary aesthetic cultures from a plurality of sources — thus 'locality' is not simple, rooted and bounded. The new assertions of the importance of culture seemed to demand not only a recuperation of suppressed, repressed or even erased local identities, but also entailed more 'Westernisation' (if that is the word we want[27]) as well as some forms of 'Asianisation' from outside the city-state, in order to obtain what might be called as 'other experiences of the present' apart from the PAP state's version of it. There arose a desire for *differences*, which the state had attempted to erase, to a large extent successfully.

The 1980s started with a theatre scene that was slowly but firmly burgeoning, led principally by The Theatre Practice (TTP), The Necessary Stage (TNS) and TheatreWorks (Singapore), among the first three professional theatre companies in recent times. TTP's Kuo Pao Kun (1939–2002) was the major enabling personality. He had been detained without trial between 1976 and 1980 for alleged communist activities. Kuo bounced back into prominence in the 1980s, with his moral and cultural authority enhanced by the detention, and with plays that examined cultural memory, the destruction of culture and the possibility of trans-ethnic understanding and a common Singapore identity. He also broke the mould of single-language theatre and created plays (e.g., *Mama Looking for Her Cat* [1988]) that encompassed a range of the languages spoken in Singapore, and was starting to explore the importance of extra-national identity when he passed away.[28] Kuo was a natural institution builder able to harness the energy of not only theatre practitioners but also visual artists involved with newer arts practices such as performance art — introduced to Singapore by visual artist and 1999 Fukuoka Cultural Prize winner Tang Da Wu — and thereby helped pioneer a multidisciplinary contemporary art scene that vigorously explored local identity issues.

The three companies created adventurous theatre productions, often formally bold (many of the plays were 'devised', with the scripts created in a workshop setting), dealing with issues of memory, ethnicity, gender and other identity issues. As indicated, these were artistic reactions against the singular, top-down disciplinary modernisation which had allowed little space for reflection on cultural or historical issues. What was notable of 1980s to mid-1990s theatre was how 'difficult' theatre — even if text-based — became the mainstream of theatre, even given the relatively checkered and uneven history of English-language theatre.[29] Devised theatre even coexisted with fledgling, indigenised Broadway-style musicals within the companies. Gender issues were noticeable by the early 1990s. Whatever the shortcomings were of early professionalism in the theatre, they were invigorating years. With regard to the visual arts scene, the return of Tang Da Wu from London in 1988 (after the best part of 20 years in England, with occasional return trips) led to his founding of a group called the Artists' Village in 1988, in an abandoned village in a then-rural area called Sembawang. This deliberate ruralism also seemed to function as a critique of the petit-bourgeois urban society that Singapore was becoming.[30]

The contemporary and anti-commercial art that arrived with Tang was an eclectic 'contemporary' that arrived helter-skelter. Suddenly, there were dynamic experiments in conceptual art, performance, installation sculpture that also used Duchampian 'found' objects, figurative painting that had German expressionist antecedents (but executed with personal rather than historical references), pop art, and 'happenings'. A museum director has observed that '[t]hrough Artists Village, Tang became more influential than any Singapore artist in introducing fresh approaches to the usage of material and space', and that the village itself 'was a dynamo in fostering alterity in Singapore as the artists lived and worked together in a close community'.[31] While these contemporary art formations may be generally described as 'postmodern', there was no resuscitation of aesthetics and the issue of beauty, which are linked to some aspects of postmodern art. There had been earlier intimations of such artistic possibilities, but they were just that — intimations.[32] Not surprisingly, these experiments transpired without definitive reference to their origins and the disagreements that had existed between their original practitioners.

Even if, by the mid-1970s, a conceptual art in the West was either popular or stale, and was to be followed by a very plural visual culture that had an unpredictable diversity, their corporate 'arrival' in Singapore, along with other contemporary visual arts forms, was both confusing and energising. These forms arrived at a moment when younger artists appeared bored with the prevailing abstract modernism and watercolours of the Singapore River and Chinatown. The various ethnicities of the predominantly young artists Tang encouraged also made for a challenging experimentation with themes that implicitly or otherwise critiqued the state's imposed bland identity and urban modernity. Thus environment, sexuality, violence, identity and rebellion became valid areas for enquiry. The world of abstract modern art that dominated the local arts in the 1970s was exploded. The creative release of the 1980s and the early 1990s brought critical judgement into the aesthetic-cultural realm, and offered new means by which local identity issues could be explored and defined,[33] though a chilling moment occurred in 1994 when the state's security apparatus was turned on contemporary artists.[34]

More recently, from the 1990s, film has developed as an embryonic art form. Eric Khoo's *Mee Pok Man* (1995)[35] — the 'noodle seller'[36] — was the first recent major attempt at making local art film, followed by his *Twelve Storeys* (1997).[37] Both of these films, it is generally acknowledged, have tried to probe 'deeper under the surface of the country's conspicuous wealth and success, focusing on the forgotten, the hidden, the problematic and the bizarre aspects of Singapore life'.[38] The first film deals with an intellectually challenged noodle hawker's fascination with a young prostitute called Bunny. Both are trapped within a society with cloned public housing and a top-down demand for success. Bunny gets run down by a car, and the lonely hawker brings her home to his small flat within a poorly maintained housing block, where he cares for her. However, she dies — but the hawker goes on trying to care for her. Individual autonomy is brutally limited for those at the extreme margins in the city-state, the film asserts, and people must make-do the best they can. The film is infamous for an extended sequence, some eight minutes long, in which the hawker has propped up the corpse in his kitchen and strokes her hair, with tufts of it coming out. *Mee Pok Man* went on to win two Special Jury prizes at the Singapore International Film Festival, a Special Jury prize at the ninth Fukuoka Film Festival and received Special Mention at the Pusan International Film Festival in South Korea in 1996.

The title of Khoo's later film, *Twelve Storeys*, refers to the number of floors many public-housing slab blocks have (see Fig. 4.1). HDB estates are once again the urban space in which the expansion of human affectivity is checked. Though not a commercial success, the film has the distinction of being the best-known film up to then to emerge from the city-state. It had two full-house screenings at Cannes in 1997, the very first Singapore film to be screened there.[39] The film deals with a China bride's refusal to sleep with her Singapore-Chinese husband, an older brother's domineering and prurient obsession with his teen-aged sister's relationship with a brash, déclassé young man, and an overweight single woman's daily torment by her aged Cantonese-speaking mother, all of which take place in the same block of flats. A Chinese man who inexplicably commits suicide at the start of the film returns and is present throughout the film as a silent spirit who witnesses and at times directly sympathises with the housing block's cheerless denizens.

In regard to the last element, the *Twelve Storeys* may be a partial adaptation of Wim Wenders's *Wings of Desire* (1987). In that film, a trench-coated angel, Daniel, wanders through the derelict urban wilderness that is Berlin's Potsdamerplatz in the mid-1980s (now transformed beyond belief) and falls in love with a mortal. Partial imitation *Twelve Storeys* possibly may be, but it indicates the West not unnaturally serves as an artistic resource for thinking through the modern Singapore that Khoo wants to depict.

Singapore's built environment appears, in both of Khoo's films, as a disjunctive and claustrophobic space to which individuals have to adjust to emotionally — unsuccessfully. They attempt to get away from the oppressive blandness of efficient Singapore, within which intimacy and individual autonomy are restricted. Khoo has admitted to being influenced by Martin Scorsese's *Taxi Driver* (1976); he has said, he has been 'attracted to characters who don't function too well and have to exist within society's rules and regulations'.[40]

Other attempts to show stories at odds with the pristine surface of the Lion City followed, the most successful being the low-budget comedy *Money No Enough* (1998),[41] which despite its relatively low production values was the second-highest grossing film in Singapore, in 1998, behind James Cameron's blockbuster, *Titanic*. The film questioned the *arriviste* materialism in Singapore life, and like *Twelve Storeys*, got past the state censors with the use of the proscribed Hokkien-Chinese (or *minnan hua*; the state has promoted Mandarin-Chinese as standard Chinese since the 1960s, though this intensified from 1979). The film looks at the financial problems of three friends of different class backgrounds, though none is especially privileged. One is a middle-class manager who, because of his lack of formal qualifications, is not promoted and decides to leave his job, only to be faced by a barrage of debt problems. Another gets entangled with a loan shark, and the last is a coffee-shop assistant who thinks buying a mobile phone will elevate his social status. The three are played by Chinese-language comedians well-known from local television, and they bring a populist *brio* to the roles.

The protagonists emerge as authentic figures from the so-called 'HDB Heartland' (the PAP tends to shy away from direct class ascription), showing how the Chinese-speaking could suffer in an urban society the politically dominant 'English-educated', as they were called until the 1980s, created. As is generally accepted, 'Much of the film's slice-of-life quality is due to the dialogue which is an authentic mix of Hokkien[-Chinese], Mandarin and Singlish [local English] with 80 percent of the dialogue in Hokkien.'[42] The use of Hokkien-Chinese, given the government's work at suppressing it in favour of Mandarin-Chinese, has been called the return of the repressed.[43]

There was also Kelvin Tong's and Jasmine Ng's *Eating Air* (1999);[44] I shall return to this film.

As a medium of art, cinema has been international from its beginnings. While Hollywood dominates this medium, Chinese film from Hong Kong mainly, and more recently, to a lesser extent, Taiwan and China have made — admittedly in limited ways — more two-way the cultural flows of globalisation to and fro the USA and Western Europe. But how strong is the cultural exchange involved here, given Hollywood's homogenising hegemony?

While this large question applies to Singapore films — which certainly have no real capacity at the moment to penetrate the West (though there is a limited impact in parts of Southeast and East Asia), save in art-house circuits — it should not stop us from seeing that the problematisation of the utopian promises of the standardised and (over-)sanitised Singapore cityscape and the desire to explore the city's darker side as a way to expose local situations hidden by the superimposition of the happy if bland modernity has been thematised by Singapore film producers. Public housing itself appears almost as a character in its own right. Euro-American film history (which included the exploration of aesthetic modernism's complex and fraught relationship to the city), along with a certain Hong Kong urban film genre as represented, in its arts-house incarnation, by Wong Kar-wai's *Chungking Express* (1994), offer various ways this dark side can be investigated. More of the West, certainly, but with a different trajectory from the government's version of it, and with more of East Asia as well — the Taiwanese Edward Yang and Malaysian-Taiwanese Tsai Ming-liang have often explored alienation in the urban environment — in the interrogation of the city culture the PAP has created.

However, because models for such urban interrogations do exist, another question might be asked: do these films portray the *actual* immediacies of HDB estate lives untainted by the cinematic images of the Euro-American and even socialist failures in adopting high-rise public housing? Do they portray thin versions of the less-salubrious aspects of alienation in Hong Kong's crowded urban zones, so unlike the carefully spaced-out and neat HDB blocks? Eric Khoo's films, for example, have been criticised as being inauthentic, as being plutocratically condescending in its presentation of the Hokkien-speaker's sub-culture. He unremittingly depicts those who live in the exotically sterile blocks as being exotically unhappy. Sociologist Chua Beng Huat and literary critic Yeo Wei-Wei charge that an 'absence of entry into the inner lives of … marginal people in a national success story is, perhaps the consequence of Khoo's own financially very upper class background for whom fascination with the poor stems from a fascination with the Other rather than empathy for the Other, making his cinema disturbingly voyeuristic'.[45] The *auteur*-director unwittingly reveals his cosmopolitan-oriented gaze into working-class Chinese life. Is this 'local' view of the city really different, in that case, from Koolhaas's view of the city-state?

The concern that arises here may be that while both Hong Kong and Singapore as former colonial societies culturally have translated the West, such translation cannot be taken as a general theoretical question removed from their contexts. In terms of the East Asian cities most open to postwar capitalism, especially since the 1980s — Tokyo, Hong Kong, Seoul, Taipei, and Singapore — it strikes me that Singapore seems the most uncomfortable with itself. Tokyo of course is the queen of the East Asian cities in the way it has made the West its own. It reigns as more or less the chief Asian disseminator of youth fashion styles and also mass culture, alongside Taiwanese and Hong Kong pop music. The presence of 'J-Pop' (Japanese pop music) and Japanese television soaps directly in Taiwan, Hong Kong, Singapore and Bangkok in the 1990s,[46] and more indirectly through youth and young adult fashion influence in the region demonstrate as much.[47] Hong Kong's film industry since the late 1970s — with major names such as Wong Kar-wai, Tsui Hark, Ann Hui and John Woo emerging as part of the Hong Kong New Wave, working in both 'serious' and more action-oriented genres — in a number of ways has made the city more confident and no longer quite the 'cultural desert' that it was once said to be.

It may be, as cultural critic Ackbar Abbas argues, that a 'new sense of how it was local [Hong Kong] ingenuity and professionalism more than the imported talent that brought about the city's great success came with the force of a revelation. In other words, it was a growing confidence in Hong Kong's international viability that led to a recovery of the local.'[48] Singapore — ironically, with much more extensive usage of English, the international language of commerce, than any other city in East or Southeast Asia (Kuala Lumpur and Manila would follow next) — lacks such a confidence. It perhaps is precisely *because* the Anglo-American West can come in directly, with less need for literal translation and thus mediation, that Singapore's West is, so to speak, more 'Western' and less local. After all, why not directly copy? This is an issue of comparative translation that cannot be addressed here in any detail, but deserves more investigation.

In some ways, the city that emerges in Khoo's films *is* a version of alienated life in the Euro-American metropolitan, and Taipei's and Hong Kong's *demi-monde*. We might then attribute part of *Money No Enough*'s unexpected box-office success to the fact that it looks far more realistically at the socially and culturally disenfranchised Chinese-speakers' struggle to survive economically in the 'Chinese' and supposedly Asian-Confucian city. The action takes place in the bright, daytime-set city created by the English-speaking elite, rather than the extreme, dark, alienated HDB cityscapes that Khoo depicts.

Nevertheless, while Khoo, Tong, and Ng, derive their film art from various external models that deal with the city's *noir* recesses, they *do* use the West and East Asia for the purpose of re-asserting local cultural diversity. *Eating Air* — a literal translation of a Hokkien-Chinese idiom that means, roughly translated, 'going for a leisurely ride' and having the wind in your hair, as it were — is a 'motorcycling/kung fu love story' (as given in the publicity blurb) that does imply new opportunities for cultural production for Singaporeans. This is partly due to the less-psychologically extreme plot when compared to, say, Khoo's *Mee Pok Man*, and to the deft use of working-class youth culture.

The 'city of the night' that the main characters Boy and his friend Ah Gu wander through is a city of empty HDB ground-floor decks (called, suggestively, 'void decks') and roofs, dated 1970s-era shopping centres, amusement arcades where less 'respectable' youths hang out, and roadside news stands. It is a world peopled with ill-educated youth possessing multilingual skills that won't obtain them a corporate job in the English-speaking financial centre. Living in the smaller of the HDB flats, Boy and his gang of friends look for space — for escape, as expressed spatially by their idling on the roofs of their HDB blocks (see Fig. 4.2). The motorcycles so important to Boy and Ah Gu represent the literal means by which they 'go for a ride'; they also become the ineluctable symbols of this desire for a larger world. Ah Gu borrows money from a loan shark — an *ah long*, in Singapore Hokkien-Chinese parlance — and (perhaps inevitably) cannot outrun the loan shark's thugs. Boy is loyal to Ah Gu to the end, and pays the cost of youthful idealism.

In this particular environment, Chinese-language comics, influenced by Japanese comics (or *manga*), dealing with kung fu masters and sword-wielding macho Chinese heroes are popular,[49] and it is a world that simultaneously co-exists with local cosmopolitanism zones such as Mohamad Sultan Road, one of the best-known Singapore zones in the late 1990s for dance clubs and bars, and the young yuppie wannabes who function as poster-youth for the state's desired globalised status. ('Who says we can't have fun?') These latter zones are conspicuously absent in *Eating Air*.

The world of adapted *manga* becomes the structuring device that Tong and Ng use to parallel the actions Boy and Ah Gu go through to find their space. Boy imagines himself as a heroic swordsman with ninja-like skills as he struggles with those who would oppress Ah Gu; unfortunately, the grim ending for the swordsman is also Boy's ending. *Manga* culture in Singapore is widespread, as it is among the Chinese overseas in Taiwan and Hong Kong:[50] it forms a distinctive form of regional Chinese youth culture that the English-speaking and 'English-educated' directors dragoon in to create their Singapore film with its Mandarin- and Hokkien-Chinese script. The genuine appreciation of *manga*-inspired animation, as witnessed in the drawings that appear in the film, alongside an original soundtrack of ballads, electronic dance music and industrial rock music in a variety of languages (Singapore-English; Mandarin-Chinese; Hokkien-Chinese), show a firm and unpatronising grasp of working-class, Chinese-speaking youth culture.

In one scene, after a scuffle with gangsters that Ah Gu has foolishly become involved with, Boy and Ah Gu are together on a high-rise rooftop, with the world of the Central Business District and its environs in the background. What relationship — apart from the merely spatial — do they have with that world, the film asks? Does the view they have give them an outlook on individual freedom? Significantly, Boy comes to a nasty end in the bowels of the city, in a part of the Central Expressway tunnel close to the downtown core: his motorbike metaphorically and otherwise cannot take him away from a constrained city life (see Fig. 4.3).

The localised Western-East Asian cinematic forms combined with the working-class comic culture deployed to interrogate the local-global city-state indicate an emerging double consciousness that may enable younger artists to represent a locality that also shares a unique cultural nexus with non-Singaporeans, but one that avoids being transformed into a shallow universalism. The double consciousness of being local-global inside a statist local-globalism with a more narrowly functional economic outlook may turn out to be a significant cultural identity development not to be nullified by the global packaging of lifestyles that continues to gain strength in the city-state's urban culture, despite Southeast Asia being weakened by the 1997 Asian economic crisis. The very fact that the initial independent films in the 1990s came about as an attempt to counter the PAP state's homogenising socio-cultural engineering as manifested in its urbanism suggests that such attempts at totalisation have their limits, even in the city without geometry. But more ominously, it may also signify that by the 1990s, the culture of economy had hollowed out enough of the cultural pluralism and energy that was Singapore up to the 1960s that this hollow now could be 'filled in' by new artistic culture.

The PAP now asserts that the passive citizens of a Singapore Inc. are no longer desirable. The moral is: be careful of what you wish for, as you may get it. In the place of state-sanctioned passivity is now a new official desire for 'messy' creativity, for something less conformist that can spur Singaporeans' ability to maintain the city-state's 'hub' status within global capitalism. The contradiction entailed clearly is significant: the interventionist state now hopes to tell its citizens how to be individually creative and non-conformist.

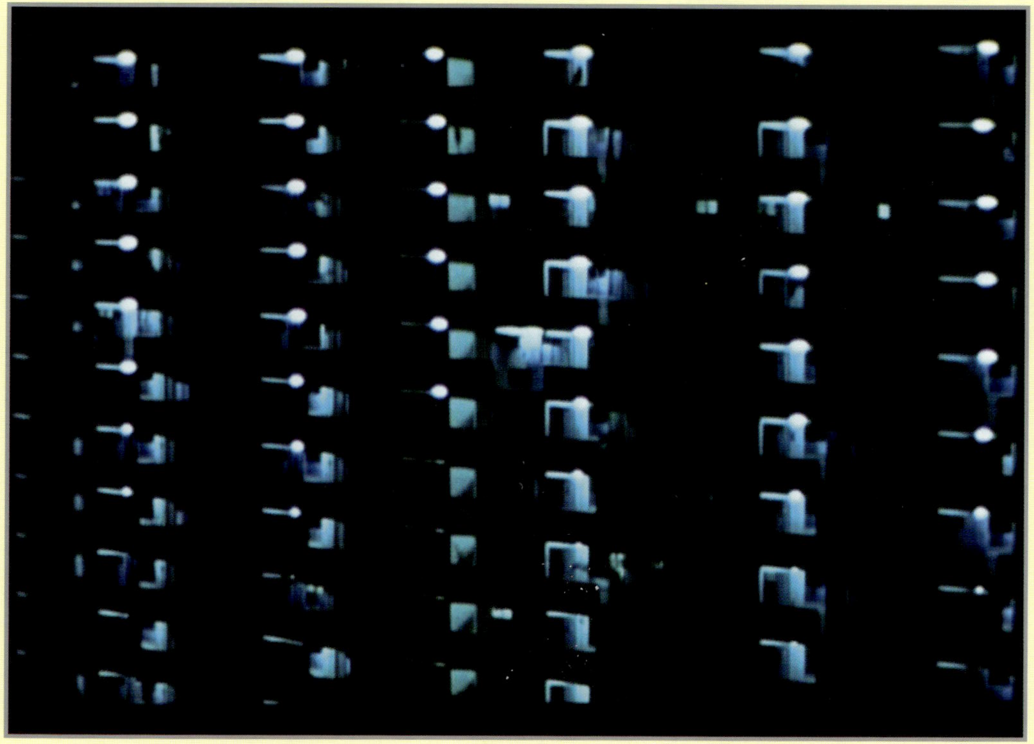

Figure 4.1
Public housing at night. From the opening sequence of *12 Storeys*, directed by Eric Khoo (1997). © Zhao Wei Films.

Figure 4.2
High jinks on the rooftop of a public-housing block. From *Eating Air: A Motorcycle Kungfu Love Story* (1999), directed by Kelvin Tong and Jasmine Ng. © Multi-Story Complex Pte. Ltd.

Figure 4.3
Death in the traffic tunnel: no way out of the city-state. From *Eating Air: A Motorcycle Kungfu Love Story* (1999), directed by Kelvin Tong and Jasmine Ng. © Multi-Story Complex Pte. Ltd.

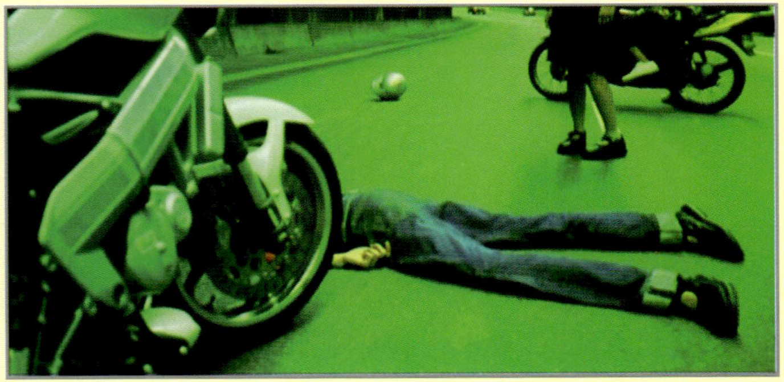

Figure 6.1
The contemporary yuppies becoming descendants of the eunuch admiral. From Ong Keng Sen's production of *Descendants of the Eunuch Admiral* (1995). © TheatreWorks (Singapore) Ltd. Photo by Lawrence Siow.

Figure 6.2
The Older Daughter talking to the Old Man. From Japan Foundation Asia Center's production of *Lear*, directed by Ong Keng Sen (1998). © Japan Foundation.

PART 2

Reterritorialisation

5

The State, Ethnic Identity and Capitalism

... capitalism is continually reterritorializing with one hand what it was deterritorializing with the other.

– Gilles Deleuze and Felix Guattari, *Anti-Oedipus: Capitalism and Schizophrenia* (1984)

Thus far, my discussion has examined how the demand for 'progress' in Singapore has led to industrial modernity itself becoming the metanarrative which frames the city-state's immediate post-independence national identity. The modernity that Lee Kuan Yew and the other first-generation People's Action Party (PAP) leaders wanted was not exactly the same as, but also not one alternative, to the advanced economies' versions of modernity. Indeed the Anglo-American West, broadly taken as either a neutral or universal culture, could be a source for the island's postcolonial state formation. However, the world has changed a great deal since the late 1960s and the 1970s.

There has been increasing discussion since the late 1980s within cultural theory and anthropology as to whether global capitalism and its associated culture homogenise the world, or whether modernity is indigenised differently in various locales.[1] Also, we understand that the very resistance to capitalist forces can revivify 'tradition', in the form of — one of the most-cited instances — the misnamed 'fundamentalist' Islam. 'Culture' — that which was either suppressed or denigrated in Singapore, unless it was the culture of the economy — seems that which emerges from the margins as a contestatory reaction to capitalism.

We may ask, however, if the state's relation to culture is only that of the above. The prominent issue of culture and the state in the discussion of the 'East Asian Miracle'[2] lead to a renewed interest in the state itself and to some Asian states' cultural differences from *laissez-faire* capitalism in managing development.[3] Singapore, of course, has been part of this issue and the debates that surrounded it. Much has been made of the 'Asian values' identitarian discourse and debate that transpired in relation to the contentious claim, made in both the West and Asia, that there may be cultural causes for these economic successes.[4]

The statist experimentation with (re-)invented or 'ethnicised' cultural identities in the case of the Asian values experiments in Singapore, I contend, represent an ongoing complicity with global capital which fostered space via an adversarial style.[5] At the very least, these experiments indicate that states are capable of managing culture as an instrument to maintain national competitiveness within global capitalism and in themselves represent a shift in the city-state's local cultural values, as discussed in the first three chapters.

Dramatic changes occurred in the PAP government's cultural management through ethnicity from the 1970s, when the state had an 'ethnically neutral' policy undergirded by a rational commitment to cultural modernisation and therefore also to deterritorialisation, to the international appearance of the Asian values discourse and the 1980s re-ethnicisation of Singaporeans into hyphenated identities. It was, indeed, an attempt to *reterritorialise* Singapore in the name of Asian values, an action that also was enabled by an increasing distance from the colonial era, and therefore from the need to recognise and to remember the island-state's particular relation to the British West. In the process, the PAP claimed that an Asian modernity should be able to bridge the gap between tradition and modernity that existed in the West.

The changes in Singapore's ethnic management suggest that the universalising of capitalism's culture so as to create markets is a complex process. Slavoj Žižek has asserted that

> the ideal form of this global capitalism is multiculturalism, the attitude which … treats *each* local culture the way the colonizer treats colonized people — as 'natives' whose mores are to be carefully studied and respected …. [In any case,] the strain of particular roots is the phantasmatic screen which conceals the fact that the subject['s] … true position is the void [capitalist] universality.[6]

Singapore, as an offshore hub for global capital flows is able to take advantage of this 'multiculturalism'. The semi-peripheral, postcolonial state consequently is *not* simply or entirely disempowered when accepting contemporary capitalist formations. This chapter will investigate these questions by examining the PAP's reterritorialisation of Singapore into a part of a Confucian East Asia as an instance of the ongoing flexible statist management of culture, the economistic cultural logic that led to this 'national culturalism', as I will call it, and its impact upon the way the state managed ethnicity.

Singapore's example of managed culture also moves attention away both from cultural contestation from the margins and the idea of the West and the Rest — that is, from a question of centre and margin — to semi-peripheral states and the institutions of advanced capitalism. The larger context for this phenomenon would be the rise of the East and Southeast Asian trading economies and intra-regional integration, which has contributed to capitalism being more multicentric and also multicultural, in Žižek's sense of the term. Such developments offer opportunities for national economies to participate in the emerging global economy — but, as Singapore illustrates, this participation can create the need for alternative identity and political legitimacy foci.

'National Culturalism' and Capitalism

To begin with, we may ask how we might think through states experimenting with large-scale cultural formations within capitalism's present configuration. This question by no means indicates that the state maintains full control of its cultural experimentation: external conditions will change, and the state functions on contradictory terrain within and without its own territory. As geographer David Harvey observes, 'State power can, in the end, be neither more nor less stable than the political economy of capitalist modernity will allow.'[7] Having said this, Singapore's example indicates the scope of manoeuvre possible within capitalist modernity.

Since the late 1990s, a rational modernity seemingly free of cultural specificity dominates, or so the new era of free-market ideology is trumpeted[8] — but this is unlikely to mean the death of cultural identity politics played at the national and even regional levels. Anthropologist Arjun Appadurai is right to argue that what he calls 'culturalism' may be rife.

Culturalism 'designate[s] a feature of movements involving identities consciously in the making'; what Appadurai has in mind is less state-sponsored identities than 'movements ... usually directed at modern nation-states. ... Culturalism, put simply, is identity politics mobilized at the level of the nation-state'.[9] Subversive micronarratives can be seen in 're-emergent' Eastern European nationalisms in the 1990s, or the diasporic championing of an independent Khalistan in India. However, we could well enquire if the culturalism 'of the margins coming into representation'[10] is the most significant form of culturalism. We need not take transnational or diasporic identity politics to be the *central* manifestation of Appadurai's 'modernity at large'. The so-called globalising economy may lead modern subjectivities to 're-imagine' themselves not only against nation-states, but at the *level of the nation-state itself* — resulting in a 'national culturism', to follow Appadurai.

In Singapore's case, there are indeed 'margins coming into representation' — but it is the marginality of the semi-peripheral, postcolonial nation-state which, while not possessing the heft and significance of India, for example, are determined to enter the higher-stakes band of the capitalist game. Thus, the 'ethnicization of the national' should not be taken generally as a negative nativist reaction against 'the universal dimension of the world market',[11] as Žižek does, but as one that can reinforce the Real of capitalism. In this instance, I think that Singapore is indicative of what identity may become at the nation-state level when it wants a state-sponsored national culture continually able to mobilise the country towards the economic goal of becoming a First-World society under the conditions of a burgeoning international economy. In that sense, it is not an eccentric cultural-economic formation, but one displaying the tensions within and the cultural (il)logic(ality) of global capitalism.

From 1959 to the 1970s, the PAP leadership supposed that if what they took to be the progressive, Enlightenment-derived logic of capitalism could be managed, Singapore would be integrated into the world via a rationalising expansion that would ignore race, language, religion and entrenched histories. A rationalising capitalism — an assumption, we will see, never dispensed with, even as the PAP moved in an apparently contradictory manner from deterritorialising to reterritorialising culture — was also preferable to the other 1960s manifestation of modernity in Southeast Asia, communism. Stuart Hall observes that:

> As a consequence [of our belief in capitalism's rationalism], we have lost sight of one of the most profound insights in Marx's *Capital* — capitalism only advances, as it were, on contradictory terrain. ... And until we can see the nature of that contradictory terrain — precisely how particularity is engaged, how it is woven in, how it presents its resistances, how it is partly overcome, and how those overcomings then appear again — we will not understand it. That is much closer to how we ought to think about the so-called logic of capital in the advancement of globalization itself.[12]

With the conjuncture of a seemingly less-superior West and Japanese emergence in the 1970s, Singapore leaders began to think that part of industrial development could work through both retaining fading and even inventing aspects of 'local' specificity as a newer means to discipline the plural nation. This transition to a reinvented local, though, I have suggested in chapter 3, seems partially catalysed by the PAP's expulsion from Socialist International and a sense of betrayal by the British Labour Party. But if the region was increasingly economically successful, there was in any case no longer a need to be so directly 'loyal' to this West. A balancing act would need to be worked out where state-sanctioned 'Asian' morality could constrain both the weaknesses of and encourage a participation in a less-regulated and predictable capitalism: a contradictory 'neo-traditional modernity' is wanted. Capitalism must homogenise — it must deterritorialise — while also producing difference — it must reterritorialise — and become a 'multicultural' capitalism.

Arif Dirlik notes the increase in the 'insistence on culture areas in the mapping of the world, whether promoted by Samuel Huntington, Jiang Zemin or Lee Kuan Yew'. The cause of this, however, it seems to me, is not only the falling back to 'earlier Orientalist or nationalist reifications'[13] — though it is that too — but also the result of a direction towards a regionalism which, in the 1990s, 'represents [the] concentration of political and economic power competing in the global economy, with multiple interregional and intraregional flows'.[14] Thus, though there seem to be the regional hegemonies of the USA, the European Union and the Asian-Pacific zone, we need to see that there are other tendencies to an increasing inter-penetration of the so-called 'triad powers' as complementarities develop, along with the changes in spatial hierarchies within each triad's region (the result of uneven development), leading, for example, to newer North-South divides.[15]

Given the emerging terrain of an uneven, multicentric world order, and recognising the nation-state's ability to function is subject to capitalist modernity's politico-economic stability, we can say that the PAP government *has* flexibly manoeuvred its way through even the years of Vietnam's fall and the height of 1960s anti-Singapore feeling in the region by re-forming the nation to the needs of international capital.

Traversing Homogenisation

While the issue of ethnicity has arisen as a substantial issue in previous chapters, it will take centre stage in this chapter. A national culturalism articulating the relationship of tradition to modernity via ethnic management goes back to 1960, and the next two sections examine its origins and the changes in the international economy that helped enable the discourse on Asian values and modernity. The intellectual genealogy leading up to this national culturalism is older, with the immediate precursor model being the late-colonial cultural policy of 'Malayanisation', which meant, in practice, entrenching English as the first language of the soon-to-be postcolonial élite.[16]

PAP culturalist policy was first directed at promoting a universal society, so as to make Singapore a site in which the supposedly neutral demands of capitalism's actual *specific* cultural requirements could be met. Hence, the party reckoned early with the need to be (what is now called) a pro-active 'developmental state' with a commitment to socio-cultural engineering.

What were the probable external conditions and standards that contributed towards the early ethnic-cultural management policy? The local or internal labour needs which led to the multi-ethnic migrations to colonial Malaya and Singapore in the nineteenth century, along with this legacy's consequences for nation-building, are well known.[17] However, it is worth recalling that the resulting pluralism was itself the product of a colonial economy set within the *larger* international framework. That is to say, Singapore's economy has always functioned within international dimensions since its colonial inception. The voluntary mass migrations of the century after 1815 are unsurpassed: about 12 million Chinese emigrated to Eastern and Southern Asia, and a half million left India for Eastern Asia, South and West Africa.[18] Capitalism's needs lead to involuntary modernities that are internally heterogeneous, divided and contested — and this questions the full autonomy of the local in some contexts, while not erasing local conditions.

The postwar Western growth — also the period of decolonisation — were 'Golden Years' during which the seemingly inevitable cycle of boom and slump became a succession of mild fluctuations, an accomplishment attributed to Keynesian economics and the resultant macro-economic management. It remained for the *telos* of progress to reach the 'Third World'. This 'progress' gathered pace in Singapore after Malaysian Separation and the loss of a potential Malaysian common market. With no possibility for import-substitution, industrialisation intensified with a turn outwards to manufacture for export.

The newly independent city-state's leaders maintained a deep respect for and envy of their former colonial master. Though the Western metropole by the 1970s seemed to be crumbling — inner city decay, narcotics problems, structural unemployment — surely modernity hailed from the West. It was only in the late 1970s, with marked economic success, that the ongoing talk of 'Western decadence' in Singapore seemed translated into a new ethnic policy.

In the meanwhile, as chapters 2 to 4 have sought to demonstrate, the PAP proceeded with a modernising 'creative destruction' to homogenise and discipline local 'irrationalities' as the means to create the physical and cultural conditions to catch-up with the West. Singapore gained its rapid manufacturing development though 'imported' entrepreneurs, the multinational corporations (MNCs). In this way, the PAP 'obviated any need ... to look to the Chinese-educated and China-oriented Chinese who had traditionally made up Singapore's entrepreneurs'.[19] By 1975, wholly or majority foreign firms produced 71.3 percent of the S$12,610.1 million output of manufactures.[20]

The above represents, broadly, the external, modern capitalist dimensions and standards that the Singapore government took into account in relation to a cultural and ethnicity management policy which stridently incorporated instrumental rationalism to domesticate and if possible deterritorialise local identities. The idea of being 'modern' is at the core of the PAP's national culturalism, even if subsequent cultural re-inscriptions have an increasingly multi-layered rationale.

As for the 'racial' model we are now familiar with, the so-called 'CMIO' (Chinese-Malay-Indian-Other) model, sociologist Sharon Siddique reminds us that that was

> first articulated in the 1950s, when indigenous political leaders were grappling with the creation of a political system capable of catering to a heterogeneous political clientele. ... The political perspective incorporating these concepts crystallized in the 'Malaysian Malaysia' campaign that was launched at the Malaysian Solidarity Convention ... in May 1965.[21]

This 'Malaysian Malaysia' idea later became after 9 August 1965 the 'Singaporean Singapore' idea, an ethnically equalitarian and modernising idea of national identity associated with the late culture and foreign minister S. Rajaratnam. However, up to 1965, given the reality of Malaysian life, the idea of the 'ethnic mosaic' animated 'multiracialism'; in practice, this meant guaranteeing the Malays' 'special position'.

From the mid-1960s to the 1970s, after independence from Malaysia, the emphasis in managing inter-ethnic relations was on the creation of a 'Singaporean Singapore' as a society *not* predicated on 'retrogressive' Asian values. There was also a movement away from the accommodationist politics of the 'ethnic mosaic' with Separation and the resultant unchallenged PAP authority, along with industrialisation, to 'a new set of [common] national values conducive to such development ... [leading to] the portrayal of Singapore national identity in terms of "meritocracy"'.[22] The 'ethnically neutral' state was the result.

Singapore was further urbanised, with traditional social organisations deliberately replaced with economically rational forms based on function and efficiency which could support the universal industrial society. The Singaporean would be able to speak English as the 'neutral' language of development, have access to technology and be interested in collective consumption. By 1966, the campaign to promote Malay as the national language (*bahasa kebangsaan*) had ceased.

While the PAP was undertaking a recognisable modernist revamp of culture via capitalist institutions and practices, it is the *level* of brash confidence expressed that deepens their national culturalism's significance. S. Rajaratnam, the first-generation leadership's *philosophe*, articulates most crisply the promulgated cultural policy. He gives us the strongest early statement — in 1960 — of the socio-cultural engineering that will pervade Singaporeans' lives: 'Malayan culture, for us, is an essential part of nation-building. It is … an instrument for reshaping society along lines we think desirable.'[23] The government has 'modern methods of propaganda to persuade them [Malayans] to recognise this [common] Malayan culture and give their loyalty to it'.[24] The idea of culture as the superstructural expression of an economic base is dismissed; instead, culture will be mobilised to *create* the base.[25]

Later, Rajaratnam also articulates the advantages of embracing the new global economy — and, also, of the dangers. In 1972, he addressed the Singapore Press Club on Singapore as a 'Global City', effectively delivering an early and prescient manifesto for flexible accumulation: 'As far back as 1968, it was noted that the growth rate of internationalised production exceeded the growth rate of their exports' — and this form of production was 'only in its infancy'; by 'linking up with international and multinational corporations, Singapore not only becomes a component of [the] world economy, but ... catch[es] up or at least keep[s] apace with the most advanced ... societies'.[26] These are now-familiar goals of other aspiring global cities. The dangers? 'The political, social and cultural problems [which may result], I believe, would be far more difficult to handle [than Separation]'.[27] Therefore, 'it is up to us to equip our people intellectually and spiritually to make the Global City into the Heavenly City that prophets and seers have dreamt of since time immemorial'.[28]

The invoking of a simultaneously technologised but still humanistic Cosmopolis — indicating an overall harmony between the order of the heavens and the order of human society[29] — can only sound ironic in the light of the PAP's consistent elevation of the material over the spiritual and the humanistic in their social order. And the irony deepens for Rajaratnam, the PAP leader most committed to an authoritarian Utopia, for that 'equipping' does occur, but in a form he later found unpalatable.

In 1990, with the Asian values discourse well-entrenched in the city-state's life, Rajaratnam was forced to write in public in the *Straits Times* to voice his concern with the hyphenated form of the Singapore identity being promulgated to better culturally anchor the citizenry to the nation-state: 'At this rate, there will be a long ethnic queue of Singapore citizens proclaiming Sikh identity, ... Hokkien identity — and goodbye Singapore identity.'[30]

The Critique of the Industrial West's Universality

The 'equipping' comes about with the state's interest in 'Asianising Singapore',[31] which was a complete turnaround from the previous policing of the traditional. The attempt to universalise cultures seemed to foster 'rootlessness' — and so, it looked as if capitalist participation now required stable notions of individual and collective Asian-ness that can express grounded, inherent meanings. Public rhetoric rejecting the West as Universal Civilisation resulted, even while a discernable modernising continued. While internal cultural dissonance relating to the nation-building agenda contributed to the change, it is apparent that there were overlaps with concerns with the state's consistent external orientation and ongoing relationship with global capitalist forces. What marks the difference of PAP culturalist practice at this stage from older modernist use and abuse of collective memory is the willingness to have combined (if superficial) national and transnational/regional ideas of collective identity and memory.

I will outline the significant changes from the late 1970s, along with some of the resistances within society,[32] and then proceed to suggest some of the shifts in external factors to which the government was adapting.

By the mid-1970s, with the economy firmer, a West-toxification discourse arose, with increasing opposition being made between 'Western' and 'Asian' values. On the one hand, citizens were enjoined to abjure the heart's dictates and to encourage their children to learn English, the language of rational science and trade — and of deculturation — and to not be sentimental about the impending loss of non-English medium schools in 1987. On the other hand, families were said to be weakened by what Prime Minister Lee called 'fundamental social and cultural changes':[33] the loss of commitment to the family and to society at large for a hedonistic individualism gained from the media. The debate's élite origins are clear, as there had been no public discussion of Confucianism before 1979.[34] Nation-building now required 'cultural ballast'.

By 1982, the General Certificate of Education 'Ordinary'-level religious knowledge courses for 15- to 16-year-olds such as Bible Knowledge, Buddhist Knowledge and Confucian Ethics encouraged individual ethnic communities to 'recuperate' their individualised cultural identities. In the late 1970s, educational reform had already begun that gave a renewed role to vernacular languages and to Mandarin — not a dominant Singapore Chinese language — and to the 'Asian values' they encapsulated. While one sociologist suggests that this stood for a 'revitalization movement',[35] the religious-studies curricula that resulted filtered out folk beliefs and the more 'superstitious' elements, so that there simultaneously was a 'rationalization of religion'.[36]

Soon, ethnically delineated self-help groups were encouraged into being by the state: first MENDAKI — an acronym for Majlis Pendidikan Anak-Anak Islam, or the Council on Education for Malay Children — for the Malay-Muslims in 1981, followed by groups for both Indians and the Chinese. Also, significantly, in 1979, the 'Speak Mandarin' campaign took off, which alienated minority groups from the nation, even if their respective 'mother tongues' were encouraged.

The rationale for bilingualism (language policy was a key area of ethnic management since the 1960s), the reasoning for which in any case varied with historical context,[37] also changed in the late 1970s. Lee told the Malay Teachers' Union in 1978 that cultural homogenisation would receive less stress: 'In 1959 ... I believed we could encourage our people to unite as a society which would be more closely knit and uniform, with more or less the same ... thinking; but after five years, I came to the conclusion that if we want to develop a Singapore society of which the people can be proud, we cannot impose a model for our people'; so, instead, 'Let each language, culture, religion follow its own course.'[38] While the state's supposed *laissez-faire* attitude must be qualified, the move away from the 'ethnically neutral' state is clear. While the belief in universal and instrumental reason was not lessened, organicism, apparently rehabilitated from the 'inside', is dragooned to support an *Asian*-Singapore modern.

In January 1991, a White Paper on Shared Values — which emphasised collective behaviour in formulations such as 'nation before community and society above self' — was debated in Parliament. This change, it was hoped, would mollify the Malays, who had reacted negatively to the seeming elevation of Chinese-ness to national-cultural primacy. Still, the Shared Values project did not differ significantly in content from the religious knowledge project. It was allowed to lapse into obscurity, though issues of a deep Asian-ness in common between groups were still advanced. With a large logical leap, it was argued that Confucianism was *pan*-Asian as it was part of Japanese and Korean cultures — presumably, if cautiously articulated, this pan-Asianism could be fitted within a renewed promulgation of the old 'ethnic mosaic' pattern of plural co-existence.[39]

The 1980s national-culturalist direction was a sea-change in the management of ethnicity, suggesting that a problem had developed in what it meant to be an ideal-type 'modern' Singaporean — one deterritorialised and hence free from the past's stultifying burdens so inimical to industrial modernity — in the 1970s, at the point when economic growth had become marked.

A key moment enabling the self-fashioning of national-regional Asian identity was Japan's success, which offered the opportunity to say that the form of capitalism adhered to in the 1960s was *only* a 'Western' form. The indigenised Japanese version stressed state direction of enterprise, consensus, loyalty to the company, and so forth (elements of which Singapore had tried to use from 1981 in management forms such as 'Quality Control Circles'); such cultural differences were packaged for world consumption in Harvard academic Ezra Vogel's non-fiction bestseller, *Japan as Number One* (1979). In the same year, Herman Kahn wrote in *World Economic Development: 1979 and Beyond* of a link between neo-Confucianism and the Japanese success.

Thus, a non-retrograde ethnically *Asian* capitalist mode — an Asian modern which in the 1990s becomes *the* Asian modern — was conceivable: Orientalist conceptions of 'Asia' were reversed and married to the modern.

Also, the economic opportunities that arose in China in 1978, as Deng Xiaopeng implemented economic reforms based on the mini-dragons' success, were not lost on Lee and the PAP. The fading of communist revolution meant that Chinese-Confucianist culture could be highlighted for capitalist opportunities.[40] The older discourse on capitalist value and values could now be interrogated: full socio-cultural homogenisation may lead to decaying Western habits inimical to development.

The discussion of Confucianism eventually did move away from the inoculation against Western values to Confucianism offering a positive work ethic appropriate for Asian capitalisms. And as the discourse moved towards the more generic Asian values enshrined in the Shared Values project, the key influential book became George Lodge and Ezra Vogel's edited *Ideology and National Competitiveness* (1987), which posited two ideal-types, the communitarian and individualistic national ideologies. Lodge in 1991 became the Lee Kuan Yew Distinguished Visitor. Yet another irony surfaces here: Asians now 'learn' from the 'West' what the 'West' in turn 'learned' from Asia. Lodge and Vogel write: 'Can the West learn from the Asians for so long as they learned from us?'[41]

Thus the Asian values positioning was enabled by shifts in the global economy since the 1970s which allowed for a multicentric economic order. As I mentioned in chapter 3, a 'flexible' regime of accumulation came about, versus the more nationally rooted, standardised mass production of the oligopolistic corporation predicated upon the labour practices, consumption habits and the technological innovations of 'Fordism-Keynesianism'. Companies started setting up factories in developing countries with cheaper labour. Developing societies also began to export substantial manufactures back to the advanced economies. Transport and communications growth meant tiny, semi-peripheral units like Hong Kong and Singapore became hubs in the new capitalist flows. Japan, as the first modernised Asian country, became the (problematic) first country (given memories of the Second World War) of the 'New Asia'.

Other chinks in the West's industrial armour could be seen. The collapse of Bretton Woods and the OPEC oil crisis produced volatility in the major economies. US involvement in the Vietnam War also created instability. Manufacturers and financial institutions compensated for domestic instability by seeking wider outlets during the inflationary 1970s, leading to large Third World bank loans. Acceleration in the internationalisation of the financial markets took place via market deregulation in the late 1970s, though the Louvre and Plaza Accords reined other volatile currency markets in the 1980s. 'De-industrialisation' occurred in the UK and the USA, and long-term unemployment in Western Europe, leading to the weakening of the welfare state which had promised security for all, and had been (in theory at least) a model for many postcolonial leaders.

As noted, Singapore's 'emergence' occurs in the 1970s, in the midst of the above changes, and the timing of the emergence carry important implications for the change in earlier national-culturalist policies. Despite the government's strong industrialisation push, for the second half of the 1960s, the economy still relied heavily on staple exports, rubber and petroleum. It was not until 1973 — when the industrial West's ability to represent itself as the unquestioned development standards becomes uncertain — that direct manufactured goods exceed primary commodity products (excluding petroleum).[42] And thus, the point when Singapore firmly transcends Third Worldism is also when cultural distinctiveness becomes incrementally and increasingly marshalled to sustain competitiveness.

Negotiating Homogenisation and Differentiation as Neo-Traditional Modernity

What were the practices that constituted a neo-traditional modernity? The newer economistic national culturalism included a simultaneous homogenisation and differentiation. Ethnic groups were further differentiated and the cultural opposition between 'East' and 'West' emphasised. However, there was an attempt to rationalise each ethnic group and the interior of their traditions, mainly among the Chinese. And while cultural memory now had a role, it was circumscribed so that a selective historical amnesia could still be encouraged. A neo-traditional modernity hence required the irrational be suitably domesticated to be truly modern, indicating a continuity in the state's flexible national culturalism, even as it traversed new terrain.

The incorporation of the 'irrational' was possible because, arguably, many basic values and structures of an industrial-consumerist society had been internalised by the population by the 1980s. That is to say, in key ways, Singapore had been completely modernised. An Asian values discourse and hyphenated-subject strategy which promised a non-deracinating modernity — a wish to have one's cake and eat it, if ever — was presented to citizens, whose collective resolve had to be further emboldened to continue the modernity race. The Institute of East Asian Philosophies was started under Dr. Goh Keng Swee's auspices to give academic weight and intellectual conviction to the endeavours.[43] The contradictions show a modernist mentality functioning in a fragmented world, desiring harmoniously organised masses and order even if, by the late 1990s, the state started planning for a less-regulated, post-industrial economy in the shape of knowledge-based industries, and for the 'creative', individualist freedom to encourage such industries.

Lee Kuan Yew's preface to the *Report on the Ministry of Education 1978* indirectly admits that turning of Singapore into an industrial-consumerist society 'has resulted in startling social transformations. This makes more important the teacher's role as moral and social anchormen'.[44] A major goal now was: 'No child should leave school after 9 years without carrying the "soft-ware" of his culture programmed into his consciousness.'[45] Lee's well-known modernist-scientific imagery is now applied — jarringly but fittingly, given the desired neo-traditionalism — to that which is usually thought of as that opposite to the mechanistic: 'culture'. The teaching of 'mother tongues' would *re-create* local identities and values, though Lee thought of it as reinforcing such value systems: 'The principal value of teaching the second language is in the imparting of moral values and understanding of cultural traditions.'[46]

The major first-generation PAP leaders were well-aware of industrialisation's problems. Dr. Toh Chin Chye, once deputy premier, wrote that 'as technology spreads the cultural differences between cosmopolitan cities tend to narrow. ... It is the rate at which modernisation spreads that produces "culture shock". It creates problems of adaptation'.[47]

Lee's antidote to deculturation also entails a selective blending of traditional and modern cultures:

> The best of the East and of the West must be blended to advantage in the Singaporean. Confucianist ethic, Malay traditions, and the Hindu ethos must be combined with sceptical Western methods in the search for truth. We have to discard obscurantist and superstitious beliefs and practices of the East, as we have to reject the passing fads of the West.[48]

Despite the commitment to 're-racination', the Orient is *still* seen as superstitious, pre-modern and therefore partially irrational.

Part of the need for change seemed to be that the universal meritocracy of the 1970s was not in itself a viable long-term nation-building strategy — the dominance of English did not satisfy those who supported Chinese-medium schools,[49] and social mobility eluded the Malays. A new national socio-ethnic containment rationale had to be formulated that could sustain the stability for development; thus the oddly rational emphasis on the primordial in the shape of local cultures and history. The actual Goh *Report* reiterates this emphasis: 'One way to overcoming the dangers of deculturalisation is to teach children the historical origins of their culture. Chinese pupils could be taught in the Chinese language in secondary schools early Chinese history ....'[50] Language usage, tied into a notion of history, therefore was to be key in neo-traditional modernisation in the late 1970s and the 1980s. Mandarin was promoted at the expense of other Chinese languages (also known derogatively as 'dialects') as part of this move towards a neo-traditional modernity, and this led to widespread dissatisfaction, given the emotional identitarian baggage involved.

One of Lee's calls to make Mandarin the Chinese *lingua franca* occurred in March 1978, in similar addresses to crowds at Tanjong Pagar (his constituency in Chinatown) and a *Chap Goh Mei* (Chinese new year fifteenth day) gathering at the Istana (or 'palace', the former Government House): 'Heaven forbid that we lose our own cultures and fail to absorb the [deeper] culture, the spirit, the values, the philosophy of life of the English-speaking civilizations.'[51] But, in order to achieve this biculturalism — as we've already seen, a sign of the modern in our midst — bilingualism must remove children from their parents' dialects, or we get a 'fractured multilingual society'. That is, an *internal homogenisation* was required, retooled for a more literate — and docile — Chinese-ness: 'To be literate, they must be Mandarin-speaking, able to read the books, ... so that they know what a good upright man should do ....' Further, 'why cut him off from the wider world of Mandarin speakers and workers beyond Singapore' — a gesture to a trans-local Chinese-ness (and business opportunities) unthinkable during the Cold War of the 1960s, indeed unthinkable before China's economic reforms. The state's economic rationality had not simply gone soft.

By December 1978, the government announced that nine élite 'Special Assistance Plan' (SAP) schools were to be created, with Chinese and English to be taken at the same level. This, the press noted, was an effective admission that Chinese education as it was no longer would exist, given the number of important Chinese-medium schools that were selected to take part in the Plan. Journalist Ilsa Sharp noted the irony involved in preserving a modicum of Chinese education when, in the 1950s, the Chinese commitment to social involvement had led to riots by the Singapore Chinese Middle School Students' Union: 'Perhaps paradoxically, it is for this very sense of social involvement that Mr. Lee Kuan Yew and his colleagues feels [*sic*] the Chinese schools should be valued, and he himself recalled the historical background in his speech at this year's National Day Rally.'[52] Lee had said that in the traditional Chinese value system 'society takes first precedence over everything else'. With leftist Chinese-ness increasingly dissipated, we can now desire this part of the past.

With the above, we get an implicit critique of Western 'individualism' — in some way, the progressive and collectivist British West Lee once admired had let him down, degenerating into hedonistic individualism, and Singapore must re-invent itself apart from this failed West. Sharp quotes Lee saying that he hopes his proposed new Singaporean would say, as he described his own son saying, 'I am me: I have come to learn your science, your technology and how you made this breakthrough into industrial production .... I have not come here to have long hair, ... [and] wear T-shirts with strange slogans on them.' And thus, Lee allows in the Asian irrational so that we can be *really* modern: 'young

Singaporeans need the protection of traditional values, including religion, to protect them against the perils of their increasingly affluent society' — in order that they may become more affluent. The race to be modern is run, it can be said, on a treadmill.

It becomes clear that neo-traditional modernity itself is part of the global revamping of Liberal economics and values that the Reaganite and Thatcherite revolutions signified. The rebirth of 'Victorian values' which stressed self-help was the equivalent of the rise of Asian-Confucian values, along with the dream of Victorian free markets (see chapter 3). Singapore's own cultural history, naturally, is mediated by British imperialism and thus British history. What sort of past and tradition did these three ideological soul mates — Lee Kuan Yew, Ronald Reagan and Margaret Thatcher — look for through the 1980s? If Britain at the turn of the nineteenth century saw Socialism, as a political theory and movement, with some obvious success replace Liberalism, because Socialism had a critique of Liberalism which appealed to a level of social explanation the latter lacked, then what we have in the 1980s is a sort of reversal of this transformation. Lee, unlike Reagan or Thatcher, though, still was interested in some form of collectivism, even while he did not want 'lazy' welfarism. However, as collectivism was discredited in neo-liberal discourse, it needed to be sneaked back in by Lee, albeit in a weakened communitarian conception of Asian values.[53]

In December 1983, the government announced the impending arrival of 'national stream' schools using English as the first language and the eventual elimination of non-English-language medium schools, though bilingualism remained important. Thus another intensification of the tension in a cultural formation that is to help citizens survive the technological era: *more* Asianisation with *more* English-language usage under the umbrella of national integration. One of the prime minister's responses to the expected dissatisfaction allows us to unearth his notions of culture and history undergirding his neo-traditionalism.

To parents at a Chinese New Year's dinner in February 1984, Lee asserted that 'A culture [in an anthropological sense] incorporates all the shared knowledge, expectations and beliefs in a group. Language gives access to the literature which expresses a culture, but language is not culture.'[54] This flatly contradicts the Goh *Report*'s rationale for language learning. Thus, though Chinese could no longer be the first language of instruction, that was not the end of 'profoundly traditional Chinese values'. The question is more how historical values are to be transmitted. The Chinese have no strong religion with a universal core which, in the case of Christianity, remained 'the same faith' even though the bible is translated into 'hundreds of languages'. Most Chinese are folk religionists who 'neither read holy books nor say prayers every day'. In that sense, they have a weak culture, not one — we may observe and note — as modern as the West's.

The nexus of tradition (and thus of culture) lies, unsurprisingly, in placing 'the interests of the family and society above those of the individual': such values are 'crucial to the continuity of any civilisation'. Lee adds: '[Chinese people in] Hongkong, Taipeh [*sic*] and Guangzhou are different ... but there are common features in all of them.'

What tradition is *not* is the cultural memory of a previous way of life, of 'old Chinatown, the bustle of lights of the street hawkers packing the roadsides selling New Year fruits and flowers': 'There are more fundamental attributes in our way of life than the sound of crackers, ... however much joy these memories may bring.' This history is not real history but an-always-already sepia-toned nostalgia and therefore a 'soft' view of cultural identity.

Among the weakest links in transmitting culture are women, freed by economic empowerment from the home: 'Working mothers who do not spend enough time with their children, plus the break-up of the extended families — these two changes are the real dangers to the transmission of our traditional values, our culture.'[55]

PAP ideological pragmatism is, with Lee, married to what many would consider a dodgy social biology: families and mothers — these are the sources of values and identity, not history or culture. This would contribute towards understanding why, without any intended irony, the city core's various historical districts, where many older markers of Singapore's collective urban memory are gone, with some 'surviving' older buildings have in fact been torn down and then 'reconstructed' — one set of colonial-era urban structures were demolished to build an underground car park, then rebuilt and covered under air-conditioned canopies[56] — can be said to bear the signs of the nation's pioneering poverty-stricken migrants, and even while there is a stronger emphasis than ever in the nation since 1997 on a multi-ethnic and national rooted-ness. The 'real' past lies elsewhere.

Re-Emphasising the Nation and the Universal

While the changes in Singapore's flexible national culturalism seem confusing, what remains consistent is an economic rationality, even while difference via the ethnicisation of the national is produced. In a sense, this is not contradictory at all, for global capitalism in a multicentric order that affirms universal capitalism's production of difference in the name of competition.

However, the 1980s governmentality that combined the formation of a disciplinary society with an idea of pan-Asian capitalist culture had started to weaken by the early 1990s. Still, in a quieter way, save for then-senior minister Lee Kuan Yew's globally proclaimed opinions, national culturalism still proceeded — but now via a simultaneous affirmation of the national in conjunction with the *global*, rather than the *regional*. This was prescient, given how problematic the Asian-Pacific 'triad power' was about to become in the wake of the pending Asian economic crisis, and given an already poor community sense in the Pacific.

In September 1996, during the Teachers' Day Rally, then-prime minister Goh Chok Tong spoke of the need of a 'National Education' programme in schools. A newspaper survey indicated that the younger citizenry's consciousness of Singapore's post-Second World War trials and tribulations was not strong. Goh argued that the 'basic facts' of nationhood, and the principles of meritocracy and multiracialism have to be rediscovered and a national symbology firmly foregrounded for the young to see.[57] Issues of ethnicity, history and meritocracy now became removed from the realm of Asian regional identity and re-inserted into the realm of the national. Of course, there was no discussion of the state's socio-cultural engineering role in the national amnesia.

The launch of the National Education Plan took place in May 1997 under the auspices of Lee Hsien Loong, the deputy prime minister (since 2004 prime minister). He told school principals and teachers that one key part of the national memory *not* to be erased was that of thorny, past inter-ethnic relations: 'Amnesia is not an option.'[58] In general, the plan is 'to equip ... [the young] with the basic attitudes, values and instincts which make them Singaporeans'. This Lee calls our 'common culture', and says it is the 'DNA to be passed from one generation to the next'. The concept 'common culture' — with its organicist implications, as with the senior Lee, still jarringly used for a rationalist commitment to cultural identity formation — is continued from the Asian values discourse. A multicultural and historicised sense of nationhood, and the PAP's established ideology of economic survival, seems to be at the core of National Education.

At the same time, Singapore campaigned hard to host the first ministerial meeting of the World Trade Organisation in December 1996. And as the Asian currency crisis broke out in July 1997, the PAP government demonstrated without any doubt its official commitment to a universal neo-liberalism and the institutions of the global economy, despite widespread criticism of the International Monetary Fund's (IMF) handling of the crisis. The national and the global become linked concerns.

It would have been hard, in any case, for Singapore's leadership to have regional solidarity with all three affected Southeast Asian countries. While Thailand responded to their IMF package stolidly, Indonesia did not, and displayed erratic economic and political behaviour in the midst of the crisis.[59] Senior Minister Lee Kuan Yew himself (since 2004, 'minister mentor'), while not personally abandoning his commitment to Asian values or the relevance of regional institutions such as the Association of Southeast Asian Nations

(ASEAN), acerbically responded to a *Time* magazine interviewer's statement that public officials' corruption occurs 'because this is the Asian way': 'Then you have this kind of crisis.' Lee affirmed the need for universal business standards: 'If it is the best way of doing business, it doesn't matter where it comes from.'[60] So, what emerges from the crisis is an affirmation of the nation and its place within contemporary, universal capitalism. The production of national identity and culture must not shut down borders and be seen as irrational (as former Indonesian president Suharto's behaviour was seen to be). Overly rooted identities may scare off free-floating capital. In fact, the crisis has led the PAP government to further (if cautious) de-regulation of the banking sector.

A major if not the only concern that underlies the National Education thrust thus is the balance of identity versus economic survivalist concerns. Former information and arts minister George Yeo has spoken of the need for 'cultural reserves' in the face of globalisation trends — though no retreat from that process was possible.[61] And Teo Chee Hean, then the education minister, during the Budget Debate in March 1998, indicated that '[p]roviding a good education' is, more than ever, an 'investment': 'The currency crisis and its ripple effects underscore the importance of good fundamentals.'[62] And National Education as part of 'good fundamentals' will 'help our young understand the challenge and constraints confronting Singapore'.[63]

Thus, a final irony: the National Education plan and narrative returns us to the type of specificity and memory that the PAP initially wanted to get away from through its national culturalism, though of course the national narrative preferred entrenches the PAP as an essential part of the nation. One guesses that the PAP government has discovered that building a national identity erected on the basis of multinational investment attracted and protected by a developmental city-state, any more than some abstract notion of a 'global community', may not work in driving a people on after the obvious marks of underdevelopment are eradicated. National culturalism must remain flexible so that it can offer the 'moral' or the 'spiritual' to further sustain discipline for a labour force that competes within global capitalism.

It can be said that in Singapore, in order to catch-up not only with the West, but also with later modernisers like Japan, the PAP government embraced the destabilisations of capitalist modernity for a place in what turns out in the end to be the neo-liberal sun. By the 1980s, this came to mean that the earlier national-culturalist experimentation with a more definitively universalist orientation became a peculiar simultaneous denial of and encouragement for the search for roots. That is, the state learnt that forging ahead in the game of free-market neo-liberalism required Asian difference (and *différance*, it could be added), with the result being an official (postmodern) pastiche Asian identity and identities overlaid on a universal, modernising project committed to capitalism as the Real.

To follow from the last statement, a final question at the close of this chapter may be: does Singapore's national culturalism transcend the level of pastiche and become a significant site of cultural practice and transformation? Singapore itself cannot be seen merely as pastiche, even given the comments often made of 'the city resembles a clean and efficient theme park', the result of deliberate, non-organic nation-building. At many levels, the nation self-consciously coheres as a society.

The *larger* discourse on modernity enshrined in the national culturalism used by the PAP government does represent, I believe, a significant site of cultural practice. The transformative power of the *specific* East Asian or Asian values discourse in the 1980s–1990s national culturalism is less clear, though even that should not be ruled out — predicting the future is always tricky.

It has been argued that the historical juncture we find ourselves at is one in which economics has come to overlap with culture, and that culture itself has become profoundly economic or commodity oriented. It seems likely that within such a context, in a world where 'delinking', as Samir Amin calls it,[64] seems increasingly difficult, *arriviste* societies such as Singapore will find future opportunities to use the signifier 'Asia', with its manifold meanings, to continue to function distinctively within the web of global capitalism. The Asian success stories have given many countries a taste particularly of the consumerist pleasures and modern conveniences connected with 'advanced societies', and it is unlikely that many newly arrived or arriving societies will in the long-run desire to return to the older ways of national being, whatever the difficulties of the present.

6

Staging Cultural Fragments, the Singaporean Eunuch and the Asian Lear

In the Introduction, I observed that one way of the ways economic and political power functions is through a global West. Capitalism's development in the 'imperial present', as Fernando Coronil puts it, has led to the West's 'invisible reterritorialisation in the elusive figure of the globe[, and this] … conceals [the] diffuse[d] transnational financial and political networks that integrate metropolitan and peripheral dominant social sectors'.[1] The consequence is that 'the image of a unified globe dispenses with the notion of an outside'.[2]

A number of East and Southeast Asian nations from the 1980s actually have benefited from the shift by the West into the globe — not only the capitalist mini-dragon Singapore, but also the not-quite-post-socialist Vietnam and, along with them and above all, post-World Trade Organisation China. They desire a continued or new part in the current global order. Such desires do not in themselves lead to a lessened sense of the present imperialist modality of domination — even if such 'domination' now also requires collusion from their 'victims'. These countries of course relate to the 'West' dispersed into the globe in varied ways, and with varying levels of comfort, but common to all of them is a willingness, to a greater or lesser degree, to participate in the transnational financial and even political networks that connect metropole to semi-periphery.

The economic and cultural dispersal of the West into the globe itself engenders new forms of cultural difference and production that can link various regional identities into what are (still) limited cosmopolitan versions of 'Asia' that attempt to contend with their subordinate positions within the global West, and also the cosmopolitan culture related with it. Western cosmopolitanism, it has been noted, 'is *local* while denying its own local character' — indeed, such cosmopolitanism serves 'as a relay for the center's values'.[3] The values here naturally are the values of the Western metropole, urban centres with an intellectual and cultural predominance because of their wealth and imperialist history. The (now-defunct) East Asian Miracle gave some Asian urban centres the increased confidence that perhaps they could now be influentially cosmopolitan in the same way. The previous chapter discussed how at the state level, tiny Singapore during the 1980s–90s had been reterritorialised and re-ethnicised in the name of Asian values after a decade and a half of active cultural deterritorialisation. This state-led culturalism contributed towards such an alternative cosmopolitan identity of 'East Asia'.

This chapter will examine two Asian theatre practitioners — that is to say, two actors at the non-state level — who, to a significant extent as a reaction to the Singapore state, have created 'limited cosmopolitan' versions of regional Asia that are connected to but simultaneously contend with the global West and the People's Action Party (PAP) state's version of Asia. That is to say, the two attempted a *counter-reterritorialisation* and re-imagining of the entity Asia, along with the city-state's place in it. They are Singapore's theatre doyen, the late Kuo Pao Kun (1939–2002), and the rising intercultural theatre director, Ong Keng Sen. Kuo's play, *Descendants of the Eunuch Admiral* (1995), written both in Mandarin-Chinese and English, worked to extend Singaporean cultural memory in the face of culturally fragmenting economic development by envisaging a fractured, non-statist Singapore-Asian and, indeed, global humanism, even as the playwright depicts the inescapability of servitude to the state and global markets. Ong directed the English-language version of *Descendants* in 1995 and 1996, and thereafter proceeded to direct a hugely ambitious 'intercultural' Asian *Lear* project. In a way, Kuo's *Descendants* and intellectual reflections and Ong's self-conscious status as an Asian 'modernised' into speaking English as his native tongue enabled the Asian *Lear* that the Japan Foundation Asia Center (JFAC) produced in 1997 and 1999. JFAC financed its first play to the tune of US$1.2 million as a way of conceiving a 'New Asia' out of various traditional Asian components. This was not a recapturing of a pre-modern past, but imagined a 'present moment of the past'[4] and a 'mind of Asia' more problematic than even T. S. Eliot's attempt at recuperating a war-fragmented 'mind of Europe'. Producer Hata Yuki[5] wanted 'Asian artists to present a new direction for Asian theater'[6] and Ong, hailing from modernised and multi-ethnic Singapore, with the oldest official multicultural policy in the region, seemed the obvious choice to help show the way.

The relative success, challenges or difficulties of such theatrical attempts to imagine such a cosmopolitan Asia must be considered within the already existing constraints of the logic of dispersed Western-now-globalised capitalist modernity in relation to culture. *Lear*'s thrust, in particular, transpires within the desire of wealthier Asian nations to take their cultural place in the New World Order. This is to say, both Kuo and Ong have ironically 'benefited' from the state's authorisation of culture that came about in the PAP government's strategy of deploying culture via their identitarian Asian-values discourse as a means to maintain competitiveness within global capitalism.

While the production of *Lear* critically exceeds the consistent instrumentalist logic of culture and race, as managed and homogenised by the PAP state in the interests of becoming modern, and also indicates some of the impasses in this statist identity politics, it does not subvert the state's identity strategies either in its earlier deterritorialising or later reterritorialising formats. Still, *Lear* is an *intra-Asian* (if not a South-South) rather than a North-South attempt to ground a pan-Asian space utilising a cultural practice that tries to transcend national notions of collective memory and create cross-cultural connections. This means that while we should not think of the world in terms of the West and the Rest, neither should we think of it in any overtly direct way as 'the West is all-in-all'. Globalisation dialectically fosters multiple cross-cultural and cross-border dialogues out 'there' by Asians within a potentially emerging Asian metropole in relation to the modern-capitalist part of the West inextricably in their midst.

Modernising/'Westernising' Singapore

Chinese-educated but bilingual and bicultural playwright-director Kuo Pao Kun was born in Hebei province, China, in 1939 and immigrated to colonial Singapore in 1949. Ong Keng Sen, in contrast, was born in Singapore in the 1960s, and is (what used to be called) 'English-educated'. Despite the differences in cultural background, there are common strands in their work, the result, to a large extent, of functioning in the distinct experiment in modernisation that is postcolonial Singapore. The inexact epithet 'Westernised' — once a synonym for 'modernisation' — is often used to describe the city-state's Anglo-Asian cultural nexus. While we perhaps do not quite yet have a lexicon to get past that and another unsatisfactory term produced by postcolonial cultural theory in the 1980s, 'hybrid', what can be said is that Singapore is part of that 'global' sphere that the West has dispersed itself into. Kuo's and Ong's locations within this experiment in modernisation/'Westernisation' is crucial to understanding how an idea and cultural ideal of the global and of 'Asia' can reach out of the former British colony.

Kuo's moral and authoritative stature among visual and theatre artists comes from his combined activist and artistic record. He was a minor high-school activist in the turbulent 1950s, against the Cold War backdrop of the Malayan Emergency. In 1958, he attended the National Institute of Dramatic

Arts (NIDA), Sydney. Returning to Singapore in 1965, the year Singapore left the Federation of Malaysia, he set up the Singapore Performing Arts School (later renamed the Performing Arts Studio, and thereafter the Practice Theatre School). In 1976, along with his wife, Kuo was interned without trial for allegedly being a member of the Malayan People's Liberation League.[7] Among other things, he had had a radical social-theatre practice that engaged with the displacement and the exploitation involved in modernisation.[8] The PAP government released him in October 1980, but did not reinstate his revoked citizenship until 1992 — and then only upon application.

Both Kuo and Ong were involved in the early attempts to culturally relocalise deterritorialised Singapore. After his release, Kuo moved away from a singular approach to theatre based on the need to reform society to a more plural comprehension of art's relation to society, one not tied in to specific ideological goals,[9] even as he continued experimenting with a multilingual form of theatre first started in the mid-1960s.[10] A groundbreaking multilingual theatre that re-imagined the multi-ethnic Singapore past to include the possibility of trans-ethnic understanding (*Mama Looking for Her Cat,* 1988) was one result. Other plays examined the destruction of culture, cultural memory, and identity in the wake of a totalising statist modernisation (*The Coffin Is Too Big for the Hole,* 1985; *Lao Jiu,* 1990[11]). Apparently without any irony, the state awarded him the national Cultural Medallion in 1989, while he was effectively stateless, and in 1997 he received the French Ordre des Arts et des Lettres.

Ong Keng Sen read law at the National University of Singapore and later had Kuo as an early mentor. He then studied performance at the Tisch School at New York University. His present career follows that of some German directors: Ong is 'king' as director, and the text becomes the vehicle for his interpretative concept. Apart from *Descendants,* he also directed Kuo's *Lao Jiu* (1993) and *The Spirits Play* (2000). The artistic director of TheatreWorks (Singapore) since 1988 — one of the three earliest professional theatre companies formed in the 1980s — he started off his career with the then-innovative, camp, nostalgic and partially indigenised Broadway-style musical, *Beauty World* (1988),[12] depicting a risqué 1960s Singapore. Ong then proceeded to translate Singapore-Asian multicultural issues (which he classifies as artificial differences produced by the state) into highbrow and multicultural (later intercultural) 'postmodern' theatre that made increasing claims to represent a 'New Asia ... defined by Asians'. To transcend the differences that make up 'Asia', Ong says he eschews the 'pursuit of the authentic[, for that] is an illusion. ... To portray Asia, you need to represent the complexity of today, where purity is no longer the truth.'[13] The generational transition from Kuo's rooted-but-exploratory and open Chinese-ness to Ong's deliberate Asian cosmopolitanism indicates how the absorbed

West has effectively reformed locality and culture, such that Ong is comfortable as a native English-speaking Asian living not in the metropolitan West but in Southeast Asia.

The PAP government, without understatement, can be described as the Southeast Asian socio-cultural engineer *par excellence*. Since 1959, it has been involved in the radical attempt to create a society erected upon industrial modernity. State interventionism, as we have seen thus far in this book, was put in the service of capitalism.

The prioritisation of economic development via the attraction of foreign investment led to the suppression of leftist Chinese-speakers within the PAP itself, strong-arm action to quell communalism, clearing people off land to build new housing projects and industrial estates, and the 'modernising' of education (for example, the hacking back of the classical curriculum in Chinese-medium schools). After the 1963 general elections, with 47.4 percent of the vote, the PAP increasingly was in a better position to advance their development agenda. In the 1968 general elections, as the opposition withdrew from electoral politics, the PAP made a clean sweep of parliamentary seats. Development became more 'orderly', and Singapore became an early beneficiary of the systemic mutation of the older monopoly capitalism of the imperial era into the new high-tech, finance-driven and multinational form of capitalism. The ongoing eradication of the old colonial city became an expression of the spatial will-to-power of PAP modernisation (see chapter 4). The city-state's transformation into a hub for capitalist flows also was an escape from its limitations as a hinterlandless, mainly Chinese city 'stranded' in volatile Southeast Asia.

What of 'culture'? The state's *petit-bourgeois*, philistine modernity, with its objectifying, analytic, and pragmatic modes of thought, meant that high or mass art, history and memory at best played a weak role in transforming society until the 1980s, when commodified, official 'Asian traditions' were put on public offer. More recently, Americanised cultural forms that serve the PAP's utopian New Economy hopes have emerged. The concerted standardisation — even Taylorisation — was also the result of a conviction that over-strong cultural identities were inimical to modern life; they needed to be homogenised and sanitised, and the (officially delineated Chinese, Malay, Indian, and Other [CMIO]) races kept apart in the management of communalism.

Singapore's post-independence cultural development is at variance with that of both Western Europe and many plural postcolonial societies, where states maintained a 'national' material and immaterial historical heritage. In contrast the PAP state re-organised the body of cultural and symbolic significations for the logic of the commodity, while denying the importance of that body of meanings.

In the 1980s to the mid-1990s, it was discovered that the irrationality of 'race' and ethnic identities — instead of just being suppressed as that inimical to industrial development in the 1960s–70s — could be objectified for advancing development via an 'Asian values' discourse, asserting a neo-traditional modernity that was used to make more 'space' within global capitalism for Singapore (see chapter 5). 'We' in Asia apparently could have a modernity that was not alienated from our 'traditional' selves, unlike the West, and have a neo-traditional modernity. This turnabout in the state's thinking on 'culture' meant that whatever the profoundly shallow instrumentality that actually existed in this culturalist policy, it nevertheless authorised a less-constrained space for thinking through 'Asian' identity. The cultural identity and memory practices that emerged from the 1980s among visual arts and theatre practitioners — above all, in Kuo Pao Kun's multidisciplinary theatre practice from the mid-1980s onwards — was to a noticeable degree in reaction against the above-discussed complex modernising practices.[14]

Kuo, while recognising the real gain in national wealth, sees the modernising process as initiating a 'crisis'. He is known for the view that Singapore's multi-racial citizenry have been for 150 years 'racial outcasts, economic marginals and cultural orphans',[15] the result of a liberal colonial capitalism. The ruling political party exacerbated this colonial legacy through an ethnic management policy that separated the groups to maintain the peace; this strategy, while effective, also led to gulfs of ignorance and indifference. As Singapore was not 'radically homogenised by the English language or European culture', and since schools used English, Mandarin-Chinese, Malay, and Tamil, it was a shock in 1979, when for pragmatic reasons linked to the access of technology and information, Kuo said at a 1996 Australian theatre conference, English was made 'the national first language, relegating all ethnic ones to second language status. ... Has any other majority population ever committed such an extraordinary act of voluntary uprooting, preferring to its own language (a major world language) one which its former coloniser forced upon it?' (US, 168).

Despite Kuo's critique of the city-state's cultural policy that has led to the fragmenting of its various local ethnic cultures, his primary question for the arts remains a positive, humanistic one: can the 'creative energies of the people' now find embodiment through the cultural practices he chooses to call 'the Theatres that Remember, that Recreate, that Activate and that Transcend', for 'these will be the chief makers of the nation's new culture' (US, 174).

By the theatre that 'Remembers', Kuo refers to earlier forms of theatre — Chinese opera, folk theatre, etc. — that now are fatally wounded: the rational or 'pragmatic English-based education system' (US, 170) has turned the cultural and literal landscape into a *terra nullius*, hindering the re-discovery of this past.

But there is still the emerging theatre that 'Recreates', often done by young people, mixing symbols from the past and present, things Western and Asian, and various languages; this 'is the most rebellious and creative theatre in Singapore' (US, 171). The theatre that 'Activates' is the progressive theatre that existed from the 1930s to the 1970s, now gone because of substantial depoliticisation. However, it is the theatre that can 'Transcend' that will go beyond the barriers of 'race, culture and language' (US, 172).

Rather than bracketing sensitive interests, Kuo thinks that in order 'to consolidate [the] unity of pluralistic people, it is necessary to explore the complexity of life in greater depth and in greater vigour' (US, 172), if necessarily, in another dramatic format, that of 'allegorical' theatre. This is an important position to note if we are to understand the Asian-cosmopolitan desires of both *Descendants* and *Lear*. Allegorical theatre transcends not only state censorship, as we might expect, but

> also has the capacity to transcend specific reality because it uses symbols and signs, usually from classical sources, that enjoy some measure of universal understanding. The allegory extends to a cultural framework which relates it to a larger understanding. In such a context in Singapore where a number of major civilisations and cultures meet, the makers of Allegorical Theatre are likely to delve not only deeply but also broadly into world mythology, world history, world literature and world art, looking for a figurative idiom, an image which can be meaningful to a wide, if not universal audience. At the time of writing, my most recent play, *Descendants of the Eunuch Admiral*, explores the theme of castration. (US, 172–73)

From local present pasts, with memory links to older Asian homelands that Singaporeans are no longer part of, to universal or more global cultural possibilities: can we stitch our cultural memories together with other cultures for that which can transcend the sum total of Singapore's cultural fragments? It is a large humanistic articulation, arising from the midst of a narrowly modernised 'cultural desert' comprised, many critics charge, mainly of shopping centres — arising, in fact, *because* of that condition. This articulation will become the foundation upon which Kuo's *Descendants of the Eunuch Admiral* will be erected.

Kuo furthers the above position in his essay 'Contemplating an Open Culture' (1998). Singaporeans, he argues, should consider producing 'a new cultural parentage for themselves' *elsewhere* as well: 'History has proved that there is no way [Singaporeans] could reconnect to their parent cultures per se. However, having lost their own — cut loose and therefore set free — they have thus become natural heirs to all the cultures of the world.'[16] Deracination can serve as an impetus for the new. Such an extended 'Open Culture' indicates — despite the cost paid — an open-ness on his part to the creative possibilities of globalisation and the information age. The new catch phrases of the government — '*Creativity, Information Technology, Global Networking, … Rootedness …*' — represent concepts that 'can[not] be adequately addressed, not to mention resolved, without relating to one's attitude and treatment of culture(s)' (OC, 59).

If the mid-1980s saw a homogenised generation starting to produce 'fictions with sweeping perspectives of inter-racial landscapes … [and the] visual arts breaking barriers of traditional forms' as key manifestations of a nascent interest in '*memory search*' (OC, 55), then we can now 'desire to enter into other cultures and take them as part of one's own as well as extending oneself beyond one's own culture to evolve a larger, diverse one' (OC, 56). Ironically, eradicated memory and hypostatised ethnic identities lead Kuo to a startlingly anti-organicist if still humanistic proposal for cultural reinvention — one that values the virtues of fragments, the local and the subjugated, while not advocating a simple 'return' to them or to autonomous cultural spaces protected from colonial or Western modernity.[17] The starting question here becomes less 'whether one must first study one's own natural racial language[, though this concern is not dismissed,] but whether one is *deeply rooted in any culture*' (OC, 57). While modernisation is complete, and history and local 'mother' languages and cultures in their original condition are gone for good, this does not mean we must settle for the contentless and depthless-image versions of the postmodern.[18] Singaporeans should *positively* recuperate history and culture from *elsewhere*, if necessary — a transnational and trans-ethnic view on cultural development.

Kuo is no simple romantic, recalling a prelapsarian world where culture and society were 'organic', untouched by the bourgeois, postcolonial powers that be. Instead, his post-romantic vision suggests that what has been lost in the modern translation of Singapore may open up a direction leading elsewhere, a direction in which we, the translated objects of a late or catch-up modernity can become *subjects* potentially inhabiting a new cultural-historical space, one possibly even free from the ambiguities of nationalistic and territorial identities managed by the modern state. This is a space that is hard to delineate — Kuo seems only to gesture towards it; but it is a space not discontinuous with other historical patterns of identity formation, and his humanistic belief in art's role in helping to show the way forward remained intact in his post-romantic view of art itself. Kuo's notion is neither a universally normative ideal, nor is it a dematerialised idealism: he knows culture is not free of the determinations of politics and economics — the very postcolonial formation that is 'Singapore' is predicated on a consciousness of the inequality of the global order.

Ong, while responding to the same forces as a member of the new, homogenised generation, presents a different face from Kuo. One commentator notes that Ong's work 'is highly self-conscious, deeply Asian [in serious aspiration at least, I would qualify], and undeniably marketable with its high gloss — even glib — post-modernism'.[19] He is aware of postcolonial and postmodern theory and talks the talk of occupying multiple positionalities: Ong says he is at odds with his 'own hybridity — as a Chinese-Singaporean who speaks Chinese with my parents but conceptualises [his art] in English. Or going to a Methodist school and then praying at a family altar.'[20] Like Kuo, there is no simple return to before-modernisation; instead, Ong revels in claiming the contemporary and the West:

> *We have to be careful not to stereotype what is meant by 'Asian'* — that it has to be traditional or that it has to be filled with history. These definitions of Asian would immediately exclude you and I in the sense that we are English-speaking and completely contemporary. ... It is important to expand the meaning of 'Asian' rather than to limit it.[21]

While he shares a culturalism broadly similar to Kuo's, Ong manages to be both more and less ambitious in his culturalist goals: *more*, in his attempts to advance a New Asia agenda not only within Asia but into the West itself, questioning the latter's centrality and claiming aspects of it as part of his multiple identity; *less*, in his lack of Kuo's fractured if broad-based humanism.[22] Such differences give a pungency to Ong's *Descendants*, indicating a cross-cultural dialogue between a rooted Chinese intellectual reaching out to the world and a 'hyphenated' and 'deracinated' Chinese intent on staging an 'in-your-face' New Asia in English—an Asia without the need for the sort of ritualistic 'authenticity' that can be said to be part of Peter Brook's monumental *The Mahabharata* (1985), for instance.

Ong's and Kuo's moves towards re-conceiving Singapore's diverse cultures within a formative global culture — towards what I have called a limited cosmopolitanism, but one that is explicitly cognizant of the dominant Western cosmopolitanism — represents the need to reconfigure the separatist and official Chinese-Malay-Indian-Other multiculturalism of the PAP government and the Singaporean identity question itself, along with the sort of present pasts artistic work might employ as a panacea to the present cultural-historical deficit, the result of a now-irrevocable modernisation/'Westernisation'. In this respect, both in their own ways approach what Bruce Robbins has spoken of as the need for a scaled-down and less-privileged version of cosmopolitanism, in which there is location and embodiment, as 'a reality of (re)attachment, multiple attachment, or attachment at a distance'.[23] How this works out, in artistic terms of possible access to and possession of Asian or alternative high cultures are acutely embodied in *Descendants*.

Castration, Cultural Fragments and the Search for the Cosmopolitan

Descendants of the Eunuch Admiral evokes the relevance — the present moment of the past — of the cosmopolitan and mythologised traveller, the Grand Eunuch Admiral Zheng He (a.k.a. Cheng Ho, 1371–1433), who, during the expansive period of the Ming dynasty, reached not only Southeast Asia but East Africa. While *Descendants* is grounded in the specificity of the Singapore commitment to modernisation and the containment (and rationalisation) of ethnic identities, its multi-levelled, epic allegory also examines man's ability to rise beyond the violence of a larger world committed to economic progress. Ong's English-language version played in Singapore in 1995 and 1996 and travelled to the Cairo International Festival of Experimental Theatre (1996), the International Summer Festival, Hamburg, and the Haus der Kulturen der Welt, Berlin (both in 1998), the final location as part of an Asian avant-garde programme. The production thus contributed signally to Ong's emerging international profile.

Descendants is a powerful play, both as a script by Kuo and as directed by Ong. It is structured as a series of monologues and dialogues — deliberately given without any stage directions or settings, thereby ensuring the director is forced to 'collaborate' with Kuo in interpreting the text — which draw explicit parallels between the history of Zheng He and contemporary man, and the cost to be paid for service to the state and to capitalism (allegorically referred to in the play as 'markets'). If some voluntarily submitted to the literal and symbolic castration necessary for such service (albeit as a result of poverty), Zheng He was violently set upon by the state and cut off from a Muslim identity and future for the Chinese state, as others have been in other cultures and times: 'But of course Zheng He didn't chose like this. He was summarily cut and cleansed by his masters when he was barely a teenager—because there was a need, a huge need for eunuchs. You see, eunuchs seem to have started fulfilling a very important aristocratic need since many thousands of years ago' (scene 5).[24]

Ironically for Zheng He, the moments of transcendence beyond his present condition come about *only* during the voyage to realms and markets away from China, while representing the glory of the Ming emperor. 'Home' and 'identity' are tortured matters for Zheng He.[25]

In any case, how does one find one's 'self' or 'home' in a terrain that is physically and culturally changing? Thus, in the epic *Descendants of the Eunuch Admiral*, the Zheng He character says, at the end of the play: 'Departing is my arriving / Wandering is my residence' (scene 16). This quotation can be compared with the following lines from Kuo's earlier play, *The Evening Climb* (1992):

> I just couldn't find my home. There were houses everywhere … they all looked like my home. I tried with my keys on the doors but couldn't open any one. I knocked on the doors but nobody answered. I got so frightened I started to sweat all over. I can't do anything but keep on trying. Trying to open up with my keys and knocking to get some response.[26]

The markets in *Descendants* — the allegorised capitalism — become a sort of prelapsarian capitalism and the cosmopolitan contact zones for an expansive Asian globalism, zones offering the genuinely marvellous and wonderful, that which exceed the confines of alienated life in the modern nation, with the potential for cultural exchange still alive.[27] The circumscribed reality of castration, deracination, and entrapment by service to the state remains though; but man *must* search *because* of the reality of a seemingly universal capitalism that continues to fragment local spheres. Zheng He's emasculated Muslim-Chinese life itself — as fractured as Singapore's cultural life — suitably only comes through in fragments; when we try to add them up to a whole, we see how the one missing piece has animated this life.

Kuo's post-romantic vision though, also reveals a commitment to human aspiration and imagination. He notes in the 1995 programme of Ong's production:

> we have not totally lost the capacity to wonder. And I am beginning to feel that the affluence has produced enough frustration to make wondering an increasingly inevitable impulse. … Zhenghe [*sic*] is especially inspiring to Singaporeans on many levels and … dimensions. As a minority Chinese (ethnically, religiously and culturally) and as a eunuch rising to the pinnacle of power and achievement, Zhenghe mirrors our existence in many ways.[28]

Ensconced amid the bleakness of Our Condition Now is a humanistic assertion is that we must begin imaginatively to know ourselves if we are ever to be free. And this 'knowing' means imbricating the present with the past, via the evocation of a near-mythic Chinese character with a physical disability that is allegorised, and seeing even our reconstruction of past myth as potential present identity to be 'process' rather than 'product'. This process may help us to avoid the objectifying/commodifying logic of capitalism that pervades contemporary life and art — the hope is that this process may give us back a more empowered subjectivity, one to a noticeable extent lost to capitalism.

Ong's production is exemplary in the way his management of spectacle highlights the parameters of statist and capitalist modernity within which the play's protagonists struggle. He emphasises the poetic in Kuo's script and parcels out the monologues to four players, maintaining the ethereal and abstract quality of the text, while turning it into a deliberately ritualised frenzied, yet restrained movement-based production.[29]

The opening monologue is by a sort of 'Collective I' who says his nightly dreaming links him with Zheng He, who has 'has become the centre of my life'; dreaming itself is a state that finds one 'Alone, painfully alone, and floating away' (scene 1). The 'terrible insanity' of the dream makes it both escapism and an alternative reality, 'Haunting. ... But promising.' The four main characters — two 'yuppie' men and two women dressed in business suits — slowly crawl up to the stage on a small bridge that connects to the front of the stalls, over the orchestra pit, as the monologue unfolds. They are on the way up the ladder, and indicate that the play exists in the present. They will learn, as the Collective I speaking is horrified to learn, that 'we were related, closely related — so closely related that I had to be a descendant of the eunuch admiral' (see Fig. 6.1).

The four characters become the everyman/woman in the corporate world of New Asian/East Asian Miracle Singapore. The monologues and dialogues, except for those of the dreaming Collective I, are split up between them and presented in a trance-like and ritualised declamatory mode. A sort of living shadow of Zheng He comes on the stage with them, a ghostly male in vaguely (neo-)traditional white Chinese attire. He is with them as they consider all the forms of traditional castration possible. Castration itself is partially symbolised by various red scarves and bolts of cloth he plays with. The ghostly Zheng He becomes the unspeaking presence of the past in implicit dialogue with the present. These yuppies, in speaking the various monologues, stage a recovery of their terrible precedent in a processual manner.

The lure of capitalism is imaged in the very gorgeousness of the dream-like set and the lighting, designed by Kuo's daughter, Kuo Jian Hong, juxtaposed against the contained yet histrionic delivery of the lines.[30] Various shelves with glass jars, after the initial scenes, start to appear at the back of the stage, and the numbers increase as the play progresses, indicating the increasing sense of horror at one's mutilated self. The players lose their clothes, starting with their trousers/skirts, and finally putting on robes similar to the ghostly Zheng He's.

The emotional centre of the play is scene 13, revealing the market's potentialities for civilised cultural expansion at its best. Against the bright and calmly reassuring singing in Gabriel Fauré's *Requiem* in D Minor, three characters in their robes start to whirl continuously — the market constricts but does not entirely destroy freedom — and the woman, in a ringing but de-individuated voice, expresses wonderment at the cross-cultural possibilities that exile from home and servitude can offer the not-quite 'Chinese' eunuch admiral as he reaches an ideal trading post in the Western Ocean.

It is a morning scene, and therefore a scene of beginnings:

> Early in the morning before sunrise, the emissaries from Zheng He's armada are getting ready to bring their goods ashore for the great trading festival — silk, brocade, china of many varieties such as vases, plates, bowls. The grand eunuchs, the junior eunuchs, the generals, the officials and officers and errand boys and soldiers ... a flotilla of people and goods began their joyous journey to the marketplace. ...
>
> Zheng He's armada, and the festivals and markets and gatherings brought together all sorts of people: there were Buddhists, Muslims, Hindus and Taoists — children of parents of a great description of people .... They brought fabrics made of jute, of cotton, of silk; they brought metalwork made of gold, of silver .... All of them were priced beforehand and the gentlemanly exchange that takes place becomes more a festival, a celebration, a meeting of friends thirsting for each other's goods and each other's presence and the great coming together.
>
> Soon after the exchange, the festivities began. Food galore, of all colours, tastes and descriptions. But there was neither beef nor pork, and a great amount of vegetarian food — a mutual show of respect between the Muslims, the Hindus and the Buddhists.

It is a scene of positive euphoria that all can participate in, regardless of race, language, religion or rank, where the market seems benevolent ('gentlemanly') and a harmonious Asian (and implicitly Singaporean) multi-ethnic and genuinely multicultural gathering takes place. The goods exchanged are not mere commodities but cultural crafts. The process is mercantile but also social: people relate to each other, and peace and friendship are achieved and cultural and other boundaries bridged during an expansive period of Ming history that need not be considered only as imperialist. The liberal-humanistic wonder of connecting with Others lingers on as the admiral's entourage leaves, for 'the departing visitors knew that their hosts were still on the shore listening to the drums and flutes coming from their boats'. Thus, the admiral 'blaze[d] the glory of the Middle Kingdom. Never did he expect to leave a trail of splendour that would seep into the lives of so many people in so many ways over so long a time ....' Zheng He thus shows the young business people (and Singaporeans) 'in limbo' what can be gained even from a nether cultural or physical status that elevates an imperial centre, as it offered him the chance to look 'for his own paradise' (scene 14). As the speaker finishes the monologue in scene 13, the ghostly Zheng He figure has joined in the whirling, indicating the freedom he has attained.

And it seems that Zheng He finds paradise. In scene 14, we are told that during a storm in the Indian Ocean near Sumatra, his armada take refuge in an apparently exemplary and free 'land where the Buddha walked' — the 'jewel of the world, ... formed by a drop of the Buddha's tear' — where the ruler, the *raja*, 'had ruled for 20 years and then voluntarily stepped down and forbade his children and relatives to succeed him'.[31] The ruler became a holy man, and the country became called by some 'the country of rulers — *negara rajaraja* [—] because all the people became their own rulers ....'

But it is only a dream, or a fantasy, in this case, revealing the deeply ambivalent status of those who dream of Zheng He as the way out of limbo, and of finding a territory untouched by the Fall. The loss of one's own *baobei* (the 'treasure' of the penis) is unforgettable, and scene 15 deals with the 'ultimate castration'. The chilling monologue relates how a trained nanny will crush a young boy's testicles by massaging his private region over a period of time: 'Apart from the absence of perceived pain, ... the greatest merit is that it is received by the subject as comforting, enjoyable and even highly desirable. ... The only difference is that life will come to an end after he has lived his own; there will be no after life ....' In the final scene, scene 16, the four players wail, in their deep understanding of the negative aspects of Zheng He's cosmopolitanism: 'Nameless, sexless, rootless, homeless / Everyone's a parent to the orphan / Every god's a protector to the wanderer / Every land and sky and water is home / It's forever *Zaijian* [Mandarin-Chinese], *Selamat* [Malay], *Vanakkam* [Tamil], Farewell.'[32] The search for paradise must go on in a cultural Asia outside of the local home. The final male player crawls through a slit in the backdrop curtain, and despairingly affirms: 'The sea, the land, the sky is waiting / The Market is calling me!'[33]

Cultural identity and history are hard to protect against the politico-economic realm — but the eunuch *must* strive to find deeper meaning. The call is to transcend this violence to the realm of culture, and to transcend the Singapore locality that practised such violence and strive towards the 'Open Culture' Kuo has elsewhere written of, painful as such transcendence is. Any person who serves the state and the global markets must face this challenge. Multiple cultural attachment and identity are offered as a goal to aspire to rather than a problem resolved in *Descendants*.

Transcending Singapore in the Asian *Lear*

While Ong Keng Sen's thinking on cultural production overlaps with Kuo Pao Kun's, an important difference is the former's less broad-based humanistic inclination — a New Asia (contesting the global West, as we shall see) is his goal in *Lear*. Thus, a director who has benefited from the PAP's modernising and wealth-creating deracination (itself really a re-orientation for the cultural needs of a modern economy), who also is comfortable with the world of multinational capitalism, finds their economic and multi-racial logic narrow. The answer to Singapore's being in thrall to the West and the destruction of cultural roots is to expand the idea of 'Asia', but not in a way that obliterates a contemporary, heterogeneous identity.

While Ong is right to deny the easy return to the exotic Asia of colonial-mentality essentialisms, the danger exists of producing a depthless Asian multiculturalism or identity politics (rather like a Benetton advertisement), as the PAP government's 1980–90s 'Asian values' discourse did. While Ong avoided that trap in *Descendants*, he does not quite manage it in *Lear*, his non-statist attempt to territorialise that empty entity, 'Asian'. He has a critical awareness of the problem of conceiving Asia in its diversity[34] — but never quite reaches a solution. *Lear* was a project with many potential traps.

At a 1998 conference on 'Looking Back at Singapore Theatre',[35] Ong spoke of TheatreWorks' second 'Flying Circus Project', a genuinely ambitious intercultural research and performance programme which brought together 50 Asian artists in theatre, dance and music for workshops and classes, and encouraged creative strategies to regenerate traditional arts in contemporary performances.[36] Ong wants artists to be able to 'enter' other Asian people's cultures to have a vision for a larger Asian and not only Singaporean culture. He argues that the national framework Singapore theatre worked within in the 1980s–1990s is now inadequate, and possibly parochial.

Lear, Ong commented at the conference, was so situated at the cultural border, via the performances of six Asian artists, that no one in Singapore wanted to 'own' it, so to speak. The JFAC production premiered in Tokyo in 1997, appearing in Singapore only in January 1999.[37] *Lear*, Ong argued, is still Singaporean because *he* is Singaporean. By this, he seems to mean that as a Singaporean, he possesses some knowledge of intercultural negotiations and the plural nature of the contemporary — local 'intra-Asia' experiences lead to the possibility of a larger intra-Asian imaginary. A descendant of the eunuch admiral might not have a literal afterlife, but still might have a *cultural* afterlife, and it is one that champs at the bit of the cautious and parochial, petit-bourgeois cultural agenda of the PAP state and the society — and thus also the theatregoers — it helped foster.

As a cross-border East and Southeast Asian cosmopolitan imaginary that could conceivably compete with intercultural theatre heavyweights such as Peter Brook, *Lear* is an imaginative product that a Singaporean-Asian artist, with his/her uncomfortable sense of being deterritorialised, is uniquely qualified to attempt. This postcolonial need to match the West which made Ong modern leads him combatively to write, after attending the 'Touring East and Southeast Asian Arts in Europe' conference in London in 1998:

> Today, Asia is modern. It is coping with the urban experience. Its art is not necessarily meditative or spiritual, it can be as anarchic and radically-chic as its European counterpart.
>
> Perhaps this is what Europe cannot face. Europe would prefer to have Asia on its terms. Europe would prefer to continue consuming Asia's exotic heritage. Europe may not want to hear about Asia's reinvention on the cultural front.[38]

Lear, presumably, is that cultural reinvention that can also transcend the limitations of an authoritarian Asianism for a definitive postcolonial, urban-metropolitan Asian identity free from the 'cultural cringe' of the philistine Singapore state that when it thinks of 'high culture' at all, is still in thrall to Western standards.[39] *Lear* was scripted by Japanese feminist playwright Kishida Rio, though with significant feedback from Ong.[40] They investigate the themes of patriarchy, gender roles and tradition, moving outwards, as in the original play, from the family to the kingdom, and then to the cosmos. The Lear figure — 'Old Man' in the reconfiguration — and the Mother (Lear's absent wife) were played by a Japanese Noh actor; the Older Daughter (Goneril and Regan collapsed) by Beijing Opera actor Jiang Qihu (in his first attempt at playing a woman); the Younger Daughter (Cordelia) by Thai dancer Peeramon Chomhavat; and the Fool, transformed into a Japanese tourist, by Katagiri Hairi (the only woman in a main role, and the only contemporary character).[41]

English-speaking Singaporean Lim Yu-Beng played the Loyal Attendant, though he had to speak Indonesian Malay — 'Western-ness' was only directly allowed in through pop musician Mark Chan's music and Rosita Ng's synthesizer score. Malay-Singaporean Abdul Gani Karim played the Older Daughter's Retainer. Japanese, Mandarin, Thai and Indonesian Malay were used, and English surtitles projected for the audience — 'the overall hermeneutics of the production was regulated through English'.[42]

The plot was simplified from the original, and the most suggestive revision lay in the insertion of the Mother as a symbol of universal salvation who affirms the need for love. The Old Man and the Mother are both played by Noh actor Umewaka Naohiko to indicate the possibilities of redefining traditional gender roles. In the concluding scene, after the Older Daughter has performed patricide (a castration rather like that in *Descendants*), the Absent Mother's shadow appears to embrace the Daughter, and the Mother herself comes to stand behind her. Having killed the Old Man and transcended the father, the Older Daughter, who, according to Ong in the programme notes is the representation of the New Asia (despite her misogyny and lasciviousness), is herself consumed by her Ambition, Unpredictability and Vanity. She can only say, three times in Mandarin-Chinese, 'Who is behind me?'[43] as the light fades. We are left with an oddly pessimistic assessment for a New Asia in a play that is supposed to offer us a putative cultural formation in which, in a reversal of Second World War history, a 'Chinese' daughter symbolically kills a 'Japanese' father. Here, we start to find ourselves asking whether Asia really can free itself from the cultural-historical detritus of past regimes and gain a new cosmopolitan identity, or is there only the consequence of becoming whom we kill?

Despite a beautifully and brilliantly staged polyphonic vision, *Lear*'s polyphony is not held together by enough of a consciousness of its inherent contradictions and tensions. The play remains an élite montage of cultural fragments of Asian high traditions fitted into the contemporary world, one 'in which women are marginalized ..., even as they are metaphorized as icons of a future Asia',[44] rather than an intercultural project with semi-voluntarist negotiations of culture, though Ong's culturalist attempt to join the present and past cannot be thought of simply as cultural pastiche. Still, he is unsuccessful in breaking out of older national-modernist uses of cultural memory so as to re-configure various high cultures into a regional identity.

Lear seems more a striking 'timeless' mythic or universal morality play rather than the allegory of an emergent 'New Asia' it is advertised to be. However, with the mythic quality on offer, the New Asia proffered becomes part of a larger essentialist, multi-ethnic/Asian-regional framing of culture into a Chinese-Japanese-Indonesian-Thai (or 'CJIT') multiculturalism,[45] which echoes Singapore's official CMIO multiculturalism, along with the national-modernist use of cultural memory just mentioned. The Anglophone Singaporean who does not have to struggle with cultural authenticity under direct violent assault — that is more the experience of artists and intellectuals of Kuo Pao Kun's generation and language group — who is already part of a dispersed West that valorises reason as a totalising principle experiences the pitfall of moving too easily into intercultural expression. A lack of a trenchant self-reflexivity of the play as (a problematically postmodern) spectacle forgets Kuo's fractured humanistic call for culture to work against the constraints of the neo-colonial dimensions of global capitalism through the processual exploration of trans-cultural connection. *Lear*'s identity politics becomes an objectified cultural product.

At its best, *Lear*'s visual virtuosity holds together and negotiates the juxtaposition of different performing traditions. In scene 16, the penultimate scene, the Older Daughter enters the stage to the accompaniment of *gamelan* music. The Old Man stands, and turns to face her — and she brutally and suddenly stabs him. The Chinese opera performer was at his most stylised and passionate, and the Noh performer was austere in his death. A red backcloth falls, in a sort of Kabuki-theatre style, and the stage lights pick up its movement to the floor. Each performer potentially reinforces the other's action (see Fig. 6.2).

Despite such dramatic brilliance, *Lear*'s pessimistic finale offers no opportunity to imagine change, nor any gesture towards any possible transcendence of national-identity limitations, as *Descendants* did. The very mythic form Ong uses is at odds with the possibility of history and historical change: *Lear*'s characters are free-floating, with neither cultural-historical nor psychological depth.

While Ong has stated that 'Asia' needs to be thought of in complex tension between history / tradition and the contemporary, 'history', given that the genesis of his own Anglo-Asian identity has a historical nexus, cannot be *just* postmodern 'text': the play's traditional arts surface *still needs* a conception of 'referent', even if that has to follow *Descendant*'s strategy of positing historical fragments not easily recovered. Curiously, even though *Lear*'s memory and identification practices do not lament the 'burden of history', the play simultaneously will not engage with history and is trapped by the fear of historical repetition. Finally, the cultural fragments remain as fragments subjugated to national identities; they do not challenge the will-to-power of modern rationality and gesture to a newer Asian identity — however problematic.

Ong's *Lear* seems a not-fully-thought-through extension of the cultural logic used in *Descendants*: we move directly from Singapore's cultural fragments via the eunuch admiral to imagining the pan-East Asian *Lear*, while eschewing Kuo's reflections with the possibilities of a fractured-but-empowering humanism, given the reality of the political, cultural and economic forces he brings allegorically into play in *Descendants*. Whatever else may be said of Kuo, he does not have a dematerialised view of culture. Arguably, the artistic and cultural practices (and problems) at issue for Ong are the unsurprising result of a society in which the modernising state has axed the past and annexed the future, with one result being that the ability to claim the present needs a resuscitation of the past, or multiple pasts, no matter how mediated. The result is an Asian *Lear* that ironically is made possible precisely through the modernisation / 'Westernisation' — along with the English language as an inherent part of Asian-Singapore that holds the multilingual script of *Lear* together — that has allowed Ong to become a 'global cosmopolitan'[46] and assert an Asia that is modern-traditional. This is an 'Asia' that struggles with the West now reterritorialised into Coronil's 'elusive figure of the globe'.[47]

Lear's results suggest that the rational, capitalist West in Singapore that has re-inscribed Ong's Asian-Chinese 'roots' is something that he has come to sharper terms with. If a dialogic exchange with the West within and without him cannot be better established, the result might be yet another monologue with 'Asia', or — at best — a dialogue only with modernised Japan, which only started to 're-Asianise' itself in the 1980s, instead of a contestatory postcolonial cultural practice to envisage a 'mind' of intra-Asia. It is not so easy — and why should it be? — for Ong to decentre the modern rationality that is part of contemporary Singapore and Ong himself.

Japanese Asianism and the New Asian *Lear*

From one perspective, the Singapore-Japanese cultural dialogue that *Lear* stands for is not surprising. In related if not the same contexts, though importantly linked by a common history of Western domination, both societies are now wealthy, modern societies that worked through the meaning of 'Asia' amid the calls for East Asian regionalism. Singapore's relation to 'Asia', though, in the end, is a fairly simple one: as has been acutely observed, given the city-state's small size, and despite its spectacular economic achievements since the 1960s, 'it is of strategic economical and political importance for Singapore to insert itself into a large[r] piece [of territory, as it were]. Asia may not need Singapore, but Singapore needs Asia'.[48]

It is a fact of modern Asian history that Japan has been aggressively anti-Asian. Japan starts re-inventing 'Japan' by the late-nineteenth century — during which the Japanese found proof of progress in the ability to become as Western as the West, leading to Western-style imperialism over Korea and China[49] — and proceed to updated versions of 'progress' in the form of modernisation[50] in the postwar era, becoming America-centric in the process. The 1980s 're-discovery' of Asia, to a large extent at the official levels, surprised some when it transpired. Singapore's history is shorter, but one in which those who took over from the British colonialists completed the modernisation process in a thorough-going style, and without the famed (stereotyped and sometimes factitious) delicate need to conserve 'heritage' of their former colonial masters.[51] The difference between the two societies (size apart) is that many in Singapore are now comfortable with English as an Asian language, with colonial cultural transformation, and in being part of the West in the middle of Southeast Asia.

There are, naturally, 'hard' politico-economic considerations for Japan's role in an emerging Asian regionalism that, unlike the European experience, is not based on an exclusivist institution-building orientation, but which instead prefers inclusive networks. Having been forced out of Southeast Asia at the end of the Second World War, the Japanese reappeared in the late 1950s, and their economic influence spread again, resulting in an informal form of regionalism.[52] By the 1980s, the massive presence of Japanese foreign direct investment (FDI) in Asian Newly Industrialising Countries (NICs) and the Association of Southeast Asian Nations (ASEAN) led to increased trade. Also, the level of technology transfer had risen. This technological dependence heightened rather than diminished economic hierarchies. The *keiretsu* structure of the large Japanese corporations led to re-built supplier chains abroad. Medium-sized firms also expanded, with a resulting regional economy that centred on Japan.[53] Japan also became a major market for NIC and ASEAN manufactures. However, given that international norms as well as the domestic structures of many Southeast Asian states militate against any closed form of regionalism under Japanese or Chinese leadership, the political definition of East Asian regionalism remains open.

Having said this, there are other historical and cultural impulses to consider in relation to Japanese 're-Asianisation'[54] — the question of Japanese cultural influence and a 'Greater Asianism' (*Dai-Ajiashugi*). This Greater Asianism leads us back to the Meiji period, when issues of being modern and Japan's inferior status vis-à-vis imperial Europe existed.[55] Then, it was the 'escape from Asia' to link with the West. China — formerly at East Asia's centre, and a long-time source of Japanese cultural insecurity — struggled to adapt to the modern world, while Japan forged ahead, with consequences for the rest of East and Southeast Asia.

While we should not assume too easily that the concerns that drove the 1940s Co-Prosperity Sphere are the same as those now — Japan does adhere to the 'peace constitution' — it is clear that concerns of being modern and equal to the West still exist within the 'New Asianism'. Japan may be different from Asia — the century of estrangement reduced feelings of commonality with Asia — but breaching such differences in recent decades seems attractive for the differences with the West seem larger. Having said this, while there has been since the late-1980s more talk of the Asianisation of Asia further sped along by the various movements of national re-definitions after 1989 and the end of the Cold War — until the 1997–99 Asian economic crisis, along with the accompanying denunciation of 'Asian values' as corruption, collusion, and nepotism derailed such talk — we need to keep the national specificity and the twentieth-century past in mind behind such talk.

What of Southeast Asia and 'culture' in this re-construction of Japan? In 1972, Prime Minister Fukuda Takeo set up the Japan Foundation under the auspices of the Foreign Affairs Ministry. Fukuda 'also called [in the same year] on the ASEAN countries for the "heart to heart" dialogues with Japan and initiated a programme of cultural diplomacy with them. His basic idea was that "economic cooperation" alone was no longer sufficient, that more extensive cultural exchanges and dialogues would be required to create the needed "special relationship".'[56] The view on Southeast Asia took on a more statist orientation after Fukuda's ASEAN visit in 1977, after which 'ASEAN' as a term replaced 'Southeast Asia' in political usage. In 1990, the ASEAN Cultural Center was set-up within the Foundation to introduce the cultures of Southeast Asia to Japan and, in 1995, the Cultural Center's brief was expanded, becoming the Japan Foundation Asia Center.

While the point is not to cast sinister aspersions on JFAC — it has funded a prodigious number of worthy academic and cultural causes, and in a real way has helped to curate and document into existence something that now can be described as 'contemporary Asian and Southeast Asian art'[57] — it is important to be aware of the complex cultural and politico-economic history behind it and its possible problems for arts and cultural matters.

An official JFAC publication tells us its mission: 'a basic understanding of one another's cultures [in Asia] ... is essential to the promotion of peace and stability'.[58] Further, the new wealth in the region 'is nurturing the emergence of an urban middle class with a new culture of its own. At the same time, traditional cultural and social values are either crumbling or undergoing painful changes.' Such ills indicate that: 'Efforts must be made to promote balanced mutual exchange and foster relations of trust through exposure to the best of Asian arts and cultures, and to encourage a more comprehensive grasp of Asian languages, histories, and societies.' The JFAC's arts priorities thus include the 'creating [of] new, shared values ... through such endeavors as promoting the co-existence of different ethnic groups; [and] the harmonization of traditional and contemporary culture.'[59]

With the above in mind, we can consider JFAC's *Lear* producer Hata Yuki's statement in Hong Kong that 'Although our modern [Asian] theater is deeply influenced by the West, we also have our own traditions. The theater in new Asian culture should be searching within its own traditional culture.'[60] Cross-cultural theatre that leads to 'a more comprehensive grasp of Asian, languages, and histories' is a solution to resisting a globally influential Western high culture that already has a role in Japanese theatre.

In the case of an Asian *Lear*, the trans-cultural takes on the conflictual burden of being intra-Asian and *not* universal (while based upon a major Anglo-Western canonical literary text), and being contemporary (though maintaining some harmony with tradition). The problematics of creating such neo-traditional fusions that breach national boundaries have been brought up in various critical responses, including the critique that what is transpiring is more 'cultural co-option' than intercultural exchange.[61] Hata notes that in order to avoid choosing a literary text biased towards any Asian culture, they chose one 'that already enjoyed a universal existence. ... Although it would have been fine not to do a play by Shakespeare, we were also interested to see how Asian artists would dismantle and re-assemble the work', so as to force 'everyone to think seriously about how to view tradition, or the old order, from a new perspective.'[62]

Ong Keng Sen seemed the obvious choice for this neo-traditional and trans-cultural or intercultural production. Hata observes: 'For nearly 10 years, we had watched him journey from the question of what it means to be Singaporean in a young and multiracial country to the broader question of what it means to be

Asian in today's world. We wanted the perspective of his generation ....'[63] All the key elements mentioned in JFAC's mission statement can be met because of Singapore's uniquely fractured and reconstructed modern Asian cultural identity.

While Hata appears uncertain over the regional orientation of *Lear*, Ong is less concerned with the Western-Asian tension than with the tradition-modernity dyad of the Asian-regional: 'Working with [playwright] Rio Kishida on the themes of the play, I was particularly interested in looking at new Asia as it grapples with history. ... "Contemporary" can be seen to be a redefinition of tradition.'[64] *Lear* was a perilous undertaking, given the dangers of being co-opted by possible Japanese cultural ambitions and Singapore's desire to continue to be 'global' while being 'Asian'. The Singapore Tourism Board's (predictably instrumental) motto until 2004 was: 'Singapore: New Asia' — only a slight updating of the Board's older 'Instant Asia' slogan. Ong's *Lear*, without doubt, critically exceeds a statist Asianism while not managing, however, to subvert it.

The dialogue on a New Asia is facilitated and mediated by a mutual, if differing and ambivalent or hesitant possession by Ong of the analytic-rational-capitalist part of the West. New Asia cultural production is the result of disjunctive cultural positions that proclaim 'cultural difference', *even* as it also records that the polycentric world of metropolitan postcolonial theory proclaims now exists is in many important respects a mirage: Ong and his New Asian modern discard the need for the Other's 'authenticity', only to discover that the hybridity and discrepant cosmopolitanism that claim a part ownership of the West are hard to sort out in his own particularist cosmopolitan envisioning of 'Asia'.[65]

What perhaps can be said is that the 'West' can no longer simply be called the enemy, though obviously this does not mean that the economic domination of Asian economies by the Euro-American transnational institutions of the global West somehow vanishes. Kuo Pao Kun's work explicitly recognises how the postcolonial state has been recompradorised, and that though the self has been fractured, there is no turning back; but neither should there be only a passive response to this reality, whatever the constraints there may be on cultural agency. At the very least, understanding the 'West within' may enable us better come to terms with the cultural violence and costs it took to become modern Asian societies.

Epilogue

Disciplinary Modernisation, the Asian Economic Crisis and Re-Invention

To speak of 'limits of growth' under a capitalistic market economy is as meaningless to speak of the limits of warfare under a warrior society.

– Murray Bookchin (1990)

A major assumption in this book has been that economic and political power has shifted away from a geographical location called the 'West' to a less identifiable position in the 'globe'. One thing the 1997 Asian economic crisis reveals is how for the former Asian 'Miracle' and up-and-coming Southeast Asian Newly Industrialising Economies (NIEs) there indeed may be less and less of an 'outside' to capitalist modernity. At the start of the new millennium, 'Renaissance' Asia[1] *still* consisted of semi-peripheral societies oriented towards a weakened Japan saddled with debt since the 1990s and the US market — though the presence of China loomed, and India was economically more noticeable than before. Even Singapore, despite its being less affected by the crisis, offers proof of the reality of the structuring and integrating forces of transnational capitalism.

The city-state's initial development process from the 1960s to the 1990s might be described as a 'disciplinary modernisation' that functioned within the ambit of an already reterritorialised 'West' within the 'globe' of that period. An Anglicised, bourgeois leadership scornful of 'retrograde' Asian cultural identities and traditions and believers in a quasi-authoritarian capitalism transformed society. In the process, they limited the procedural and other mechanisms that would allow for strong participation and expression of the plurality of socio-political and ethnic forces.

What resulted was a partial welfare state adapted from the home model of the departing British colonialists that both provided public subsidies in services and housing and invested social relations in their entirety. It became a capitalist society that practised interventionism within its boundaries but supported liberal free trade outside it. Singapore's small size allowed the People's Action Party (PAP) to force a great deal of society and most of its productive and reproductive articulations under the control of the local state, in connection to the requirements of multinational capital. The government was committed to re-tooling the subjectivities of its citizenry as a largely uni-dimensional function of economic development as the means to catch-up with the island's erstwhile colonisers. Japan's neo-mercantilism — if not its nationalism — also offered an example of how such late development could be achieved.

The post-economic crisis question left the PAP state with the question, 'Whither the protective-interventionist state?' that the West had once allowed. The emergence of a multicentric world order with an Asian-Pacific zone by the 1980s had allowed aggressive talk, as we have seen, of an indigenous trans-local/regional relationship between culture, cultural values and capitalist modernity. However, the Asian values discourse that at times belligerently proclaimed a 'neo-traditional' and alternative modernity and cultural identity Other to the West's had subsided in Singapore by the mid-1990s, save for qualified pronouncements by Lee Kuan Yew, a champion of Confucian values. The fact that globalisation does not homogenise cultural imaginations, that even 'when nation-states declare themselves most faithful to an assumed universal modernity does *not* mean, conversely, that when the universal is being foresworn, that something simply Other to "a powerful discourse [that] has emanated from Europe and North America" is developing'.[2]

The Asian-values discourse was a nationalist-culturalist fantasy of difference, an essentialism apparently contesting a capitalism that the PAP itself takes to be *global*. While we need not take 'global' to mean 'universal', it is, at the same time, as Stuart Hall observes, and as the PAP recognises, 'not nation- or society-specific either'.[3] As the 'West' had dispersed itself into the globe, the PAP thought it necessary to take on more aspects of 'them' that would best prepare Singapore to prosper economically.

With the weakening of the 1990s multicentric economic order, can the PAP government continue its established format of economic disciplinary-interventionism within the realm of free-market ideology predicated upon US economic practices dominated by services and information? In a post-communist era, when old-style Western-European social democracy is weakened? Within its own borders, the PAP has hastened, if cautiously, economic de-regulation and urges its citizenry to be more 'creative'. There now needs to exist new, less-conformist subjectivities and a vibrant socio-cultural life. The government hopes this will result in a productive population that will become an autonomous mass with intelligent productivity. These are hopes clearly at odds with the favoured disciplinary modalities of rule. The fear exists that intelligent productivity may lead to democratic power; and yet the ongoing re-invention of Singapore, the government itself argues, depends on the very creation of the autonomous forces of productive co-operation supposed to be the *sine qua non* of the New Economy.

This epilogue explores these modalities of disciplinary governance, and argues that the PAP state is trapped between the society and culture it created and the society and culture it says it now desires. By and large, the party remains faithful to its core mission since 1965 of matching up to the modern West, using all relevant socio-cultural engineering tools to bring that goal about, with the assumption that culture and thus subjectivity or consciousness itself are instrumentalisable, non-autonomous realms. They will not or, possibly, *cannot* recognise that more than ever, their earlier assumptions of the polarised oppositions between political economy and culture, the material and the discursive, are obsolete. Having so much subjected local society and culture to external conditions, they now would like the local to be more dynamic, so that it may interact better with the global as a means of economic advancement. This is an admission of Singapore's subjection within neo-liberal globalisation, and also why anthropologist Aihwa Ong is able to say that the 'Singapore case is larger than the island itself, since the pairing of neoliberal logic and authoritarian control in Asia has produced some of the most radical experimentations in social engineering'.[4]

Globalisation may in principle, at least, stand for the equality of all cultures within a universality that promotes diversity, but it does not seem a principle that the city-state is inclined or able, for the moment, to affirm.

Statist Modernisation in Its Disciplinary Mode

Before we can understand the current PAP hopes for Singapore as a hub for transnational capital flows, we must think through the earlier state-oriented paradigm of modernisation.

The city-state's immediate economy has its origins in the mid-1960s. The region's instability, the city-state's small size and the sense of a beleaguered 'Chinese' identity in the region have become persistent themes in the government's reminders to its citizenry of Singapore's insecurity. Consequently, the argument runs, tight national discipline under a centralised bureaucracy must be maintained in the interests of political and economic survival. Two Singapore authors, literary critic Geraldine Heng and public commentator Janadas Devan, argue that

> by repeatedly focusing anxiety on the fragility of the new nation, its ostensible vulnerability to every kind of exigency, the state's originating agency is periodically reinvoked and ratified, its access to wide-ranging instruments of power in the service of national protection continually consolidated. It is a post-Foucauldian truism that they who successfully define and superintend a crisis, furnishing its lexicon and discursive parameters, successfully confirm themselves the owners of power, the administration of crisis operating to revitalize ownership of the instruments of power even as it vindicates the necessity of their use.[5]

The PAP's response to political, ethnic and social instabilities in Southeast Asia that were either released or triggered by the Asian economic crisis were circumstances that confirm the above analysis. The government could again invoke 'crisis' as a rallying point for more self-discipline, given the scale of the regional problems. Investors since have steered away from the region towards China, for instance, which compromised the immediate efforts to return to pre-crisis growth rates.

Other, more international problems loomed on the horizon at the end of the century. The likelihood of a new and successful World Trade Organisation (WTO) round of trade talks seemed diminished at the end of 1999[6] — bad for a city-state that stakes its future on free trade and itself had hosted the first WTO ministerial meeting in 1996. Another difficulty was the slowdown of the US economy and thus the strength of its market to absorb manufactures from Asia at the start of 2001.

The above discussion raises two related matters to be explored. The first is the issue of governance: is there really Foucauldian governmentality in Singapore, and to what extent is it more important than a direct, statist disciplinarity? Heng and Devan's argument privileges the former, while not denying the existence of the latter. The second is a need to investigate how the governing of Singapore and the management of crises relate to the outside world. How sovereign was the postcolonial Singapore state within the politico-economic parts of the global West it chose to participate in? Was statist modernisation in its disciplinary mode part of a specific — now historical — global context?

Let me begin with the first issue, that of the significance of governmentality in Singapore. A key part of Michel Foucault's work is a critique of the concept of power as a unitary system — see, for example, *Surveiller et Punir: Naissance de la prison* (*Discipline and Punish: The Birth of the Prison* [1975]). He considered power, as Arnold Davidson puts it, 'as a domain of strategic relations between individuals and groups, relations whose strategies were to govern the conduct of these individuals'.[7] The question then is, 'how do we relate to ourselves?', for such ways then contribute to the manner in which our subjectivity is constituted and experienced. Foucault's emphasis is less on the familiar aspects of state power, but instead on the *immanence* of the art of government. He contends that this sort of power, with its sixteenth- to eighteenth-century European origins,

> is essentially concerned with answering the question of how to introduce oeconomy, that is the correct manner of managing individuals, goods and wealth within the family (which a good father is expected to do in relation to his wife, children and servants) and of making it thrive — how to introduce this meticulous attention of the father toward his family, into the management of the State.[8]

It is therefore a mistake to equate sovereignty, as many political theories do, with the state and its apparatus of direct controls; instead sovereignty has been removed from any real political location, and is now more complexly mediated.

In Singapore, governmentality in Foucault's sense functions in conjunction with the more direct state apparatus to make society amenable to capitalist development. They have been used jointly to create the subjectivity, cultural values and, thus, the very ways of life necessary to become a modern society. Capitalism itself is a cultural form (or forms), and for capitalism to be embedded in ways amenable to multinational companies, more proletarians have to be formed out of subsistence farmers, consumerism has to be encouraged, education has to be widely available, and so forth. The PAP, in effect, first used state power to *enforce* a strong rationalising modernity, in keeping with the universalising and culturally homogenising and therefore deterritorialising teleological thinking of the 1960s that was the cultural logic of capital that underlay modernisation theory. One example of the latter process is the extensive learning of the English language to link the new nation with the international economy. State power, however, was, and still is, significant. Singapore's small territorial size enabled a top-down elimination or at least suppression and management of 'recalcitrant' cultural identities that signally contributed to the rephrasing of capitalist modernity within the framework of a global capitalism with all its ruptural forms and formulations.

Therefore, what has *not* happened, despite the emergence of disciplinary and regulatory power relations where power relations are disseminated through more extensive social networks, is the *removal* of what might be called the 'principle of sovereignty' from a real political position — the government and its representatives in the form of the civil service. Foucault argues that: 'At bottom, despite the differences in epochs and objectives, the representation of power has remained under the spell of monarchy. In political thought and analysis, we still have not cut off the head of the king.'[9] In Singapore, both the 'monarch' and the disciplinary regime exist, but the first refuses to disappear so that governmentality will be ascendant.[10] For instance, in 1992, then-senior minister

Lee Kuan Yew (now the 'minister mentor'[11]), was able — quite rightly — to claim he 'does not believe that democracy necessarily lead[s] to development'; instead, 'what a country needs to develop is discipline more than democracy'.[12] Singapore economist Linda Low subtitles her 1998 book 'Government-Made Singapore'.[13] And a former information and arts minister, George Yeo, at a 1998 conference on civil society starkly asserted society's lack of independence from the state, even while contending that the economic demands of the next century call for a more pro-active civil society: 'Although Singapore society was largely created by the state, it has to be Singapore society which ensures the state's long-term existence.'[14] Singapore's 'illiberal democracy', as Singapore sociologist Chua Beng Huat has described it, does not perhaps fit so well into Foucault's model of governance — all the charges of 'authoritarianism' in Southeast Asia levied by various critics suggest this.[15]

This leads me to the second issue, the question of the statist-disciplinary regime in relation to the wider world. If a state's sovereignty is weakened by contemporary capitalism, as is popularly argued,[16] then when the Singapore state re-tools its culture for national development, does it do it independently or under the indirect or direct duress of larger conditions? The answer seems to be that while choice did matter, that choice was made *within* the larger context of the at-least-incipient governmentality of the 'West' disseminated into the globe. The agency of the state here does matter, and this came in for renewed attention with the position some analysts think industrial policy played in the 'East Asian Miracle';[17] but it is also a circumscribed agency, if one that functioned well for a number of decades.

During the period of worldwide decolonisation, there was a gradual decentring of production in the advanced economies. According to Michael Hardt and Antonio Negri, that entailed

> the spread of disciplinary forms of production and government across the world. ... The ideological model that was projected from the dominant countries (particularly from the United States) consisted of Fordist wage regimes, Taylorist methods of the organization of labor, and a welfare state that would be modernizing, paternalistic, and protective. ... The high wages of a Fordist regime and the accompanying state assistance were posed as the workers' rewards for accepting disciplinarity, for entering the global factory.[18]

Singapore was part of this development. Fortuitous circumstances (the island's geographical location as a crossroads; and its early entrance to the field) and the strong-arm sovereign state made it more successful than other aspirants to become a Fordist and Taylorised factory-society that was paternalistic and protective.

Lee Kuan Yew, in the wake of the Asian financial crisis, spoke of why free capital flows do not work for all smaller economies to the *Los Angeles Times'* Nathan Gardels at the 1999 World Economic Forum in Davos: 'Handling the "financial herds" is not easy for a small country. It takes years to train competent bankers and managers. Most countries won't have the capacity for one or two generations. ... If you haven't got the circuit breakers and can't monitor and contain power surges, then don't plug in.'[19] The very machine imagery Lee (typically) uses is indicative of the state-created Fordist-Taylorised subjectivity he aimed for in Singapore, with the result that the city-state has survived the consequences of the weakening of the Asian miracle.

The crisis has led to the city-state trying to internalise the perceived Outside of multinational capitalism that framed its success *even more* thoroughly — thus no more political articulation of the supposed local of 'Asian values' and an Asian modernity within the global. Though much of the Association of Southeast Asian Nations (ASEAN) waffled over the proposed ASEAN Free Trade Area (AFTA), Singapore pursued bilateral trade arrangements with the USA, Europe and Japan to 'leave' the region, as it were; its first two-way trade treaty was signed with New Zealand in December 2000. Free trade talks began with the USA under Bill Clinton in December 2000, with a third round in May 2001. The PAP government now further 'plugged' the island in to what one commentator has called 'an authoritarian mode of liberalism'[20] that poses problems for the existing model of governing Singapore and the requisite subjectivity once thought to be sufficient in maintaining an ultra-modern status.

Out with the Old Economy, and in with the New ...

The PAP government has acknowledged for some years that the Fordist-Taylorised machinery of disciplinary modernisation that it had so successfully used was starting to creak. While the reshaping of the old paradigm began before the Asian economic crisis started, that has hastened change; the result is an insistent parading of the buzzwords associated with the 'New Economy', possibly making the PAP unique as a political party that dares to ask its grass-roots supporters to accept the undisputed domination of global capital.[21] The major obstacle to change is that the entrenched utilitarian-pragmatic mentality of the protective-interventionist state that, not surprisingly, plagues the very idea of less-conformist subjectivities and a vibrant socio-cultural life that is thought will provide the 'creative' intellectual and entrepreneurial support for an 'Information Society'.

In November 1996, then-prime minister Goh Chok Tong announced that a thorough review would be made of competitiveness over the next ten years; the

Committee on Singapore's Competitiveness was then formed in May 1997. In November 1998, Goh discussed the Committee's findings and recommendations. The fundamental policy recommendation was that the island-state must become an advanced knowledge economy in the next decade, with manufacturing and services being the twin engines of growth. Needless to say, a skilled workforce would be requisite. The role of traditional labour and capital becomes less important than what can be described as immaterial labour, along with 'intellectual' capital: 'We are putting in place the capabilities that will enable us to compete effectively and capitalise quickly when the region recovers.'[22]

While the Committee's report makes the necessary gesture to supporting the region's economies, what is most important is the location of Singapore within the global-regional world-economic map: 'Singapore should position itself as a critical hub which MNCs [multinational corporations] and local enterprises use as a base to manufacture high value-added products and provide manufacturing-related services, including headquarters services, to the satellite plants in the region, especially South-east Asia.'[23]

While business remains the main focus of the report, business now has less tangible dimensions as to what makes for a remunerative dynamism. The social fabric must be 'cultural' in a manner less tied in to the earlier post-independence sense of ethnicity and traditional culture, or even to the 1980s Asian-values sense. The *Straits Times* paraphrased the report thus: 'Add some fizz into local entertainment by setting up an Arts Marketplace for interactive arts activities, similar to Melbourne's Sunday Market and Montmartre in Paris. To boost tourism, build more theme parks and study the feasibility of building a new cruise centre.'[24] As with the best global — meaning Anglo-American — versions of metropolitanism, we need to enhance the city-state's stature as a 'hub'. Since the late 1980s, the PAP has tried to have a cultural policy, setting up a ministry of information and the arts, later renamed the ministry of information, communications and the arts (MICA); by 1992, the concept of Singapore as a 'Global City of the Arts' had been articulated.[25] The 'pragmatic' state felt it now needed a broader realm of culture than before.

What we have — as with many other places in the world now — is an unexceptionable fantasy of Americanisation, despite the references to Euro-Western centres, and even to Australia. The fact that the English language of the island's colonial inheritance is now widespread helps the ongoing process of gaining access to the United States, given its privileged position within the global West. In cultural identity terms, a sense of a pastiche postmodernism may come through, save for the fact that the PAP government's consumerist kitsch is never playful but always serious.

Lee Kuan Yew himself, in 1999, has admitted — at the prestigious World Economic Forum in Davos, Switzerland, where world political and business leaders meet, no less — that the seemingly 'Unlimited growth' of the Japan-led East Asian pattern of export-oriented industry is gone:

> Countries like Singapore, Korea or Taiwan that have successfully followed the Japanese model in the past did not have to contend with the vast reservoir of cheap labour of China and India now that they have entered the global economy. ... [T]hey have to [further] educate their workforce ... and find niches of higher value-added production to keep going.
>
> Singapore, Korea and Taiwan, in effect, must now compete with Ireland, Spain and Britain. ... [T]hey must offer a social infrastructure that foreign managers will find attractive, lifestyles to which they are accustomed at home — good health care, a clean environment, concerts, symphonies, boutique restaurants.[26]

This admission is significant in that Lee himself — not known for his belief in the immaterial, given a petit-bourgeois vision of capitalist modernity — now articulates that a place exists for 'culture', however indirectly referred to or loosely used. The 'hardware', as it is called in Singapore, now needs a 'software upgrade', not only in terms of what can still be pragmatically understood like healthcare or even the environment, but also in terms of what one suspects Lee (still) takes to be window-dressing. The difference between the metropolitan West, with their chi-chi high-cultural centres, and who 'we' are now, now must be eradicated further. We now need *lifestyle capitalism*, as it might be called, to attract the foreign know-how to assist local development.

How do we 'upgrade' subjectivities to be like *American* subjectivities and thereby 'possess' the USA's supposed can-do individualism? Deputy Prime Minister Dr. Tony Tan and a Singapore delegation visited the Research Triangle Park in North Carolina in April 1999. A journalist who accompanied Tan seemed confused between desire and fantasy, and wrote of Singapore as an insistently genuine simulacra: 'Singapore too, with its proactive government, has its research parks, and has a multi-billion dollar plan to build a science hub in the Buena Vista area, which includes the National University of Singapore.'[27] The city-state is the virtual copy that needs a new subjectivity to make its wishful virtuality literal.[28]

The push to be 'global' in general has resulted in a two-pronged strategy, one more international, in which the city-state strongly supports the actions of the international financial institutions. The second is aimed at re-inventing the subjectivity of the island's citizenry.

On 6 May 1998, a year after the Asian crisis started, the other deputy prime minister, Lee Hsien Loong, now in the forefront to push for change in the economy, spoke to an American audience in Washington, D.C. on 'Whither Globalism — A World in Crisis'. Lee encouraged the USA and affected Asian countries to stay the course for free trade:

> Globalisation did not cause ... [Asia's] problems, and [nationalistically] closing their economies will not solve them. ... The solution is not to retreat from globalism, but to strengthen their economies and businesses to hold their own against global competition and to be able to weather ups and downs of international markets.

The US role in this system of global capital is pivotal, for '*Pax Americana* allowed Asian countries to concentrate their resources on development and peaceful economic competition'. Global capitalism's benefits, in the end, flow both ways: 'The alternative is not just less competitive industries or lower standards of living, but a world in which countries will be less secure, and more prone to conflicts.'[29]

Such a strong championing of the neo-liberal agenda also, in the end, subjects the city-state to the imperatives and rules of 'authoritarian liberalism', even if there is a clear sense that it needs to be carefully managed.[30] To be sure, while Singapore can be accused of being a comprador regime, the present regional instability that partly drives the affirmation of global rather than regional capitalism is real enough. There has been a loss of capital inflows to China, North American Free Trade Area (NAFTA) and India. Indonesia still struggles with the authority vacuum left by Suharto's departure, ethnic strife and the December 2004 tsunami disaster; the Philippines has a weak government; and Thailand's political direction, along with the Islamic 'problem' in the south of the country, is uncertain. ASEAN was unable to provide leadership during the East Timor struggle for independence from Indonesia. Overall, Southeast Asia has a weakened influence in the world.

One consequence of the above, along with the slow evolution of AFTA, already mentioned, is that the city-state is working out bilateral trade agreements. No one would suggest that the protective-interventionist state is dead, but it is not as confident as it used to.

At the local level, the PAP government gradually is trying to become more financially and economically transparent (though this does not quite apply to the political realm) to the international financial world. Lee Hsien Loong, in his previous capacity as chairman of the Monetary Authority of Singapore (MAS), effectively the city-state's central bank, announced in February 1999 that the state was reviewing all restrictions in the domestic retail sector for foreign banks. Competition was the only way to develop strong local banks that could measure up to international standards. Lee Kuan Yew himself apocalyptically warned that the state's ability to protect local banks will, in any case, 'be gone in 10 years or less. So, unless we move forward, and fast, ... [w]e'll be marginalised in our own domestic base.'[31] The state will not — possibly *cannot* — protect the local the way it used to. Efficiency must be higher.

The government also came out with a surprise announcement in January 2000 that the entire telecommunications market was to be fully freed up from

April of the same year, even though they had granted the company StarHub[32] a basic phone licence to compete with Singapore Telecommunications (SingTel) on the basis that there would be no new entrants until April 2002.

Liberalisation has also been extended to the 'suitable' form of labour as well — meaning those who can work in high-end financial services, though the island also has a noticeable contract-labour pool from Bangladesh, Indonesia and the Philippines — described by the government rather unfortunately as 'foreign talent'. In fact, despite many public reservations about the weakening 'protective' element of the protective-interventionist state, Prime Minister Goh in 1999 stressed that the regional slowdown was no reason for the recruitment of foreign talent to let up: 'Rather, we should concentrate on how to make the economy grow faster and stronger, using talent, local and foreign, to do so.'[33]

There is also an attempt to encourage the large government-linked companies (GLCs) that dominate the city-state and are themselves extensions of the interventionist state, to expand by spreading into the region, rather than by crowding out private investment and intimidate possible smaller competitors in the city-state, as they long have been accused of in the past.[34] The regional response to such expansion, though, has been suspicion about the sort of liberalisation and internationalism is being advocated to cream off the profits from the neighbourhood.

The above, in general, indicates that the PAP is saying 'you in the local arena *must* be more independent of us', even if they refuse to process the entirety of what is being argued. 'Creativity' and 'innovation' become key words that represent the desire to reconstruct the nature of labour, and in the increasing imbrication of the material and the social. Significantly, the idea of culturally and educationally 'passive Asians' has become a widespread and not only a Singapore perception of Asians. *Asia Magazine* during the crisis cited Vice-Chancellor Edward Chen of Lingnan College, Hong Kong, on this issue: 'Nations in Southeast Asia ... need to strike a balance between the technical education which has been traditionally given them in the past, and the more Western-style liberal education which has helped form many innovative and creative minds.' The same issue also cites Prime Minister Goh from his opening address in June 1997 at the Seventh International Conference on Thinking: 'We must ensure that our young can think for themselves, so that the next generation can find their own solutions to whatever problem they may face.'[35] Others, too, rush to embrace the 'new individualism' of market modernity, as Third Way guru Anthony Giddens calls it.[36] As one might guess, politically apathetic, unadventurous and complacent youth are sometimes cited as stumbling blocks to the New Economy gaining strength.

Overall, the PAP government recognises that there are trends in the world tending towards cultural pluralism and democracy, and with demands for political accountability. The (admittedly uneven) emergence of international civil society is hard to ignore. But while they see these changes, they are also reluctant to recognise that governmentality rather than strict direct government would better suit the New Economy and even moderate the stronger expressions of these new trends in their favour. There is, in any case, no effective or credible threat to PAP political dominance. Despite this, the party leadership continues in the contradictions of their desire for 'managed change'. In 1998, during the first year of the crisis, with growth rates starting to decline, the *Straits Times* polled 1,000 readers. It received responses that responded positively to the statement, 'I trust the Government's ability to run the country' (88 percent), along with 'The Government should consult me beforehand on policies affecting me' (67 percent) and 'There is freedom of speech here' (25 percent).[37] What was politically remarkable was that the population did not blame the government for the crisis — a sign that the hegemonic compact for delivering economic prosperity in return for political acquiescence still held — while indicating more and more to the PAP that not only had the outside world changed, but that the local population had too.[38]

The recognition of changed circumstances, though, is not missing. Lee Kuan Yew told his audience at the Singapore Techventures 2000 conference on 9 March, in San Francisco, that: 'The strength of the American system is that it has always embraced change and creative destruction.' The government has actually become aware that they literally have been *too successful* in their efforts in 'creatively destroying' Singapore since the 1960s — they got the pacified society they desired. Lee himself sees that: 'For us, the change [in the way society and the economy are to be managed] means the abandonment of rules which have served us well for 30-plus years.'[39] The fundamental problem, as perceived not only by the foreign media, but also by local commentators such as Simon Tay, a former nominated member of parliament, is that: 'The PAP is willing to liberalize without democratizing.'[40] They will not see that greater democratisation and its possible relationship to a 'ground-up' entrepreneurial and cultural dynamism can co-exist and, possibly, flourish while being kept within limits in their favour with the tools of governmentality, in immanent relationships of domination, which is the way capitalism itself functions in the 'globe'; instead, the PAP still practises a transcendent application of the sovereign state's apparatus of control — an approach their own rhetoric declares will not support a desired Information Society. Old habits die hard.

Singapore occupies a specific place within global capitalism. During the Cold War, and as the sun set on the British Empire, the PAP government used a disciplinary modernisation that managed to draw in Western — especially American — and Japanese FDI to transform Singapore into a Brave New World in the midst of the decolonised Third World. The fall of the Berlin Wall, though, slowly led to changes in the way the city-state could function.

Bruce Cumings has argued that Japan's emergence in the postwar international system as a secondary power — despite Tokyo's increasingly 'mercantile spirit and the strong role played by the state in its economy',[41] elements at odds with much US economic thinking — was enabled by the USA as part of a strategy to contain the communist enemy. The revived Japanese economy helped make Japan self-supporting and led to interdependent economic links in hot spots such as Southeast Asia. It is within this system that Singapore was established as a disciplinary-interventionist state that supported free trade; and it was a state that was willing to retool the subjectivities of its citizenry for the needs of economic development to achieve a catch-up modernity. As Cumings notes, 'with the end of the cold war, the question of Japan's [and, by extension, the Little Dragons'] compatibility with a new era of free-market ideology was bound to arise'. The 1997 crisis offered an opportunity for the American boot to be put in via the International Monetary Fund's (IMF) rescue packages.

The upshot is that the PAP government is trying to re-invent the city-state again, and create less-conformist subjectivities for a so-called 'Knowledge-Based Economy' that, with the 2001 dot.com/high-tech crash in the USA, at least temporarily ran aground. It is also a world in which China is now part of the WTO, and will continue to offer new economic challenges to the rest of East and Southeast Asia. The paradigm shift that the government is trying to effect is necessitated by circumstances — but the question remains: will the PAP leadership let the old heavy-handedness die, so that the new can be born?

Past History's Last 'Post' ...?

A final reflection on culture and capitalism. What might be significant, I have suggested in the Introduction, in the utopian Singapore experiment is that while because of its size, it is not a representative experiment in capitalist development, its small size has made it a bellwether of some capitalist currents in recent decades. This is also true too of the city-state in the 1990s, and perhaps in the start of the new millennium. With the demise of the USSR, capitalism seems to lack a vision of the future — lacking a Second-World modernity to define itself against, having won that ideological battle — and it seems to even revel in a short-term pragmatism, as if that were an alternative for a lack of vision. Singapore's casting about since the late 1990s for new directions in which to progress is part-and-parcel of that uncertainty.

Of course, when the Cold War ended in 1989, it was supposed to be a triumph, according to Francis Fukuyama, as it also offered the occasion for announcing the end of ideological conflict and the triumph of a liberal capitalism; this also apparently signified the end to politics, to the antagonism between two systems of social and political ideals that made competitive truth claims. The 'triumph of the West', Fukuyama opined, was the victory of 'the Western *idea*'.[42] We now inhabit a realm that has seen the end of history — a post-ideological world. Humankind has arrived.

In this regard, the city-state, one could say, was effectively a *post-ideological state* before the end of the Cold War — it was 'ahead' of its time. By the 1980s, it was confident of its entrenched position within a booming globalised capitalism. Having chosen which side it was on by the 1960s, and with the Cold War itself becoming less threatening by the 1980s, the strongly anti-communist city-state could proclaim a modernity *culturally different* from the Anglo-American model it had already assimilated and adapted. As literary critic Walter Benn Michaels has observed, it was 'the replacement of *ideological* by cultural difference that marks the coming of the new [world] order'.[43]

Fukuyama's essay, in Michaels's thinking, was the prototype for the much more notorious 'The Clash of Civilizations?' essay by political scientist Samuel Huntington, who argued that 'the fundamental source of conflict in this new world will not be primarily ideological .... The great division among mankind and the dominating source of conflict will be cultural.'[44] The city-state's leaders proclaimed an essentialist cultural identity in the early 1980s until the mid-1990s it did not entirely believe in — and performed the alternative identity of an Asian capitalist modernity. During the key years of the 1960s to the 1970s, though, when communism was a clear and present danger in Southeast Asia, cultural identity — what your society was — was simply an absurd issue; what mattered was whose side you were on: 'Ideological conflicts are universal ... precisely because, unlike conflicts of interest, they involve disagreement, and it is the mere possibility of disagreement that is universalizing.'[45] The years of the East Asian Miracle had afforded the city-state the confidence and the assurance that it could indulge in an early version of Fukuyama's and Huntington's 'post-historicist' thinking, resulting in (seeming) cultural conflict with the USA and its human-rights agenda. But even before September 11, 2001 (which gave a more ominous inflection to Huntington's warning about civilisations clashing, and after which, the much-trumpeted stability of the New World Order tottered), and even before the Asian economic crisis of 1997, the PAP state retreated back to 'the Western *idea*', giving up its (bizarrely) postmodernist valorisation of cultural difference and identity of the 1980s. Asserting cultural difference is all very well, but it may not actually advance economic growth beyond a certain point.

However, at the same time, as mentioned in the previous section, the PAP state found another use for culture: high culture, the culture industry and lifestyle consumption, taken in toto, can bolster the city-state's economic attractiveness. Singapore at the start of the new millennium had been transformed from a colonial city into a modern but unifunctional premier 'world city' with a puritan work ethic, and into an economic centre for business in Southeast Asia and in the Asia-Pacific region.[46] The pressing question is whether it can become a multifunctional cultural metropolis, given increased regional and international competition from other aspirational world cities. The need for more autonomy also applied to artistic and related cultural developments. The city-state has been working out how this freedom and autonomy can be wrought by the disciplinary state. As is apparent, assessing irony, whether intended or not, is not one of the stronger points of the city-state's politicos — or its senior civil servants.

By 2006, the permanent secretary of MICA,[47] Tan Chin Nam — effectively if not literally, and even if unintended — was proclaiming that the sacred nation-state concept was dead, or perhaps transcended. 'Singapore,' he writes, 'is seen as a country with a positive brand', and the difference between the 'branding' in the immediate post-independence years and in 2006 is this: 'In tandem with the continual re-invention of the economic and social landscape ..., the Singapore "brand" has shifted from a focus on "hard" aspects such as costs, efficiency and technology to "softer" aspects such as lifestyle, experience and innovation.'[48] He goes on: 'Sacred cows of the past are being slaughtered with the development of two integrated resorts which will transform our entertainment industry.' By 'integrated resorts', Tan refers to two entertainment complexes, one of which one will arise in a new downtown core, with casinos in them (which the PAP government had never allowed in the past, for fear of the social consequences), but also with additional upmarket shopping and a possible art museum. What of the citizens of the branded city-state, then? Their role is to be 'ambassadors of the nation. Our people will also have to meaningfully engaged to be co-creators of the Singapore brand.' This 'branded' city-state, one could speculate, is one consequence of using a deterritorialising modernity as a metanarrative to try to ground post-independence developments, of the instrumentalisation of cultural identity.

An article next to Tan's is entitled 'Why Nation Branding Is Important for Singapore'. The writer — a 'full-service' consultant — offers Singaporeans this reworking of the *patria*, the classical national project of a territorially defined 'people', and even of the nation as comfortable hearth and home: 'Few things are as complex as a nation. There are many elements contribute to its identity: its history, people, traditions, political system, economy, location and so on. These things collectively make up that elusive thing that is a nation's *de facto* brand, its identity in the minds of its people.'[49] This definition turns cultural difference and historical traditions into components of a national logo. I suppose we could ask if a 'brand name' can be an essential(ised) identity that can truly drive a call say for national sacrifice in the face of adversity?

Singapore's assorted strengths must be marketed coherently, for uncoordinated marketing by the various state agencies will 'fracture Singapore's overall identity'. The solution is to conceive of 'a metabrand that embodies the essence of Singapore's identity', for this 'provides a collective vision ... and supports the agendas of all key stakeholders, including the ministries and organisations seeking to market themselves abroad'. In September 2006, a tender bid was put out by the government for a consultant to create this 'metabrand', and '[a]ccording to the tender documents, the consultants will have to suss out the global marketing efforts of competitors like Dubai, India, China, Hong Kong and Thailand'.[50]

The arts and entertainment come in as support mechanisms for this post-Brave New World being wrought, as part of that which can create the image of global chic and cool. The article next to 'Why Nation Branding' informs us that Singapore will host the 2006 annual meetings of the board of governors of the IMF and the World Bank Group, and that this all occurs under the auspices of a larger campaign called Singapore 2006, 'Global City, World of Opportunities'. The 16,000 delegates to come will get a taste of Singapore 'through various programmes such as the [inaugural] Singapore Biennale 2006 [SB2006]'.[51] The biennale event was actually proposed in 2005 as part of the larger staging of the IMF–World Bank meeting. Indeed, the visitor's guide to the Singapore Biennale highlights SB2006 being the 'anchor cultural event'[52] for the meeting. The biennale, the guide also informs us, will further highlight 'Singapore's prominence as an international contemporary arts centre'. Such a statement would raise eyebrows now, but in, say, 1994, the year of the PAP state's crackdown on the arts,[53] this statement would have elicited outright astonishment among the city-state's citizens.

International visual arts biennales have become part of the global circulation of high culture. Such art events and also art exhibitions in a similar 'globalised' mould have come to operate 'within the dimensions of attraction and entertainment, on the one hand, and critical reflection and subversion, on the other'.[54] Many voices have alleged that 'the ever-extending rhizome of international biennale exhibitions'[55] have become part of postmodern cultural tourism and lifestyle culture, of what John Urry calls 'consuming places'.[56] The 1980s saw the emergence of an international circuit of biennales, and the 1990s the appearance of Asian or regionally mounted biennales such as the Fukuoka Asian Art Triennale (formerly the Asian Art Show in the 1980s) — 'conceived primarily for viewers in Asia[, where an] Asia-centric paradigm replaced Euro-American centricity':[57] the state-driven Asian modernity discourses were not the only Asian culturalist outcomes of the 1980s–90s Asian Miracle — and the Asia-Pacific Triennials at Australia's Queensland Art Gallery. The PAP state wants to be part of this Asian cultural bandwagon.

The Singapore state's present (and somewhat belated) development strategy is in itself not surprising, given a now-increasingly established pattern of what it means to foster a competitive global city that will lure and retain capital flows and foreign direct investment. It is the bluntness of and lack of nuance in its articulation by the very highest state officials that catches the reader off-guard, given the near statement — whether intended or otherwise — that the citizens are now really minor equity holders in an enterprise rather than a nation-state. National culture and the arts themselves become commodities in the process of creating the suitable brand. As with earlier 1980s–90s manifestation of what anthropologist Arjun Appadurai influentially has described as a 'modernity decisively at large, irregularly self-conscious, and unevenly experienced',[58] the city-state manages to bring into sharp focus — in this case a revelation if not revealing distortion of — certain culturalist aspects of the present version of the modern.

It is important to reiterate in this epilogue that a central position in this book is that the 'modernity at large' of the globalisation processes of the past two decades have not only brought about, as Appadurai thinks, a subversive culturalism of 'micronarratives of film, television, music, and other expressive forms, which allow modernity to be rewritten more as vernacular globalization', as 'identity politics mobilized at the level of the nation-state',[59] but also state-driven macronarratives of regional identity that reinforce the position of capitalism. If the imagination in the post-electronic world, as he argues, has broken out of special expressive space of art, myth or ritual to the ordinary person in the quotidian space, it has also been claimed by states to re-imagine national and regional identities. Appadurai has since registered that *Modernity at Large* (1996) has been critiqued 'as being insufficiently attentive to the darker side of [1990s] globalization', and has moved on to examining the culturally driven violence that marks the contemporary moment, which he links back to the increasingly weakened position of the nation-state: the 'virtually complete loss of even the fiction of a national economy ... now leaves the cultural field as the main one in which fantasies of purity, authenticity, borders, and security can be enacted'.[60]

We cannot assume, though, that the process of globalisation will carry on in the way it has in the 'high period' of the 1990s. The current circulation of knowledge, mass-mediated images and sensations — even if there are 'disjunctures' between various kinds of flows, say of ideologies, goods and people[61] — and the possibility of envisioning a knowledge-based post-industrial economy was the consequence of the Uruguay round of trade talks of the 1980s and the 1990s. During that period, the advanced Western economies and Japan, to a lesser degree, were able to get their way on a free-trade agenda with the less developed economies, which could be bullied or otherwise persuaded. The USA in particular was a key defender of the multilateral negotiation of free trade. The difficulties the Doha round talks, which began in 2001, suggest that such multilateralism promoted by the advanced economies, especially the USA, may change with the economic challenges coming from China (which became a full member of the WTO in 2001), but also from India.

Developing economies also have started to work more in concert against liberalisation processes not in their favour, and in 2003 managed to scuttle the WTO meeting in Cancún. Martin Jacques rightly notes that:

> The irony of Doha is that it is being killed by the West's lack of interest in the face of growing power of the developing world. The rise of China and, and to a lesser extent India, is likely to be accompanied by a parallel irony. The West, which has been the traditional defender of free trade — because free trade always favours the most powerful and advanced economies — is likely to put up protectionist barriers, unable to cope with the political, social and economic implications of the rise of China.[62]

Of course, fortune telling has its pitfalls, and the USA remains a resilient society and economy thus far. However, there is also no doubt that China's re-emergence onto the world stage as East Asia's 500-pound gorilla that has overtaken the place of Japan and the Tiger economies in the 'Asian Century' and in the new millennium will affect not only the flows of global capital, but also how culture and cultural images will flow, and — one would expect — what knowledge will be deemed as important. Singapore and the region at large have entered a stage of transition, but what the 'emergent', as the late Raymond Williams would call it, might be is not at all clear.

Perhaps the above indicates that the end of the Cold War has *not* meant a world that is *posthistoire*, if by that term we have in mind Karl Manheim's understanding of it: 'It is possible, therefore, that in the future, in a world in which there is never anything new, in which all is finished and each moment is a repetition of the past, there can exist a condition in which all thought will be utterly devoid of all ideological and utopian elements.'[63] We are hardly in such a state of being; we are all, in effect, still coming to terms with what a world without the Soviet Union means, and in which 'culture clash' has come to the fore in ways not imaginable in the 1980s.

Notes

Introduction

1. Hou Hanru and Hans-Ulrich Obrist, 'Cities on the Move — London Version', in *Bangkok on the Move*, <http://www.art4d.com/bangkokonthemove/2542/London/index.html>.
2. Fredric Jameson, *A Singular Modernity: Essay on the Ontology of the Present* (London: Verso, 2002), 7. As Jameson notes, modernisation was itself not an innocent term as originally used, 'for it was an active propaganda word during the Cold War, and constituted the principle US contribution to its various Third World allies an clients and even to Europe itself during the period of the Marshall Plan' (ibid., 229, note 5).
3. The pioneering work on the idea of the 'developmental' includes: Chalmers Johnson, *MITI and the Japanese Miracle: The Growth of Industrial Policy, 1925–1975* (Stanford: Stanford University Press, 1982); Alice H. Amsden, *Asia's Next Giant: South Korea and Late Industrialization* (New York: Oxford University Press, 1989); and Robert Wade, *Governing the Market: Economic Theory and the Role of Government in East Asian Industrialization* (Princeton, NJ: Princeton University Press, 1990). The most pertinent scholarship for my purpose, though, is Manuel Castell's 'Four Asian Tigers with a Dragon Head: A Comparative Analysis of the State, Economy and Society in the Asian Pacific Rim', in *States and Development in the Asian Pacific Rim*, ed. Richard P. Appelbaum and Jeffrey Henderson (London: Sage Publications, 1992). In Castell's usage, the developmental state is one which conceives its purpose as that of ensuring economic development, usually meaning high rates of accumulation and industrialisation. This state 'establishes as its principle of legitimacy its ability to promote sustained development, understanding by development the steady high rates of economic growth and structural change in the productive system, both domestically and in its relationship to the international economy' (55). The political élite must gain ideological hegemony, so that the developmental project also becomes, in the Gramscian sense, hegemonic — a project which key players in the nation adhere voluntarily. The state, however, must enjoy relative autonomy from the major social actors.

4. World Bank, *The East Asian Miracle: Economic Growth and Public Policy* (New York: Oxford University Press, 1993).
5. Jay Branegan, 'Is Singapore a Model for the West?' *Time*, 18 January 1993, 36. All further page references will be given within brackets in the main text.
6. 'Modernity' and 'modern' are terms that of course have contrasting and layered meanings. The central focus will be to see how the set of relations between modernism (critical or experimental cultural and symbolic practices), modernisation (the socio-economic and industrial creation of modernity) and tradition (or, in the case of the book's second chapter, also the primordial), are transformed in the way modernity is mapped onto Singapore. Cf. Zygmunt Bauman, *Modernity and Ambivalence* (Cambridge: Polity Press, 1991): 'Modernity, like all other quasi-totalities we want to prise off from the continuous flow of being, becomes elusive: we discover that the concept is fraught with ambiguity, while its referent is opaque at the core and frayed at the edges' (4). I use the term 'modernity' here as Bauman does: 'I call "modernity" a historical period that began in Western Europe with a series of profound social-structural and intellectual transformations of the seventeenth-century and achieved its maturity: (1) as a cultural project — with the growth of Enlightenment; (2) as a socially accomplished form of life — with the growth of industrial (capitalist, and later communist) society" (4, note 1). I also draw upon Marshall Berman's *All that Is Solid Melts into Air: The Experience of Modernity* (1982; New York: Penguin, 1988) and Jürgen Habermas's *The Philosophical Discourse of Modernity*, trans. Frederick Lawrence (Cambridge, Mass.: MIT Press, 1987) for some of the central distinctions between modernity as an historical stage, modernisation and modernism, and also from empirical studies on the unexpected relation between cultural and socio-economic modernisation in the non-Western world, especially Latin America (Néstor García Canclini, *Hybrid Cultures: Strategies for Entering and Leaving Modernity*, trans. Christopher L. Chiappari and Silvia L. López [Minneapolis: University of Minnesota Press, 1995]).
7. On 6 September 1999, a new parliament building opened next to the old building, which has been converted to become a performing arts centre; the Supreme Court and City Hall buildings are now slated to be converted into a new Asian art gallery by perhaps 2010.
8. E. J. Hobsbawm, *Nations and Nationalism since 1780: Programme, Myth, Reality* (Cambridge: Cambridge University Press, 1990), 175. Official discourse has played up such an impression of Singapore. A Singapore journalist interviewed the then-arts minister, George Yeo, and reported the following on Singapore's 'civic life': 'Singapore was like Venice, an Italian city which had always seen itself as Italian, although its people spoke their own dialect and the population never grew beyond 200,000 .... Singapore, B[rigadier-]G[eneral] Yeo said, was defined by the way its people maintained a sense of unity while celebrating diversity' (Koh Buck Song, 'Culture Goes Regional', *Straits Times Weekly Overseas Edition*, 20 March 1993, 13).
9. Now called the Ministry of Information, Communications and the Arts, or MICA for short.
10. Ministry of Culture, *Singapore 1984* (Singapore: Information Division, Ministry of Culture, 1984), 4, 7. All further page references will be given within brackets in the main text.
11. Akhil Gupta and James Ferguson, 'Beyond "Culture": Space, Identity, and the Politics of Difference', *Cultural Anthropology* 7, no. 1 (February 1992): 7.
12. Akhil Gupta, 'The Song of the Nonaligned World: Transnational Identities and the Reinscription of Late Capitalism', *Cultural Anthropology* 7, no. 1 (February 1992): 72.
13. It is not just the official publications which announce Singapore as the very remarkable triumph or fulfilment of colonial modernity as conceived in the free trade era of English

imperial history, a triumph which the English could not possibly have expected. Here is Singapore historian Edwin Lee: 'The leitmotiv of Singapore's history is free trade. Free trade is, first of all, an idea thrust forth by the British Industrial Revolution .... The trader in pursuit of his proper objective is the exemplar of what life on earth is all about. This idea, nurtured in the mind of Sir Stamford Raffles, was translated into reality on a strategic island, Singapore, which he founded as the entrepôt for British trade in Southeast Asia. The idea, once put into effect, succeeded beyond all expectations' ('The Colonial Legacy', in *Management of Success: The Moulding of Modern Singapore*, ed. Kernial Singh Sandhu and Paul Wheatley [Boulder, Co.: Westview Press, 1990], 39).

14. Cf. Theodor W. Adorno and Max Horkheimer: 'We are wholly convinced — and therein lies our *petitio principii* — that social freedom is inseparable from enlightened thought. Nevertheless, we believe that we have just as clearly recognized that the notion of this very way of thinking, no less than the actual historic forms — the social institutions — with which it is interwoven, already contains the seed of the reversal universally apparent today' (*Dialectic of Enlightenment*, trans. John Cumming [New York: Herder, 1972], xiii).
15. Benedict Anderson, *The Spectre of Comparisons: Nationalism, Southeast Asia, and the World* (London: Verso, 1998), 15. Two of the facts are wrong: Lee's title was 'prime minister'. 'Chief minister' was used only from 1955 to 59, when the colony gained internal self-rule. He became prime minister only in 1959. Anderson also does not note that, by the late 1950s, Lee was also London's clear choice as a post-independence prime minister.
16. Renato Rosaldo, *Culture and Truth: The Remaking of Social Analysis* (Boston: Beacon Press, 1989), 217.
17. Jean and John L. Comaroff, 'Naturing the Nation: Aliens, Apocalypse, and the Postcolonial State', *HAGAR: International Social Science Review* 1, no. 1 (2000): 7–40.
18. Ezra F. Vogel, *Japan as Number One: Lessons for America* (Cambridge, Mass.: Harvard University Press, 1979).
19. Clifford Geertz, 'The Integrative Revolution: Primordial Sentiments and Civil Politics in the New States', in *Old Societies and New States*, ed. Clifford Geertz (New York: Free Press, 1963), 108.
20. As early as 1956, in the colonial legislative assembly, Lee used the word 'primordial' in relation to the gut issues that fueled the educational and identity concerns of the various ethnic groups: 'I have used the word "primordial" once and it brought a rebuke from the Hon. Mr. [G. A. P.] Sutherland [a nominated assemblyman], but that was perhaps he does not understand these [socially incendiary and complicated] things' (*Singapore Legislative Assembly Debates* 1, 12 April 1956, column 1910).
21. Ten years later, Lee's position had not changed much — and this following 1978 quotation in retrospect warns us what was to come with the Asian values discourse: 'Literature and heritage or tradition are different altogether. What is important for pupils in not literature, but a philosophy of life ... a value system' (cited in Shirley Geok-lin Lim, 'The English-Language Writer in Singapore', in *Singaporean Literature in English: A Critical Reader*, ed. Mohammad A. Quayum and Peter Wicks [Serdang: Universiti Putra Malaysia Press, 2002], 37). Lee was very public on the need for a larger value system during this period of the late 1970s–1980s (see 'Lee: Need for Value System', *Straits Times* [Singapore], 5 June 1978).
22. See Raymond Williams, *Culture and Society, 1780–1950* (London: Chatto & Windus, 1958).
23. The PAP state's national philistinism has been noted even by sympathetic observers such as the late Michael Leifer: 'Singapore is primarily about the business of business with its denizens more interested and accomplished in the art of karaoke than in the arts *per se*. Indeed, it is worth heeding the comment made by in 1976 by the head of the Department of

Philosophy in the University of Singapore that the concept of a global city had a pretentious ring, and that Singapore was not a centre from which new frontiers of knowledge would emanate. It was founded to be a trading centre "which is what it remains to this day"' (*Singapore's Foreign Policy: Coping with Vulnerability* [London: Routledge, 2000], 14).

24. García Canclini, *Hybrid Cultures*, 41.
25. Architect Tay Kheng Soon — a long-time and acute critic of the PAP government's model of a deferential, pro-Western and bland modernity — claims that: 'In the contest between [socio-economic] modernization and modernity [by which he refers to the project of fostering individuated and critical consciousness through the arts and other areas of symbolic creation] within the imperatives of [the emerging post-independence] political economy, the incipient modernity which sprouted in [colonial] Malaya was sadly truncated by the impossibility of managing ethnic imaginations without a strong referee. Ideas of the modern could not be consciously articulated but were lived through the vectors of language and ethnicity; and modernity being sequestered from consciousness was therefore ambivalent. But for a small strategic English-educated elite in Malaya, modernity could not be articulated at all. Thus, this group saw that a certain adherence to the principle of meritocracy applied to racial equality, fair play, the autonomy of reason, a critical spirit etc., could be made to work despite the passions of the times [in postwar Malaya and Singapore].' The Chinese intelligentsia in Malaya and Singapore, Tay tells his readers, were starting to 'develop an aesthetic of place in [their] growing output of works. ... The tragedy is that [anti-communist] political events prevented the growth of this new sentiment and in the independence movement and post-independence ideological struggles for political dominance, the tragic fault lines were drawn in such a manner that a shared modernity was impossible' (Tay Kheng Soon with Robbie B. H. Goh, 'Reading the Southeast Asian City in the Context of Rapid Economic Growth', in *Theorizing the Southeast Asian City as Text*, ed. Robbie B. H. Goh and Brenda S. A. Yeoh [Singapore: World Scientific, 2003], 21; 21–22). Thus, there were incipient signs of cultural modernism on the island — but they had been mown down by the state by the late 1970s. (Also see William S. W. Lim, *Asian New Urbanism* [Singapore: Select Books, 1998].) I shall return to this issue in chapter 6.
26. It is possible to take the PAP state's socio-cultural engineering itself as a particular critical symbolic act. This is the position taken by Singapore sociologist Kian-Woon Kwok and his co-author, Kee-Hong Low: 'the opening chapter of Jacob Burkhardt's *The Civilization of Renaissance Italy* (1958) is titled "The State as a Work of Art." As rationalistic as the modernism of the Singapore state has been, it is also been *culturally* subversive, having the ambition of, on the one hand, working on the premise of a tabula rasa and, on the other hand, actively projecting the next necessary steps must be taken into a future that is already present' ('Cultural Policy and the City-State: Singapore and the "New Asian Renaissance"', in *Global Culture: Media, Arts, Policy, and Globalization*, ed. Diana Crane, Nobuko Kawashima and Ken'ichi Kawasaki [New York: Routledge, 2002], 164–65).
27. Among Tu's relevant work from the 1980s–90s are: Tu Wei-ming, *Confucian Ethics Today: The Singapore Challenge* (Singapore: Curriculum Development Institute of Singapore/Federal Publications, 1984); Tu Wei-ming, *Confucianism in an Historical Perspective* (Singapore: Institute of East Asian Philosophies, 1989); Tu Wei-ming (ed.), *The Triadic Chord: Confucian Ethics, Industrial East Asia and Max Weber: Proceedings of the 1987 Singapore Conference on Confucian Ethics and the Modernisation of Industrial East Asia* (Singapore: Institute of East Asian Philosophies, 1991); Tu Wei-Ming (ed.), *The Living Tree: The Changing Meaning of Being Chinese Today* (Stanford: Stanford University Press, 1994); and Tu Wei-ming (ed.), *Confucian Traditions in East Asian Modernity: Moral Education and Economic Culture in Japan and the Four*

Mini-Dragons (Cambridge, Mass.: Harvard University Press, 1996). His work seemed to help generate a mini-publishing industry on the topic of East Asian and Confucian culture and modernity.

28. Or to put this another way, as anthropologist Aihwa Ong has: 'In our desire to find definite breaks between ... the oppressive and the progressive, and the stable and the unstable, we sometimes overlook complicated accommodations, alliances, and creative tensions between the nation-state and mobile capital .... Attention to specific histories and geo-political situations will reveal that such simple oppositions between transnational forces and the nation-state cannot be universally sustained' (*Flexible Citizenship: The Cultural Logics of Transnationality* [Durham, NC: Duke University Press, 1999], 16).
29. The 1993 Vienna World Conference on Human Rights was one of the notable clashes between (the clichéd idea of) Western 'individualism' and (the equally clichéd idea of) Asian 'collectivism', as the UN Conference followed in the wake of the 1993 Bangkok Declaration signed by Singapore, Malaysia, Taiwan and China. The central concern of this clash, as Jürgen Habermas describes it, was over 'the [East Asian] political community [being] more traditionally integrated more by duties than by [Western-style] rights. The political ethic recognizes no individual rights, but only rights that are conferred on individuals.' The real issue, however, Habermas feels, was about 'the more or less "soft" authoritarianism that characterizes the dictatorships of developed nations. ... In reality, these [East Asian] governments do not defend individual rights at all, but rather a paternalistic care meant to allow them to restrict rights that in the West have been considered the most basic' (*The Postnational Constellation*, trans. Max Pensky [Cambridge, Mass.: MIT Press, 2001], 123, 124–25).
30. Cf. Kwok and Low's assertion regarding the role of the arts in the city-state: 'But it is not the case that governments are the active purveyors and citizens the passive recipients of the effects of cultural policy. It is the spheres of the arts and social memory, in which such constructions [of the national body politic within a new globalised order] are being developed and contested by individuals — artists, cultural workers, intellectuals, citizens — that the tensions, dilemmas, and costs of modernity are explored and articulated' ('Cultural Policy', 165).
31. Partha Chatterjee, *The Nation and its Fragments: Colonial and Postcolonial Histories* (Princeton, NJ: Princeton University Press, 1993).
32. There were other related developments that year that complicated inter-ethnic relations. On 9 December 2001, the Singapore government arrested 15 men under the Internal Security Act, which allows detention without trial. The men were said to be members of the group Jemaah Islamiyah (JI), some of whom had trained in al-Qaida camps in Afghanistan. They were apparently planning to attack the US and Israeli Embassies and British and Australian diplomatic buildings on the island. In August 2002, the city-state's Internal Security Department arrested another 21 alleged members of the JI.

Chapter 1

1. For a series of broad critical views on the re-inventions of the cartographic and other identities in the Asia-Pacific region in the 1980s and the 1990s, with the rise of the East and Southeast Asian trading economies, see the essays in Arif Dirlik (ed.), *What Is in a Rim? Critical Perspectives on the Pacific Region* (Lanham, Md.: Rowman & Littlefield, 1998).
2. Dilip Parameshwar Gaonker, 'On Alternative Modernities', in *Alternative Modernities*, ed. Gaonkar (Durham, NC: Duke University Press, 2001), 1. All further page references will be given within brackets in the main text.

3. Fredric Jameson, *A Singular Modernity: Essay on the Ontology of the Present* (London: Verso, 2002), 12.
4. Marshall Berman, *All that Is Solid Melts into Air: The Experience of Modernity* (1982; New York: Penguin, 1988), 124.
5. Rob Wilson and Arif Dirlik, 'Introduction: Asia/Pacific as Space of Cultural Production', in *boundary 2* 21, no. 1 (Spring 1994): 11. Special Issue, 'Asia/Pacific as Space of Cultural Production'.
6. Perry Anderson, 'Modernity and Revolution', *New Left Review* 144 (March–April 1984): 109.
7. Cf. Ian Buruma, 'What Happened to the Asian Century?', *New York Times*, 29 December 1999 <http://taiwansecurity org/NYT/NYT-991229-Asian-Century-htm>. Buruma is rightly critical of the hubris that went into such claims to New Asia representing a new way to being modern, one in which democracy and individual rights would matter less in the face of 'development rights'. However, the misfortunes of the emerging Southeast Asian economies of course is more than balanced by the increased economic presence of China, and some observers such as former Australian prime minister Paul Keating replace the Little Tigers, Indonesia, Malaysia and Thailand with China in their view of Asia — see Keating's 'The American Era is Over: The Asian Century is Dawning', *The Age* (Melbourne), 16 October 2003 <http://www.theage.com.au/articles/2003/10/15/1065917476292.html?from=storyrhs>. And so, the debate on the Rise of East Asia continues.
8. Ashis Nandy, *The Intimate Enemy: Loss and Recovery of Self under Colonialism* (New Delhi: Oxford University Press, 1983).
9. Fernando Coronil, 'Towards a Critique of Globalcentrism: Speculations on Capitalism's Nature', *Public Culture* 12, no. 2 (Spring 2000): 353, 368. Special issue, 'Millennial Capitalism and the Culture of Neoliberalism', guest ed. Jean Comaroff and John L. Comaroff. Hereafter cited as TCG. Further page references to this article will be given in brackets in the main text.
10. Coronil contends that 'neoliberal globalization conjures up the image of an undifferentiated process without clearly demarcated geopolitical agents or target populations' (TCG, 369). During the Asian economic crisis, when capital was fleeing Thailand after the *baht* was devalued in July 1997, it was hard of course to see who exactly 'the geopolitical agents' in the various financial institutions in the West who were doing this; but the International Monetary Fund, which subsequently entered into Indonesia and Thailand to demand restructuring in return for requested bailout loans, can hardly be considered an 'undemarcated' agent.
11. Dipesh Chakrabarty, *Habitations of Modernity: Essays in the Wake of Subaltern Studies* (Chicago: University of Chicago Press, 2002), xxi.
12. Paul Rabinow, *French Modern: Norms and Forms of the Social Environment* (Cambridge, Mass.: MIT Press, 1989), 13.
13. See Catherine Hall, *Civilising Subjects: Metropole and Colony in the English Imagination 1830–1867* (Cambridge: Polity, 2002); and C. J. W.-L. Wee, *Culture, Empire, and the Question of Being Modern* (Lanham, Md.: Lexington Books, 2003).
14. The ethnic composition of East and West Malaysia combined is approximately Malays (50 percent), who are largely Muslim; Chinese (23 percent); Indians (seven percent), largely Tamilians; indigenous people groups — e.g., Kadazan, Dusun, Iban (11 percent); and 'Others' (eight percent). Singapore's ethnic composition is Chinese (78 percent); Malay (14 percent), also largely Muslim; Indian (seven percent), also largely Tamilians; and a category the state, like Malaysia, calls 'Others'. It has been the question of the role of Malays and Malay culture in national life that led to what is called Separation in 1965.

15. The former jewel in the British colonial crown has also offered us major intellectuals whose contributions play a large part in the postcolonial theorising of culture. For an acute if not entirely fair assessment of some prominent contributions in the 1980s and 1990s — especially of Indians living in the United States — see Arif Dirlik, 'The Postcolonial Aura: Third World Criticism in the Age of Global Capitalism', *Critical Inquiry* 20 (1994): 328–56.
16. See Gyan Prakash, *Another Reason: Science and the Imagination of Modern India* (Princeton, NJ: Princeton University Press, 1999), 3, 203–7 and 234.
17. Partha Chatterjee, *Nationalist Thought and the Colonial World — A Derivative Discourse?* (London: Zed, 1986), 133.
18. Jawaharlal Nehru, *The Discovery of India* (New York: John Day, 1946), 261–62.
19. Ibid., 261.
20. Ibid., 518.
21. Fredric Jameson, *The Geopolitical Aesthetic: Cinema and Space in the World System* (Bloomington: Indiana University Press, 2002), 212.
22. In 1963, with the merger with British North Borneo, Sarawak and Singapore into the Federation of Malaysia, Malaya became known as West Malaysia.
23. Ashis Nandy, *Traditions, Tyranny and Utopias: Essays in the Politics of Awareness* (Delhi: Oxford University Press, 1987); Veena Das and Ashis Nandy, 'Violence, Victimhood and the Language of Silence', in *The Word and the World: India's Contribution to the Study of Language*, ed. Bimal Krishna Matilal (Delhi: Oxford University Press, 1990); and Bhikhu Parekh, *Colonialism, Tradition, and Reform: An Examination of Gandhi's Political Discourse* (London: Sage, 1989).
24. Tejaswini Niranjana, P. Sudhir and Vivek Dhareshwar (eds.), *Interrogating Modernity: Culture and Colonialism in India* (Calcutta: Seagull, 1993); and Dipesh Chakrabarty, *Provincializing Europe: Postcolonial Thought and Historical Difference* (Princeton, NJ: Princeton University Press, 2000).
25. For a chronology of the events, see 'Babri Masjid Archive: Before and After', <http://admin.muslimsonline.com/babri/babriarc.htm>, accessed 9 March 2006.
26. Dipesh Chakrabarty, 'Modernity and Ethnicity in India', *South Asia* 17 (1994): 144, Special Issue on 'After Ayodhya' (1994): 144.
27. Joseph Levenson, *Confucian China and its Modern Fate: A Trilogy* (Berkeley: University of California Press, 1968). See, for discussions of the Confucian cultural re-invention, Arif Dirlik, 'Confucius in the Borderlands: Global Capitalism and the Reinvention of Confucius', *boundary 2* 22, no. 3 (Fall 1995): 229–73; and C. J. W.-L. Wee, 'The "Clash" of Civilizations? Or an Emerging "East Asian Modernity"?' *SOJOURN: Journal of Social Issues in Southeast Asia* 11, no. 2 (1996): 211–30.
28. Tani Barlow, Editor's Introduction, *positions: east asia cultures critique* 1, no. 1 (Spring 1993): vi.
29. Dr. Mahathir stepped down as prime minister in December 2003, and was succeeded by Abdullah Badawi.
30. Cf. one journalistic European view of some nationalistic responses to the Petronas Centre: 'The completion of Kuala Lumpur's twin tower[s] ... is a development as humiliating as that suffered by the English cricket team on its annual rounds of self-abasement against the likes of Sri Lanka. Here, for once, is an authentic skyscraper outside America .... It is an act of economic and cultural humiliation [for the United States]' (Deyan Sudjic, 'Scaling the Heights of Human Madness', *Guardian Weekly*, 10 March 1996, 23). Cesar Pelli, the architect behind the Twin Towers, and a reinventor of 1930s-style retro skyscrapers, not accidentally also was the designer of London's tallest structure, the Canary Wharf, and

the World Financial Center in New York City. Even the important, neo-liberal magazine, the *Economist*, so much ideologically at one with transnational capitalism, was not certain how to regard Dr. Mahathir's extravagant and 'macho' challenges. In 1996, a year before the crisis, Malaysia, along with Thailand and Indonesia, experienced slow export-oriented growth combined with ongoing current account deficits. Despite this situation, Malaysia did not seem likely to curb its deficit, given its drive for investment: 'This is fine to a point .... But Dr. Mahathir's plans go further. His monumental ambitions include a hydroelectric dam, a new administrative capital, the world's tallest building and a "multi-media supercorridor" covering 750 square kilometres' ('South-East Asian Economies: States of Denial', *Economist*, 10 August 1996, 57). The distaste at this postcolonial one-upsmanship is hidden under the self-righteous and seemingly disinterested rhetoric of financial rectitude. The Petronas Twin Towers were displaced by the opening of Taiwan's Taipei 101 (*Taibei Yilingyi*) building in December 2004. From the ground to structural top, the Taipei 101 is 508 metres tall, beating Petronas's 452 metres; arguably, the Taipei 'triumph' too is another version of postcolonial one-upsmanship.

31. Mahathir seems to share with Lee Kuan Yew — the latter is only a few years Mahathir's senior — a paternalistic-masculinist, anti-imperial stance that is grounded no longer in the social-democratic language popular in the 1960s, but instead in the newer language of transnational capitalism. *Ecce Papa* in the brave, new transnational world.
32. See Anwar's argument in *Time* that 'Southeast Asian Muslims prefer to concentrate on the task of ensuring economic growth and eradicating poverty instead of amputating the limbs of thieves' (Anwar Ibrahim, Viewpoint, *Time*, 12 September 1996, 24). The cover story for this issue is 'The New Face of Islam: In Southeast Asia an Ancient Religion Eagerly Embraces the Modern World.' Anwar later fell foul of Dr. Mahathir, and was sacked from the cabinet on 2 September 1998. He was charged for corruption and sodomy. In 1999, he was convicted on the former charge, and in 2000, on the latter. In 2004, the Federal Court overturned the sodomy conviction and Anwar was released from gaol, having completed his sentence for corruption, which had been reduced based on good behaviour.
33. Gavan McCormak and Yushio Sugimoto, 'Introduction: Modernization and Beyond', in *The Japanese Trajectory: Modernization and Beyond*, ed. McCormack and Sugimoto (Cambridge: Cambridge University Press, 1992), 4.
34. Japanese reaction to the policy was mixed; see Lim Hua Sing, *Japan's Role in ASEAN: Issues and Prospects* (Singapore: Times Academic Press, 1994), 1–26. Lim offers a detailed analysis of the general economic relationship between Japan and ASEAN from the 1980s to the book's publication.
35. Thang Leng Leng and S. K. Gan, 'The "Learn from Japan" Campaign in Singapore', in *Japan and Singapore: A Multidisciplinary Approach*, ed. Tsu Yun Hui (Singapore: McGraw-Hill Education [Asia], 2006), 261. For an examination of the city-state's experimentation with Japanese management techniques, see ibid., 267–73.
36. Ogura Kazuo, 'A Call for a New Concept of Asia', *Japan Echo* 20, no. 3 (Autumn 1993): 39.
37. Saito Seiichiro, 'The Pitfalls of the New Asianism', *Japan Echo* 19, Special Issue (1990): 14–19; also see Nakanishi Terumasa, 'Japan's Place in the World', *Japan Echo* 19, Special Issue (1990): 2–5; Ogura, 'A Call': 37–44; Koichi Iwabuchi, 'Return to Asia? Japan in the Global Audio-Visual Market', *SOJOURN: Journal of Social Issues in Southeast Asia* 9, no. 2 (October 1994): 226–45, Special Issue on 'Mass Media: Local and Global Positions'; and Paul Blustein, 'Japan Swings Towards Asia Away From West', *Straits Times* (Singapore), 13 December 1994, 28 (reprinted from the *Washington Post*).
38. Nakanishi, 'Japan's Place': 3–4.

39. Quoted in Iwabuchi, 'Return?': 227.
40. Quoted by Saito, 'Pitfalls': 17.
41. Shintaro Ishihara, 'Oppressed by the West, Japan's Return to Asia can Change Future', *Straits Times* (Singapore), 21 January 1995, 32. In 1999, Ishihara ran on an independent platform and was elected governor of Tokyo.
42. The scholarship debating this position became quite profuse. A few examples are: Hung-Chao Tai, *Confucianism and Economic Development* (Washington, DC: Washington Institute Press, 1989); Ronald P. Dore, *Taking Japan Seriously: A Confucian Perspective on Leading Economic Issues* (Stanford: Stanford University Press, 1987); Peter L. Berger and Hsin-Huang Michael Hsiao (eds.), *In Search of an East Asian Development Model* (New Brunswick, NJ: Transaction Books, 1988); Gilbert Rozman (ed.), *The East Asia Region: Confucian Heritage and Its Modern Adaptation* (Princeton, NJ: Princeton University Press, 1991); and Joseph P. L. Jiang (ed.), *Confucianism and Modernization: A Symposium* (Taipei: Wu Nan Publishing, 1987).
43. Ezra F. Vogel, *The Four Little Dragons: The Spread of Industrialization in East Asia* (Cambridge, Mass.: Harvard University Press, 1991), 92.
44. Vogel, *Four Little Dragons*, 90, 91.
45. Ibid., 92–101.
46. However, Mahathir did go on to co-author, with Ishihara Shintaro, *'No' to ieru Ajia*, with the title weakly translated into English as *The Voice of Asia*, trans. Frank Baldwin (Tokyo: Kodansha, 1995).
47. 'PROTON' stands for 'Perusahaan Otomobil National', or the National Automobile Industry. The fear of obsolescent cars was then at hand. On 3 November 1995, a joint venture agreement was signed in Paris between PROTON and Renault, the French motorcar manufacturer, to build Malaysia's own truck.
48. Mahathir Mohamad, Speech at the 5th Joint Conference of MAJECA/JAMECA, Kuala Lumpur, 8 February 1982; reprinted in *Foreign Affairs Malaysia* 15, no. 1 (March 1982): 38–45. For a more detailed analysis of Mahathir's Japanism, see Khoo Boo Teik, *Paradoxes of Mahathirism: An Intellectual Biography of Mahathir Mohamad* (Kuala Lumpur: Oxford University Press, 1995), 54–102. Also see the essays in Jomo K. S. (ed.), *Mahathir's Economic Policies* (Petaling Jaya: Institute of Social Analysis, 1989).
49. Gyan Prakash, 'Introduction', in *After Colonialism: Imperial Histories and Postcolonial Displacement*, ed. Prakash (Princeton, NJ: Princeton University Press, 1995), 9. Prakash's specific meaning here is this: 'The nationalist intellectual spoke of "unity in diversity"; they claimed that the colonized formed a nation in spite of social, regional, and ethnic differences. Such assertions were not merely polemical responses to the colonial rulers who resisted the nationalist demands; instead, they underscored the necessity of the stage of difference for the performance of the nation's unity' (9).
50. 'Need for Asia "To Stress Morality" in Development: Values, Traditions Important in Economic Growth', *Straits Times* (Singapore), 28 October 1993, 13.
51. The National Front subsequently gained an increased majority in the national elections of May 1995; many people have gained from Malaysia's spectacular growth over the past few years, and the general feeling is that the electorate was unwilling to 'rock the boat' even by keeping opposition strength at the previous level. The relationship between democratic development and economic growth is, to say the least, uneven.
52. Tu's work is often caricatured such that he becomes the spokesman for a (once-)triumphant Confucian-values-driven modernity in East Asia, though, in actuality, his work is more careful than that. Tu adopts an 'alternative modernity' position at a basic level not so

different from that of Dilip Parameshwar Gaonkar's (see the discussion at the start of this chapter): 'The rise of industrial East Asia, at a minimum, has significantly complicated the Weberian picture of modernization as rationalization .... Once we begin to acknowledge the compatibility of a market economy and an authoritarian [rather than liberal] state, recognize the centrality of family virtues to social solidarity, ... and employ new conceptual apparatuses such as network capitalism to understand a different kind of economic dynamics, we are well on the way to an alternative vision of modernity' ('Introduction', in *Confucian Traditions in East Asian Modernity: Moral Education and Economic Culture in Japan and the Four Mini-Dragons*, ed. Tu [Cambridge, Mass.: Harvard University Press, 1996], 7). This alternative view of modernity though, is one in which he recognises that parts of the West have become an inherent part of East Asia: 'Actually, since East Asian intellectuals have been devoted students of the modern West for several generations, the Enlightenment values, including human rights, have become an integral part of their own cultural heritage .... East Asian intellectuals, not to mention the English-speaking political elite, are more familiar with the life-orientation of the modern West than with any traditional Asian way of living' (Tu Wei-ming, *The Inaugural Wu Teh Yao Memorial Lectures 1995* [Singapore: UniPress, 1996], 27). The focus of his lecture was 'A Confucian Perspective on Human Rights'.

53. Samuel P. Huntington, 'The Clash of Civilizations?', *Foreign Affairs* 72, no. 3 (Summer 1993): 22–49.
54. Anwar Ibrahim, 'Towards Global Peace, Understanding', *New Straits Times* (Kuala Lumpur), 14 March 1995. All the following quotations from Anwar come from this speech. Ogura Kazuo's 'A Call' makes a similar if less obviously breathtaking argument: 'It seems to me that it has now become necessary to cultivate the traditional spirit of Asia in order to answer some of the major history of Europe to be overcome...?' (40). But of course, Ogura is not a major politician, and Japan does not have the particular history of ethnic tensions that Malaysia has; Singapore obviously has a similar history, given the common colonial and national histories until Singapore's separation from Malaysia in 1965.
55. Such an assertion shows us that the 'legacy' of Bandung as already weak in the year of its fortieth anniversary, 1995, the year that the 'Islam and Confucianism' dialogue was held. For a present assessment of Bandung's legacy, see the essays in *Inter-Asia Cultural Studies* 6, no. 4 (December 2005), Special Issue on 'Bandung / Third Worldism'.
56. 'S[enior] M[inister] Lee: Tide Is Rising for East Asia', *Straits Times* (Singapore), 6 February 1995, 25.
57. 'Asian Values: The Scourge of the West', *Economist*, 22 April 1995, 24. Mahbubani served with the foreign service from 1971 to 2004. He had postings in Cambodia (where he served during the war in 1973–74), Malaysia and Washington DC; he also served two stints as Singapore ambassador to the UN, and was also president of the UN Security Council in January 2001 and May 2002. Since 2004, Mahbubani has been dean of the new Lee Kuan Yew School of Public Policy at the National University of Singapore, and is the author of *Beyond the Age of Innocence: Rebuilding Trust Between America and the World* (New York: Public Affairs, 2005).
58. Kishore Mahbubani, 'Pacific Community: Fusion of East and West', *Straits Times* (Singapore), 17 September 1994, 35.
59. See Yao Souchou, 'The Predicament of Modernity: Mass Media and the Making of the West in Southeast Asia', *Asian Journal of Communication* 4, no. 1 (1994): 33–51.
60. 'Is Everyone Here?', *Asiaweek*, 22 December 1993, 12.
61. Francis Deron, 'Confucius, Mao and Business', *Le Monde* section of *Guardian Weekly*, 23 October 1994.

Chapter 2

1. Bruno Latour, *We Have Never Been Modern*, trans. Catherine Porter (1991; Hemel Hempstead, Herts.: Harvester Wheatsheaf, 1993), 71.
2. E. J. Hobsbawm, 'Ethnicity and Nationalism in Europe Today', *Anthropology Today* 8, no. 1 (February 1992): 3
3. See Ernest Gellner, *Nations and Nationalism* (Oxford: Basil Blackwell, 1983); E. J. Hobsbawm and Terence O. Ranger (eds.), *The Invention of Tradition* (Cambridge: Cambridge University Press, 1983); and Benedict Anderson, *Imagined Communities: Reflections on the Origin and Spread of Nationalism* (London: Verso, 1983).
4. Akhil Gupta, 'The Song of the Nonaligned World: Transnational Identities and the Reinscription of Late Capitalism', *Cultural Anthropology* 7, no. 1 (February 1992): 63, 73. All further page references will be given within brackets in the main text. Gupta is interested in considering how the nation-state might becoming unstable as a 'dominant organizational form' (73) and how imagined transnational communities, such as the European Community or world-wide Islam, may indicate what is to come.
5. 'Communalism' in Singapore carries the same implications that Indian nationalists ascribed to that term: 'Communalism was, in common with colonialism, the Other of nationalism, its opposite, its chief adversary, and hence a necessary part of the story of nation-building in India' (Gyanendra Pandey, *The Construction of Communalism in Colonial India* [Delhi: Oxford University Press, 1990], 2–3).
6. For an account of the Malayan Emergency by one of the lead players in the event, see Chin Peng, as told to Ian Ward and Norma Miraflor, *My Side of History* (Singapore: Media Masters, 2003). Chin Peng was the Secretary General of the Malayan Communist Party during the period of the Malayan Emergency.
7. Malaysia and Singapore's complex plural societies have been often commented upon; see, for example, K. J. Ratnam, *Communalism and the Political Process in Malaya* (Kuala Lumpur: University of Malaya Press, 1965); and Karl von Vorys, *Democracy without Consensus: Communalism and Political Stability in Malaysia* (Princeton, NJ: Princeton University Press, 1975). The present Federation of Malaysia comprises peninsular or West Malaysia (formerly Malaya), Sabah (formerly British North Borneo) and Sarawak.
8. Singapore is 78 percent Chinese, 14 percent Malay and seven percent Indian; West Malaysia — the former Malaya — is 51 percent Malay, 33 percent Chinese and 11 percent Indian.
9. Officially, Singapore has four equal state languages (English, Malay, Mandarin-Chinese and Tamil), though English is the main language of bureaucracy and Malay is the 'national language' (*bahasa kebangsaan*) which was taught as a compulsory third language in schools until the late 1960s.
10. See Gupta, 'The Song': 70; and Nicholas B. Dirks, 'History and a Sign of the Modern', *Public Culture* 2, no. 2 (1990): 25–32.
11. Cf. Etienne Balibar, 'The Nation Form: History and Ideology', in Etienne Balibar and Immanuel Wallerstein, *Race, Class, Nation: Ambiguous Identities* (London: Verso, 1991): 'The history of nations, beginning with our own [that is, France], is always already presented to us in the form of a narrative which attributes to these entities the continuity of a subject. The formation of the nation thus appears as the fulfilment of a "project" stretching across centuries, in which there are different stages and moments of coming to self-awareness, which the prejudices of the various historians will portray as more or less decisive ...' (86). The postcolonial construction of Singapore ought to complicate what Balibar has to say of

'younger' nations: 'The myth of origins and national continuity, which we can easily see being set in place in the contemporary history of the "young" nations (such as India or Algeria) which emerged with the end of colonialism ... is therefore an effective ideological form, in which the imaginary singularity of national formations is constructed daily, by moving from the present into the past' (87).

12. Anderson, *Imagined Communities*, 123.
13. Partha Chatterjee, *Nationalist Thought in the Colonial World: A Derivative Discourse?* (London: Zed Books, 1986), 21.
14. See Robert Elegant, 'The Singapore of Mr Lee: "Confucian" Ethics, Asian Values', *Encounter*, June 1990, 21–29.
15. Rajaratnam's position as a racial minority in the country may partially account (his serious philosophical conviction aside) for his being steadfastly liberal and modern, in the nineteenth-century, British sense.
16. Cited in Alex Josey, *Lee Kuan Yew* (Singapore: Donald Moore Press), 303. Josey's book is my source for Lee's speeches. All further page references to further quotations by Lee will be given within brackets in the main text.
17. Cf. Edwin Lee's view on the imperial reinscription of the structure of Singapore consciousness: 'One hundred and forty years or so of British rule have etched on the Singapore consciousness certain principles and values which have become part of the national ethos. Singapore today is a country ... where th e prime minister sets the tone of public life as the colonial governor once did, where the rule of law prevails...'. ('The Colonial Legacy', in *Management of Success: The Moulding of Modern Singapore*, ed. Kernial Singh Sandhu and Paul Wheatley [Boulder, Co.: Westview Press, 1990], 42). It sounds as if the prime minister was, say, Sir Alfred Milner of South Africa, in his ability to maintain so-called 'irresponsible government' (which, of course, Milner considered very responsible), answerable only to Whitehall, rather than the chief of a cabinet of ministers answerable to a parliament seen to be the representative of 'the people'. One question would be: how is this particular structure of consciousness maintained in the postcolonial context? Another, more fundamental question would be: what exactly is a Singapore 'consciousness', given the complexity of the ethnic and culture positions in the country?
18. Cited by Josey, *Lee Kuan Yew*, 503.
19. The British, however, still controlled defence and foreign policy even though Lee was called 'prime minister', and not 'chief minister', which was David Marshall's equivocal title in Singapore before 1959.
20. Soon to be called the University of Singapore, and then in 1980 the National University of Singapore after it was combined with Nanyang University.
21. The Chinese form the majority of the English-educated groups.
22. This celebrates the gaining of self-rule; National Day is now celebrated on 9 August, the day Singapore was separated from Malaysia.
23. Cited in Josey, *Lee Kuan Yew*, 498.
24. In December 1966, Lee tells a Tamil audience: 'Three thousand years ago, there were no Anglo-Saxons because the Saxons had not yet gone over to Britain. One thousand years ago, they were still wearing animal skins. Your people in the Deccan had by then created a literature, and so had my ancestors in China' (634).
25. See Donald E. Hall (ed.), *Muscular Christianity: Embodying the Victorian Age* (Cambridge: Cambridge University Press, 1994); and C. J. W.-L. Wee, *Culture, Empire, and the Question of Being Modern* (Lanham, Md.: Lexington Books, 2003), especially the final chapter on Singapore. Cf. Lee's 8 August 1966 National Day address on Radio and Television

Singapore: 'The [educational] system we inherited from the British was lop-sided. Too much emphasis was laid on examination and the paper qualification. We were, therefore, rearing a whole *generation of softies*, who were clever, who wore spectacles, who were weak from want of enough exercise, enough sunshine, and with *not enough guts in them*. That was all right for a British colony, because the officers came from England, who had the necessary *brawn* and *toughness*. It was they who gave the orders and our people just executed them' (497, emphases mine). The extremely examination-oriented educational system in Singapore, which garners an unbelievable number of 'A' grades in the Singapore-Cambridge General Certificate of Examination 'Advanced' Levels, that has since developed is extremely ironic in the light of this speech's emphasis on a need for a Singaporean manliness.

26. The other parties are: the Malayan (later Malaysian) Chinese Association (MCA) and the Malayan (later Malaysian) Indian Congress (MIC).
27. All else apart, the PAP's ability to realise this threat was slim, given the party's poor performance on the mainland in the one general election they participated in.
28. It should be noted that the English-educated Chinese were also the minority Chinese group vis-à-vis the vernacular- and Mandarin-speaking Chinese groups.
29. See chapter 5. The question of Lee's 'Chineseness' is a long-standing one; Alex Josey has a section in his *Lee Kuan Yew* entitled 'How Much of a Chinese is Lee Kuan Yew?' (623–45).
30. Lee Kuan Yew, *Towards a Malaysian Malaysia* (Singapore: Government Printing Office, 1965).
31. *Straits Times* (Singapore), 25 February 1990.
32. For an attempt at a more general assessment of Rajaratnam's contribution to Singapore nation-building, see Hong Lysa, 'Making the History of Singapore: S. Rajaratnam and C. V. Devan Nair', in *Lee's Lieutenants: Singapore's Old Guard*, ed. Lam Peng Er and Kevin Y. L. Tan (St. Leonards, NSW: Allen & Unwin, 1999).
33. Chan Heng Chee and Obaid ul Haq (eds.), *The Prophetic and the Political: Selected Speeches and Writings of S. Rajaratnam* (Singapore: Graham Brash, 1987), 242. Chan and Obaid's book is my source for Rajaratnam's speeches. All further page references to further quotations by Rajaratnam will be given within brackets in the main text.
34. See Chatterjee, *Nationalist Thought in the Colonial World*.
35. See Hobsbawm, *Nations*.
36. See D. J. Enright, *Memoirs of a Mendicant Professor* (London: Chatto & Windus, 1969). Cf. Raymond Williams's not dissimilar take on this regarding non-white British identity in British culture: 'it is a serious misunderstanding ... to suppose that the problems of social identity are resolved by formal (merely legal) definitions. For unevenly and at times precariously, but always through long experience substantially, an effective awareness of social identity depends on actual and sustained social relationships' (*Towards 2000* [Harmondsworth: Penguin, 1983], 195). This prompts Paul Gilroy to ask, 'how long is long enough [for a British minority] to become a genuine Brit?' (*There Ain't No Black in the Union Jack: The Cultural Politics of Race and Nation* [1987; reissue, Chicago: University of Chicago Press, 1991], 49).
37. The 'iron framework' of a 'genuine era of world politics and world economics' which he spoke of in 1966.
38. For more general assessments of Goh's contribution to Singapore nation-building, see Kwok Kian-Woon, 'The Social Architect', and Tilak Doshi and Peter Coclanis, 'The Economic Architect: Goh Keng Swee', both in *Lee's Lieutenants*, ed. Lam and Tan.

39. Goh Keng Swee, *The Economics of Modernization and Other Essays* (Singapore: Asia Pacific Press, 1972), 32. Goh's book is my source for his speeches. All further page references to further quotations by Goh will be given within brackets in the main text.
40. Josey, *Lee Kuan Yew*, 252.
41. Representative examples of such thinking can be found in Julian Steward (ed.), *Contemporary Change in Traditional Societies* (Urbana: University of Illinois Press, 1967).
42. Bernard S. Cohn, *Colonialism and Its Forms of Knowledge: The British in India* (Princeton, NJ: Princeton University Press, 1996), 14–15.
43. 'Raja Wants Revival of a "Singaporean Singapore"', *Straits Times Weekly Overseas Edition*, 17 March 1990, 3.

Chapter 3

1. Rostow was an American academic who believed in developing societies' capacity for 'self-sustained growth'. He was an assistant to both Presidents John F. Kennedy and Lyndon B. Johnson, and had an influence on US foreign policy in the 1960s.
2. *Singapore: Facts and Figures 1967* (Singapore: Ministry of Culture, 1967), 6. The same line appears as the opening entry in sections entitled either 'Historical Dates' or 'Chronology' virtually in every *Facts and Figures* (later *Facts and Pictures*) publication thereafter.
3. The Barisan Sosialis, or Socialist Front, was formed as a breakaway, or ejected, party in September 1961.
4. See Dennis Bloodworth, *The Tiger and the Trojan Horse* (Singapore: Times Books International, 1986) and 'The Plen: What Singapore Would Have Become', *Straits Times Interactive* (Singapore), 22 July 1997 <http://www.asia1.com.sg/straitstimes>.
5. As noted, the PAP's representation of national emergence also subscribes to the evolutionary developmental perspective of postwar American social-science paradigms, as manifested in the theories of Daniel Lerner and Walt Rostow. See Julian Steward (ed.), *Contemporary Change in Traditional Societies* (Urbana: University of Illinois Press, 1967).
6. See C. J. W.-L. Wee, 'The Vanquished: Lim Chin Siong and a Progressivist National Narrative' in *Lee's Lieutenants: Singapore's Old Guard*, ed. Lam Peng Er and Kevin Y. L. Tan, (St. Leonards: Allen & Unwin, 1999). See also Loh Kah Seng, 'Within the Singapore Story: The Use and Narrative of History in Singapore', *Crossroads* 12, no. 2 (1998): 1–21; and T. N. Harper, 'Lim Chin Siong and the "Singapore Story"', in *Comet in Our Sky: Lim Chin Siong in History*, ed. Tan Jing Quee and Jomo K. S. (Kuala Lumpur: Insan, 2001). 'The Singapore Story', notably, is also the title of Volume I of Lee Kuan Yew's memoirs: *The Singapore Story: Memoirs of Lee Kuan Yew* (Singapore: Times Editions, 1998).
7. In Singapore's particularist multi-ethnic society, the PAP state as the guarantor of freedoms gained would draw on existing institutions, such as the Emergency Regulations set out by the British, later transformed first into the 1955 Preservation of Public Security Ordinance, and thereafter the Internal Security Act, and restrict what it takes to be the most dangerous aspects of autonomous human action.
8. Quentin Skinner, 'Meaning and Understanding in the History of Ideas', *History and Theory* 8 (1969): 3–53.
9. J. W. Burrow, *A Liberal Descent: Victorian Historians and the English Past* (Cambridge: Cambridge University Press, 1981), 4.
10. The text 'PAP's First Ten years' is reprinted in *The Prophetic and the Political: Selected Speeches of S. Rajaratnam*, ed. Chan Heng Chee and Obaid ul Haq (Singapore: Graham Brash, 1987), 64.

11. Hong Lysa, 'Making the History of Singapore: S. Rajaratnam and C. V. Devan Nair', in *Lee's Lieutenants*, ed. Lam and Tan, 101. She refers to Dennis Bloodworth's *Tiger and the Trojan Horse* and John Drysdale's *Singapore: Struggle for Success* (Singapore: Times Books International, 1984).
12. Hong, 'Making the History', 104. She is quoting from a speech by Rajaratnam given in 1968. This returns us to the general arguments that Lee, Rajaratnam and Dr. Goh Keng Swee made in the 1960s and 1970s relating to the need for a homogenised national culture, as has been examined in chapter 2.
13. C. J. W.-L. Wee, 'The "Clash" of Civilizations? Or an Emerging "East Asian Modernity"?' *SOJOURN: Journal of Social Issues in Southeast Asia* 11, no. 2 (1996): 211–30.
14. As literary critic Philip Holden notes, 'The "economic instrumental rationality" which underlies the first-generation PAP's leadership of pragmatism has clear, and explicitly drawn connections with the colonial government rationality through which Raffles' life is narrativised. Raffles, in this narrative, founded a new order in a moment of crisis, a modern order which paradoxically permitted the operations of the natural forces of the market, and allowed individuals to subject themselves to the market's discipline. Similarly, the post-independence PAP government justified interventionist policies through the argument that it was preparing the ground for the natural operations of the market' ('The Free Market's Second Coming: Monumentalising Raffles', in *Reading Culture: Textual Practices in Singapore,* ed. Phyllis G. L. Chew and Anneliese Kramer-Dahl [Singapore: Times Academic Press, 1999], 93).
15. Hong reinforces this point: 'Rajaratnam's cosmopolitanism should be understood as a provocation to those he saw as advocating ethnic-based nationalisms in Singapore rather than as being the credo of a supra-national humanist, for his concern is unabashedly centred on Singapore as a nation and the politics that would ensure its survival' ('Making the History', 106).
16. Raj K. Vasil, *Asianising Singapore: The PAP's Management of Ethnicity* (Singapore: Heinneman, 1995).
17. Chua Beng Huat has noted the scepticism of both S. Rajaratnam and Dr. Goh Keng Swee to Lee Kuan Yew's later stance on Asian values and economic success, especially given the latter's position that the great Victorian values were the crucial values at hand (*Communitarian Ideology and Democracy in Singapore* [London: Routledge, 1995], 66). Also see Ray Langenbach, *Performing the Singapore State, 1988–1995*, Ph.D. dissertation, University of Western Sydney, 2003, 111–14.
18. The phrase itself is probably from Alfred, Lord Tennyson's 'Ode on the Death of the Duke of Wellington', completed in time for the funeral on 18 November 1852, and was in that context more militaristic than Whiggish: 'Not once or twice in our rough island-story / The path of duty was the way to glory.' Cultural items can have strange lives.
19. Peter Osborne, 'Modernity is a Qualitative, not a Chronological, Category', *New Left Review*, 192 (March–April 1992): 76.
20. *Singapore: Facts and Figures 1964* (Singapore: Ministry of Culture, 1964), 11–13.
21. *Singapore: Facts and Figures 1967* (Singapore: Ministry of Culture, 1967), 6 and 3 respectively. All page numbers hereafter will be given in brackets in the main text.
22. *Singapore: Facts and Pictures 1976* (Singapore: Ministry of Culture, 1976), 26. All page numbers hereafter will be given in brackets in the main text.
23. *Singapore: Facts and Pictures 1986* (Singapore: Ministry of Communications and Information, 1986), 19.

24. *Singapore: Facts and Pictures 1998* (Singapore: Ministry of Information and the Arts, 1998), 10–15.
25. Wong Lin Ken, 'Commercial Growth Before the Second World War', in *A History of Singapore*, ed. Ernest C. T. Chew and Edwin Lee (Singapore: Oxford University Press, 1991). Page numbers of quotations hereafter will be given in brackets in the main text.
26. Cheng Siok Hwa, 'Economic Change and Industrialization', in *A History of Singapore*, ed. Chew and Lee, 181. Page numbers of subsequent quotations will be given in brackets in the main text.
27. Edwin Lee, 'The Colonial Legacy' in *The Management of Success: The Moulding of Modern Singapore*, ed. Kernial Singh Sandhu and Paul Wheatley (Singapore: Institute of Southeast Asian Studies, 1989). All page numbers hereafter will be given in brackets in the main text.
28. This interpretation has come under question. See Anthony Webster, *Gentlemen Capitalists: British Imperialism in South East Asia 1770–1890* (London: Tauris Academic Studies, 1998), 67.
29. Alfred Milner, 'Credo', *Times* (London), 27 July 1925.
30. F. S. Oliver, *The Endless Adventure: Personalities and Practical Politics in Eighteenth-Century England* (London: Macmillan, 1930), 3. Oliver was an associate of Milner's.
31. Chan Heng Chee, 'Political Developments', in *A History of Singapore*, ed. Chew and Lee, 176.
32. The acknowledged economic architect of Singapore, Dr. Goh Keng Swee, was conscious of the Victorian colonial economic legacy. See Tilak Doshi and Peter Coclanis, 'The Economic Architect: Goh Keng Swee', in *Lee's Lieutenants: Singapore's Old Guard*, ed. Lam and Tan; and Goh Keng Swee, *The Economics of Modernization* (Singapore: Asia Pacific Press, 1972).
33. Sangeeta Ray and Bill Schwarz, 'Postcolonial Discourse: The Raw and the Cooked', *ARIEL* 26, no. 1 (Jan. 1995): 150. Also see Karl Hack, 'Theories and Approaches to British Decolonization in Southeast Asia', in *The Transformation of Southeast Asia: International Perspectives on Decolonization*, ed. Marc Frey, Ronald W. Pruessen and Tan Tai Yong (Armonk, NY: M. E. Sharpe, 2003), for a different perspective on related issues.
34. See C. V. Devan Nair (compiler and ed.), *Socialism that* Works ... *The Singapore Way* (Singapore: Federal Publications, 1976), for details of the clash. I will return to this clash at the end of the chapter.
35. These political-theoretical terms, as they were used from the late-nineteenth century to the First World War, were capitalised.
36. *International Herald Tribune*, 28 September 1998.
37. Alfred Marshall, *The Official Papers of Alfred Marshall*, ed. J. M. Keynes (London: Macmillan, 1926), 253.
38. Stefan Collini, *Liberalism and Sociology: L. T. Hobhouse and Political Argument in England 1880–1914* (Cambridge: Cambridge University Press, 1979), 129.
39. L. T. Hobhouse, 'The Career of Fabianism', *Nation*, 30 March 1907.
40. E. J. Hobsbawm, *Age of Extremes: The Short Twentieth Century 1914–1991* (London: Abacus, 1995), 280.
41. Paul Hirst and Grahame Thompson, *Globalization in Question: The International Economy and the Possibilities of Governance* (Cambridge: Polity, 1996), 6.
42. See ibid., 31.
43. We could take Brenda S. A. Yeoh's *Contesting Space: Power Relations and the Urban Built Environment in Colonial Singapore* (Kuala Lumpur: Oxford University Press, 1996) as one subaltern historico-geographical study. Yeoh's exception perhaps proves what might be

a rule. Two histories from the 'bottom up' have also been written by James F. Warren: *Rickshaw Coolie: A People's History of Singapore, 1880–1940* (Singapore: Oxford University Press, 1986) and *Ah Ku and Karayuki-San: Prostitution in Singapore, 1870–1940* (Singapore: Oxford University Press, 1993). As Warren is non-Singaporean, this too seems to prove a possible rule.

44. See C. F. Yong, *Tan Kah-Kee: The Making of an Overseas Chinese Legend* (Singapore: Oxford University Press, 1989); C. F. Yong, *Chinese Leadership and Power in Colonial Singapore* (Singapore: Times Academic Press, 1992); Richard Lim, *Building a Singapore Bank: The O[verseas] U[nion] B[ank] Story* (Singapore: Overseas Union Bank Limited, 1999); Lien Ying Chow with Louis Kraar, *From Chinese Villager to Singapore Tycoon: My Life Story* (Singapore: Times Books International, 1992); Ho Rih Hwa, *Eating Salt: An Autobiography* (Singapore: Times Books International, 1991).
45. The term 'invented' implies a sort of bad-faith articulation of political and other identities — but this implication of inauthenticity is at least partially the result of Hobsbawm's antipathy towards certain aspects of nationalism.
46. See, for example, Gavan McCormack and Yoshio Sugimoto (eds.), *The Japanese Trajectory: Modernization and Beyond* (Cambridge: Cambridge University Press, 1988); and Marilyn Ivy, *Discourses of the Vanishing: Modernity, Phantasm, Japan* (Chicago: University of Chicago Press, 1995).
47. See chapter 5.
48. Dutch Labour Party, 'Memorandum Recommending Expulsion of the People's Action Party of Singapore from the Socialist International', in *Socialism that* Works ... *The Singapore Way*, compiled and ed. Nair, 250.
49. Ibid., 262. Note that there is no reference to 'East Asia'; instead, the larger identification, apart from Southeast Asia, is South Asia. In the process of gaining economic success, both critics and supporters of Singapore jointly have created a new cartographic concept — 'East Asia' — in order to make corporate sense of the Asian 'miracles'.
50. C. V. Devan Nair, 'Statement on Behalf of the People's Action Party of Singapore Made at the Meeting of the Bureau of the Socialist International Held in London on 28–29 May 1976', in *Socialism that* Works ... *The Singapore Way*, compiled and ed. Nair, 142, 143.
51. Ibid., 142–43.
52. Ibid., 143.
53. Goh Keng Swee, 'A Socialist Economy That Works', in *Socialism That* Works ... *The Singapore Way*, compiled and ed. Nair, 83.
54. Ibid., 84.
55. Manuel Castells, 'Four Asian Tigers with a Dragon Head: A Comparative Analysis of the State, Economy and Society in the Asian Pacific Rim', in *States and Development in the Asian Pacific Rim*, ed. Richard P. Appelbaum and Jeffrey Henderson (Newbury, Calif.: Sage, 1992); see Chua Beng-Huat, *Political Legitimacy and Housing: Stakeholding in Singapore* (London: Routledge, 1997) for a specific analysis of the 'consumption' of public housing and political legitimacy
56. The intellectual heritage Goh saw himself part of, from a 1970 speech, is clearly stated: 'If we are completely honest with ourselves, I think we can detect in contemporary Singapore a strange and striking similarity of intellectual climate with Victorian England, together with much of the hypocrisies and cruelties of that age' (cited in Doshi, Coclanis, and Kwok 1999). It is within the context of such utterances that we can see his contribution to the reworking of both *laissez-faire*ism and state interventionism in relation to the global market forces.

57. W. G. Huff, *The Economic Growth of Singapore: Trade and Development in the Twentieth Century* (Cambridge: Cambridge University Press, 1994), 320.
58. Augustine H. H. Tan, 'Foreign Investment and Multinational Corporations', in *Socialism That* Works ... *The Singapore Way*, compiled and ed. Nair, 86.
59. Ibid., 95.
60. S. Rajaratnam, 'An Epistle to the Synod of the Socialist Orthodox Church', in *Socialism that* Works ... *The Singapore Way*, compiled and ed. Nair; reprinted in *The Prophetic and the Political: Selected Speeches of S. Rajaratnam*, ed. Chan Heng Chee and Obaid ul Haq (Singapore: Graham Brash, 1987), 82.
61. Ibid., 85.
62. Ibid., 86.
63. Ibid., 87.
64. Chua Beng-Huat, 'Asian Values Discourse and the Resurrection of the Social', *positions: east asia cultures critique* 7, no. 2 (1999): 583.

Chapter 4

1. Sharon Siddique, 'Culture and Identity in the Public Housing Environment', in *The City and the State: Singapore's Built Environment Revisited*, ed. Ooi Giok Ling and Kenson Kwok (Singapore: Oxford University Press, 1997), 136.
2. Goh Keng Swee, *Urban Incomes and Housing: A Report of the Social Survey of Singapore 1953–54* (Singapore: Government Printing Office, 1956).
3. Robert E. Gamer, *The Politics of Urban Development in Singapore* (Ithaca, NY: Cornell University Press, 1972), 47.
4. Rem Koolhaas, 'Singapore Songlines: Portrait of a Potemkin Metropolis ... or Thirty Years of Tabula Rasa', in Rem Koolhaas and Bruce Mau, *Small, Medium, Large, Extra-Large*, ed. Jennifer Sigler (Rotterdam: 010 Publishers, 1995), 1041. All subsequent page references will be given within brackets in the main text.
5. For more information on the OMA, see their website: <http://www.oma.nl/index.htm>.
6. See Marshall Berman, *All that Is Solid Melts into Air: The Experience of Modernity* (1982; New York: Penguin, 1988), mainly chapter 3, 'Baudelaire: Modernism in the Streets'.
7. See the essays in the section 'A Geography of Modernism', in *Modernism: A Guide to European Literature 1890–1930*, ed. Malcolm Bradbury and James McFarlane (1976; London: Penguin, 1991).
8. Koolhaas is right about the state but simply wrong about high culture *per se* in Singapore — this is a matter of lack of knowledge. The Chinese-speaking intelligentsia and arts practitioners — in dramatic, literary, and in some cases visual-arts fields — from the earlier part of the twentieth century had a strong reformist and oftentimes leftist streak drawn from, to a large extent, the May Fourth Movement in China. By the late 1970s, most of such practices had either been repressed or eliminated. The problem is how you recall the 'agony' of modernity and modernity in a society where history has been rendered unimportant. While Singapore as a society with a fairly advanced economy may not be unique in having a memory 'loss', its cultural resources are also less well-endowed to deal with such problems. Of course, such difficulties are compounded by the non-native nature of these artistic practices — how was this Chinese-inflected modernism 'part' of colonial Malaya or Singapore? This question has yet to be fully addressed in the scholarship on the arts within the city-state.

9. While I think that Koolhaas, by and large, is correct, he is here of course making his point both generally and polemically. The ascendance of the PAP over the body of the island was gained more slowly, with many unplanned circumstances that aided them, such as the Separation from Malaysia — this freed the PAP from the need to answer to the federal government and gave them complete territorial control over the island. See Gamer, *Politics of Urban Development*, chapters 3 to 5, especially chapter 4, 'Kallang: Dealing with Those Who Stood in the Way'.
10. The original publication Koolhaas refers to is: Christopher Alexander, 'A City Is Not a Tree', *Architectural Forum* 122, no. 1 (April 1965): 58–61.
11. See Fumihiko Maki, *Investigations in Collective Form* (St. Louis, Mo.: Washington University School of Architecture, 1964).
12. Kasimir Malevich (1879–1935) was the founder of Suprematism, which stood for a pure geometric abstraction in painting. While his art tried to reach the purest form (the 'White on White' series of paintings of 1917–20 embodies well his abstract approach), he did make suggestions for a utopian architecture, which later influenced not only the Bauhaus but also, more generally, modernist architecture.
13. Pankaj Mishra, 'Matter over Minds: For 500 Years East and West Have Exchanged Goods But Not Cultural Values', *Guardian Weekly* (29 October–4 November 2004), 25. Mishra here is reviewing the 'Encounters: The Meeting of Asia and Europe' exhibition at the Victoria and Albert Museum, London, held during the closing months of 2004. He is a critic, novelist (*The Romantics* [2001]) and writer (*An End to Suffering: The Buddha in the World* [2004]) who has edited some of V. S. Naipaul's writing — and therefore like Naipaul is interested in questions of culture, history and empire, though he is not a cultural reactionary.
14. Harry Harootunian, *History's Disquiet: Modernity, Cultural Practice, and the Question of Everyday Life* (New York: Columbia University Press, 2000), 19.
15. Paul Hirst and Grahame Thompson, *Globalization in Question: The International Economy and the Possibilities of Governance* (Cambridge: Polity Press, 1996).
16. Saskia Sassen, 'Detecting the Global Inside the National', *University of Chicago Magazine*, December 2000, 32.
17. The UN team consisted of Charles Abrams, Susumu Kobe and Otto Koenigsberger.
18. Harootunian, *History's Disquiet*, 17.
19. Cf. Jürgen Habermas: 'the deformations of a lifeworld that is regimented, dissected, controlled, and watched over are more subtle than the obvious forms of material exploitation and impoverishment' (*The New Conservatism: Cultural Criticism and the Historians' Debate*, ed. and trans. Shierry Weber Nicholson [Cambridge, Mass.: MIT Press, 1989], 59).
20. See Beng-Huat Chua, *Communitarian Ideology and Democracy in Singapore* (London: Routledge, 1995).
21. Rem Koolhaas, *Project for Prada Part 1* (Milan: Fondazione Prada Edizioni, 2001).
22. Ministry of Information, Communications and the Arts, Singapore, 'Press Releases: Creative Industries take Centre Stage in Singapore in November 2005' <http://www.mica.gov.sg/pressroom/press_0510051.htm>.
23. Harootunian, *History's Disquiet*, 163, note 4.
24. Ziauddin Sardar, 'Cultural Suicide, Ayoh!: Ziauddin Sardar Arrives in Singapore to Find It's Been Occupied', *New Internationalist* 333 (April 2001) <http://www.oneworld.org/ni/issue333/cultural.htm>.
25. Elsewhere, Sardar opines that the conscious Asian fake — the fake brand-name clothes and video compact discs (VCDs) you can easily buy in either Kuala Lumpur or Bangkok — are the 'genuine' signs of identity, and not the counterfeit Asian modern

of Singapore: 'Eventually, we all want to look in a mirror and see ourselves' (ibid.). His preference is for Kuala Lumpur — Malaysia's federal capital, and another former British colonial city — because he thinks that the multi-ethnic cultural synthesis there is both more disorienting and exciting; see Ziauddin Sardar, *The Consumption of Kuala Lumpur* (London: Reaktion Books, 2000).

26. Raymund Ryan, 'Urban Generations: Raymund Ryan on the Evolution of Urban Culture from Utopia to Dystopia', *tate* 24 (Spring 2001), 25.
27. Cf. Abidin Kusno, *Beyond the Postcolonial: Architecture, Urban Space and Political Cultures in Indonesia* (London: Routledge, 2000): '"Westernization" or "Americanization" ... may suggest ... a destination, a process of arrival, by replication, at some imagined place called the "West". But seen from the other [non-Western] side of the globe, ... [i]t could point to a departure, an exit from something one wants to leave behind, which does not necessarily imply that one would then arrive at, or replicate, a particular place called the "West"' (204).
28. Kuo's role in the counter-reterritorialising of Singapore culture is addressed in chapter 6.
29. See David Birch, 'Singapore English Drama: A Historical Overview 1958–1985', in *9 Lives: 10 Years of Singapore Theatre 1987–1997*, ed. Sanjay Krishnan (Singapore: The Necessary Stage, 1996).
30. In 1989, Tang is quoted as saying that: 'The main reason for being here [in Sembawang] is the isolation.' The magazine writer's response to this was: 'The psychological context of the village is earthy, rudimentary, and free of the numerous and trivial distractions normally found in the city' (Chia Ming Chien, 'The Artists' Village', *Man*, April–May 1989, 33).
31. Kwok Kian Chow, *Channels and Confluences: A History of Singapore Art*, exhibition catalogue (Singapore: Singapore Art Museum, 1996), 142, 144. For more on the Artists' Village, see Museum of Contemporary Art, *Situation: Collaborations, Collectives and Artist Networks from Sydney, Singapore, Berlin* (Sydney: Museum of Contemporary Art, 2005).
32. Kwok, *Channels and Confluences*, 141.
33. This is one Japanese curator's assessment of that moment: 'Like it or not, every country in Asia is baptized by Western modern art completely different from its traditional art. The common way by which each country accepted modern art was to depict their own unique theme (sceneries of the country, religious symbols) through the use of the materials, media (for example, oil and canvas) and styles (Cubism, Expressionism) of the Occident. In Singapore there are many works in such a manner. ... To compromise traditional painting technique and modern art — this seems too facile a way to vivify the tradition of the people. ... Just a half-baked mixture of the techniques of the West and the East will not be able to transcend either one of them. Also, in Singaporean art, it is not only the technique that is conservative but the content itself tends to be strongly so. There are scarcely any works that are suffused with message or based on social criticism. Such a conservative, luke-warm trend has been most dominant in the art scene of the 80s in Singapore [until the arrival of Tang Da Wu].' Thereafter, '[t]he art scene of Singapore has rushed into the realm of contemporary art at the end of the 1980s. As a matter of fact, younger generation has begun to make their works in international styles without sticking to their ethnic tradition. ... From the generation relying on the ethnic traditional culture to the generation not adhered to it, Singapore is now trying to make a change at a bound' (Etsuko Tsuzuki, 'Between Ethnic Culture and Intimidated Culture', in Fukuoka Art Museum, *Annual Artist Today — Fukuoka Annual V: Tang Da Wu*, exhibition catalogue [Fukuoka: Fukuoka Art Museum, 1991], 7, 8, 9).
34. For more details on arts development in the 1990s, see C. J. W.-L. Wee, 'Creating High Culture in the Globalized "Cultural Desert" of Singapore', *The Drama Review* 47, no. 4

(Winter 2003): 84–97. In the early hours of 1994, at an independent arts event, a 21-year-old performance artist presented a performance work in which he protested a police entrapment exercise undertaken against homosexual men. At one point, he had his back to the audience and cut off a bit of his pubic hair, though the audience could not see this. A picture of this — with the young man's buttocks partially exposed — was on the front page of a tabloid, and the police were called in, amid a blaze of sensationalised press coverage. The controversy thereafter was extended to a forum theatre production by The Necessary Stage, which was said to be Marxist because of forum theatre's connection with Augusto Boal. 'Marxist' is an old coded state term for 'communist' — though by 1994, such charges did not make sense anymore. Unscripted performance art and theatre work were then proscribed for many years, and some artists were brought to court. See Ray Langenbach, *Performing the Singapore State, 1988–1995*, unpublished Ph.D. dissertation, University of Western Sydney, Australia, 2003; and Lee Weng Choy, 'Chronology of a Controversy' and 'A Review of Josef Ng's Performance', both in *Looking at Culture*, ed. Sanjay Krishna, Sharaad Kuttan, Lee Weng Choy, Leon Perrera and Jimmy Yap (Singapore: Artres Design & Communications, 1996). *Looking at Culture* initially was to be an issue of the National University of Singapore Society's journal, *Commentary*. The Society panicked in the wake of the 1994 arts controversy, and stopped the publication process; the editors resigned and subsequently had the issue privately published.

35. *Mee Pok Man*. Eric Khoo (Singapore: Zhao Wei Films, 1995).
36. *Mee pok* is a flat noodle, and this is a Hokkien-Chinese term.
37. *Twelve Storeys* (Mandarin-Chinese: *Shi'er lou*). Eric Khoo (Singapore: Zhao Wei Films, 1997).
38. Jan Uhde and Yvonne Ng Uhde, *Latent Images: Film in Singapore* (Singapore: Oxford University Press, 2000), 109.
39. See Murray Hiebert, 'Cannes Do, *Lah*: A Dynamic Young Director Spurs Singapore's Sleepy Movie-Making Industry Back to Life', *Far Eastern Economic Review* (17 July 1997) <http://www.singapore-window.org/0717feer.htm>. (The article overstates the notion of a Singapore 'movie-making industry,' though.)
40. 'Interview with Eric Khoo', in Uhde and Uhde, *Latent Images*, 121.
41. *Money No Enough*. Tay Teck Lock (Singapore: JSP Entertainment, 1998).
42. Uhde and Ng Uhde, 127.
43. See Chua Beng-Huat, 'Taiwan's Present/Singapore's Past Mediated by Hokkien Language', in *Rogue Flows: Trans-Asian Cultural Traffic*, ed. Koichi Iwabuchi, Stephen Muecke and Mandy Thomas (Hong Kong: Hong Kong University Press, 2004).
44. *Eating Air*. Kelvin Tong and Jasmine Ng (Singapore: Multi-Story Complex, 1999).
45. Chua Beng Huat and Wei-Wei Yeo, 'Singapore Cinema: Eric Khoo and Jack Neo — Critique from the Margins and the Mainstream', *Inter-Asian Cultural Studies* 4, no. 1 (April 2003): 120.
46. Koichi Iwabuchi (ed.), *Feeling Asian Modernities: Transnational Consumption of Japanese TV Dramas* (Hong Kong: Hong Kong University Press, 2004).
47. In Singapore's case, it is a strongly resurgent presence from about the mid-1990s onwards, in form of both popular music and TV dramas. While the Japanese mass cultural presence was reasonably visible in the 1970s and the 1980s, it had become less visible by the early 1990s. (See Koichi Iwabuchi, *Recentering Globalization: Popular Culture and Japanese Transnationalism* [Durham, NC: Duke University Press, 2002]; C. J. W.-L. Wee, 'Buying Japan: Singapore, Japan and an "East Asian" Modernity', *Journal of Pacific Asia* 4 [1997]: 21–46; and Leo Ching, 'Globalizing the Regional, Regionalizing the Global: Mass Culture

and Asianism in the Age of Late Capital', in *Globalization*, ed. Arjun Appadurai [Durham, NC: Duke University Press, 2001].) However, this presence renewed itself with increased vigour by the mid-1990s. More recently, from about 2000 onwards, Korean popular music and, more significantly, TV dramas and films — *Hallyu*, or the so-called Korean Wave — have made inroads into the region at large. In return, though, J-pop has made surprisingly direct inroads into South Korea since the ban was lifted by Seoul on the entry of Japanese cultural products, despite anti-Japanese antipathy.

48. Ackbar Abbas, *Hong Kong: Culture and the Politics of Disappearance* (Minneapolis: University of Minnesota Press, 1997), 31.
49. This is a cultural and mythicised imaginary now a little more familiar to the West through Lee Ang's hit film, *Crouching Tiger and Hidden Dragon* (2000).
50. Much Japanese *manga* is translated into Chinese in locales such as Taipei, and then exported to places with noticeable Chinese populations such as Kuala Lumpur and Singapore. For an historicised study of *manga*, see Sharon Kinsella, *Adult Manga: Culture and Power in Contemporary Japanese Culture* (Honolulu: University of Hawai'i Press, 2000).

Chapter 5

1. See, for example, the articles in *Cultural Anthropology* 3, no. 4 (1988), Special Issue on 'Anthropology and the Analysis of Modernity', ed. Paul Rabinow; Arjun Appadurai, 'Disjuncture and Difference in the Global Cultural Economy', *Public Culture* 2, no. 2 (1990), reprinted in Appadurai's *Modernity at Large: Cultural Dimensions of Globalization* (Minneapolis: University of Minnesota Press, 1996); and Lisa Rofel, *Other Modernities: Gendered Yearnings in China after Socialism* (Berkeley: University of California Press, 1999).
2. Examples are: Roy Hofheinz, Jr. and Kent Calder, *The Eastasia Edge* (New York: Basic Books, 1982); Robert Wade, *Governing the Market: Economic Theory and the Role of Government in East Asia* (Princeton, NJ: Princeton University Press, 1990); and Linda Weiss, 'Sources of the East Asian Advantage: An Institutional Analysis', in *Pathways to Asia: The Politics of Engagement*, ed. Richard Robison (St. Leonards, NSW: Allen & Unwin, 1996).
3. Neo-Confucian champion Tu Wei-ming provocatively argued at the debate's height that a socio-historical explanation of societies 'predicated on the exclusive dichotomy of tradition and modernity [as societies are thought to be in the West] is no longer workable' ('The Rise of Industrial East Asia: The Role of Confucian Values', *Copenhagen Papers in East and Southeast Asian Studies* 4 [1989]: 92). Tu seems to have since changed his mind; he surprised a Singapore audience in 1995 by saying that industrial East Asia's rise embodied the *worst* aspects of the Enlightenment heritage of 'growth, development and exploitation': 'Japan and the four mini-dragons [are] ... characterised by mercantilism, commercialism and international competitiveness' (quoted in 'Democracy "Better for Confucian Ideals"', *Straits Times* [Singapore], 22 March 1995, 22).
4. 'Some economies — notably Japan, Korea, and Taiwan ... intervened in markets with industrial, trade, and financial sector policies. On balance, some of these interventions contributed to their extraordinary growth, but this was only possible because of highly unusual *historical and institutional circumstances*' (World Bank, *The East Asian Miracle: Economic Growth and Public Policy* [New York: Oxford University Press, 1993], 366, emphasis mine).
5. C. J. W.-L. Wee, 'Framing the "New" East Asia: Anti-Imperialist Discourse and Global Capitalism', in *'The Clash of Civilizations?' Asian Responses*, ed. Salim Rashid (Dhaka: University Press, 1997).

6. Slavoj Žižek, 'Multiculturalism, or, the Cultural Logic of Multinational Capitalism', *New Left Review* 225 (1997): 44.
7. David Harvey, *The Condition of Postmodernity: An Enquiry into the Conditions of Cultural Change* (Cambridge, Mass.: Blackwell, 1990), 109.
8. Nicholas D. Kristof, 'Asian Style Capitalism Giving Way to the Free Market', *New York Times*, 17 January 1998.
9. Appadurai, *Modernity at Large*, 15.
10. Stuart Hall, 'The Local and the Global: Globalization and Ethnicity', in *Dangerous Liaisons: Gender, Nation, and Postcolonial Perspectives*, ed. Anne McClintock, Aamir Mufti and Ella Shohat (Minneapolis: University of Minnesota Press, 1997), 183.
11. Žižek, 'Multiculturalism': 46, 52.
12. Hall, 'The Local and the Global', 180.
13. Arif Dirlik, 'Globalisation and the Politics of Place' in *Globalisation and the Asia-Pacific: Contested Territories*, ed. Kris Olds, Peter Dicken, Philip F. Kelly, Lily Kong and Henry Wai-chung Yeung (London: Routledge, 1999), 49.
14. James H. Mittelman, 'Rethinking the "New Regionalism" in the Context of Globalisation', *Global Governance* 2, no. 2 (1996): 190.
15. See Bob Jessop, 'Reflections on Globalisation and its (Il)Logic(s)', in *Globalisation and the Asia-Pacific*, ed. Olds, Dicken, Kelly, Kong and Yeung.
16. See T. N. Harper, *The End of Empire and the Making of Malaya* (Cambridge: Cambridge University Press, 1999), 274–307. The dominance of the English language was part of a continuation of a colonial modernity. See Kwok Kian-Woon, 'The Problem of "Tradition" in Contemporary Singapore', in *Heritage and Contemporary Values in Singapore*, ed. Arun Mahizhnan (Singapore: Institute of Policy Studies, 1993).
17. For example, Geoffrey Benjamin, 'The Cultural Logic of Singapore's "Multiracialism"', in *Singapore: Society in Transition*, ed. Riaz Hassan (Kuala Lumpur: Oxford University Press, 1976); and David Brown, *The State and Ethnic Politics in Southeast Asia* (London: Routledge, 1994). The other causes usually adduced for seeing the political in ethnic terms are: the political consciousness of being Chinese in a largely Malay region; and the link between what the PAP called 'Chinese chauvinism' and leftist movements. Such concerns allowed the state to promote an internal crisis mentality — an 'ideology of survival' (Chan Heng Chee, *The Politics of Survival* [Singapore: Oxford University Press, 1971]) — that helps maintain PAP political 'indispensability'.
18. Aaron Segal, *Atlas of International Migration* (London: Hans Zell, 1993), 12. The Indian migration statistics are probably underestimated. Migration and its consequences for an integrated labour market is one broad area of analysis in the history of the international economy.
19. W. G. Huff, *The Economic Growth of Singapore: Trade and Development in the Twentieth Century* (Cambridge: Cambridge University Press, 1994), 320.
20. Figures from Economic Development Board, *Report of the Census of Industrial Production* (Singapore: Department of Statistics, 1975); see Huff, *Economic Growth*, 319.
21. Sharon Siddique, 'Singaporean Identity', in *Management of Success: The Moulding of Modern Singapore*, ed. K. S. Sandhu and Paul Wheatley (Singapore: Institute of Southeast Asian Studies, 1989), 563–64.
22. Brown, *State and Ethnic Politics*, 80.
23. S. Rajaratnam, *The Prophetic and the Political: Selected Speeches of S. Rajaratnam*, ed. Chan Heng Chee and Obaid ul Haq (Singapore: Graham Brash, 1987), 119–20.
24. Ibid., 128.

25. Rajaratnam is also one member of the founding generation of the PAP who has steadfastly maintained his commitment to an ethnicity-blind multiracialism. One scholar observes: 'As the [English-language] university base expanded, and English became more widely embraced, the fast-track passport status [of the English-speaking] was diluted, and with it, the Singaporean Singapore identity. It was probably no accident that Raja[ratnam] was the proponent of this because as a Ceylonese Tamil, he was the ... the beneficiary under the colonial era' (private e-mail communication to the author).
26. Rajaratnam, *Prophetic and the Political*, 229.
27. Ibid., 231.
28. Ibid., 231.
29. Stephen Toulmin, *Cosmopolis: The Hidden Agenda of Modernity* (Chicago: University of Chicago Press, 1992).
30. S. Rajaratnam, 'Raja Wants Revival of a "Singaporean Singapore"', *Straits Times Weekly Overseas Edition*, 17 March 1990, 3.
31. Raj K. Vasil, *Asianising Singapore: The PAP's Management of Ethnicity* (Singapore: Heinneman, 1995).
32. The latter is not the primary focus; for detailed analysis of such resistance within Singapore society, see Brown, *State and Ethnic Politics*; Nirmala S. PuruShotam, *Negotiating Language, Constructing Difference: Disciplining Difference in Singapore* (Berlin: Mouton de Gruyter, 1998); and Michael Hill and Lian Kwen Fee, *The Politics of Nation Building and Citizenship in Singapore* (London: Routledge, 1995).
33. 'Real Threat to Culture: It's Not the End of Chinese Schools, but the Loss of Traditional Family Values, Says PM', *Straits Times* (Singapore), 19 February 1984.
34. John Wong and Aline K. Wong, 'Confucian Values as a Social Framework for Singapore's Economic Development', in *Conference on Confucianism and Economic Development in East Asia* (Taipei: Chung-Hua Institution for Economic Research, 1989).
35. Eddie C. Y. Kuo, *Confucianism as Political Discourse in Singapore: The Case of an Incomplete Revitalization Movement*, Working Paper No. 113 (Singapore: Department of Sociology, National University of Singapore, 1992).
36. Tong Chee Kiong, 'The Rationalization of Religion', in *Imagining Singapore*, ed. Ban Kah Choon, Anne Pakir and Tong Chee Kiong (Singapore: Times Academic Press, 1992).
37. H. E. Wilson, *Social Engineering in Singapore: Educational Policies and Social Change, 1819–1972* (Singapore: Singapore University Press, 1978).
38. Quoted in 'Lee: Need for a Value System', *Straits Times* (Singapore), 5 June 1978.
39. Chua Beng-Huat comments that the PAP first 'racialized boundaries' and subsequently homogenised the population 'to arrive at a definition of Singapore as an "Asian" nation'; he also notes: 'it is of strategic economical and political importance for Singapore to insert itself into a larger piece. Asia may not need Singapore, but Singapore needs Asia' ('Culture, Multiracialism and National Identity in Singapore', in *Trajectories: Inter-Asia Cultural Studies*, ed. Kuan-Hsing Chen [London: Routledge, 1998], 198).
40. In 1980, Roderick MacFarquhar had used the term 'post-Confucian challenge' in the *Economist* magazine, and US academic Edwin O. Reishauer the expression 'Sinic world' in *Foreign Affairs*.
41. George C. Lodge and Ezra Vogel (eds.), *Ideology and National Competitiveness: An Analysis of Nine Countries* (Boston: Harvard Business School, 1987), 124.
42. Huff, *Economic Growth of Singapore*, 312.

43. In January 1987, the Institute organised a major conference on 'Confucian Ethics and the Modernization of Industrial Asia', and in 1990, 'Confucian Humanism and Modernization: The Institutional Imperatives'. As the rationale for its being ran out, it was changed into first the Institute of East Asian Political Economy and then the present East Asian Institute, which is a part of the National University of Singapore.
44. Lee Kuan Yew, 'Preface' to Goh Keng Swee and the Education Study Team, *Report on the Ministry of Education 1978* (Singapore: Singapore National Printers, 1979), v.
45. Ibid.
46. Ibid.
47. Toh Chin Chye, 'Cultural Heritage versus Technological Development: Challenges to Education', in *Cultural Heritage versus Technological Development*, ed. R. E. Vente, R. S. Bhatal and R. M. Nakhoda (Hong Kong: Maruzen Asia, 1981), 21–22.
48. Lee, 'Preface', v.
49. In 1971, the state had even detained some members of the Chinese daily, *Nanyang Siang Pau*, because of this discontent (see Chan Heng Chee and H.-D. Evers, 'Nation Building and National Identity in Southeast Asia', in *Buildings States and Nations*, Vol. 2, ed. S. N. Eisenstadt and Stein Rokkan [Beverly Hills: Sage, 1973], 312–14).
50. Goh Keng Swee and the Education Study Team, *Report on the Ministry of Education 1978* (Singapore: Singapore National Printers, 1979), 1–5.
51. Quoted in Chia Poteik, 'Lee Explains Need to Use Mandarin', *Straits Times* (Singapore), 13 March 1978. All quotations from Lee in this paragraph are from Chia.
52. Ilsa Sharp, 'Part of a Daring Experiment ... to Preserve that "Part of Ourselves" and to Imbibe the Best from the West', *Straits Times* (Singapore), 2 December 1978. Both the quotations from Lee in this paragraph and all quotations from Lee in the next paragraph are from Sharp.
53. See Chua Beng Huat, '"Asian Values" Discourse and the Resurrection of the Social', *positions: east asia cultures critique* 7, no. 2 (Fall 1999): 573–92.
54. Lee Kuan Yew, 'Make Time for Your Children', *Straits Times* (Singapore), 19 February 1984. All quotations in this and the next four paragraphs are from this article.
55. For the relationship between motherhood, sexuality, Confucianism and race, see Geraldine Heng and Janadas Devan, 'State Fatherhood: The Politics of Sexuality, Nationalism and Race in Singapore', in *Nationalisms and Sexualities*, ed. Andrew Parker et al. (New York: Routledge, 1992).
56. The set of buildings in question were in Bugis, a downtown heritage district that is 'today characterised as a sanitised tourist attraction with a complex history'; in the late nineteenth century, the area 'was called *Bu Ye Tian* (Heaven without Night), … where itinerant hawkers enjoy[ed] a roaring business in the prosperous night market, and where entertainers and transvestites attract[ed] public audiences throughout the night till daybreak. … [The urban redevelopment that took place in this area is called] Bugis Junction[, which] formerly consisted of three city blocks surrounded by main roads and divided by four minor roads — Hylam, Malabar, Malay, and Bugis Streets. When these blocks were parcellated, tendered and subsequently sold, the U[rban] R[edevelopment] A[uthority] stipulated that the development should conserve existing rows of shophouses on three minor roads in the district. During the design process, it was determined that a large parking space would be required. … In the end, the car park was located in a newly constructed basement, which required that the shophouses built on ground level be demolished. To retain the character of the original streets, these shophouses were subsequently reconstructed. Although all the facades of the shophouses were exhaustively documented and rebuilt, the buildings'

structure and interior arrangements were altered in order to accommodate new commercial programmes. The shopping malls tracing the original streets were covered with new glass roofs, and this became Singapore's first air-conditioned shopping arcade [in 1994]' (Tsuto Sakamoto, 'Bugis: Everyday Presence/Representation of the Ideal', *Singapore Architect* 212 [December 2001], 160, 160–61).

57. Goh Chok Tong, 'Prepare Our Children Well for the New Century', *Contact*, September 1996, 2.
58. Lee Hsien Loong, 'National Education', Ministry of Education (Singapore) website, 17 May 1997 <http: / / www1.moe.edu.sg / speeches / 170597.htm>.
59. Martin Jacques, 'Suharto Has His Back to the Wall', *Guardian Weekly*, 1 March 1998, 7; John Aglionby and AP, 'Indonesia's Elite Spits Defiance', *Guardian Weekly*, 28 April 1998, 4.
60. 'Interview: Lee Kuan Yew, "Asian Values" and the Crisis', *Time*, 16 March 1998, 24.
61. Quoted in 'Key Challenge Is to Retain Some Sense of Singaporeanness', *Straits Times* (Singapore), 25 October 1997.
62. Teo Chee Hean, 'Ministerial Statement by the Minister of Education, Rear-Adm. Teo Chee Hean at the Budget Debate on 19 Mar. 98', Ministry of Education (Singapore) website, 19 March 1998, <http: / / www1.moe.edu.sg / speeches / 030697.htm>, 1.
63. Ibid., 4.
64. Samir Amin, *Delinking: Towards a Polycentric World*, trans. Michael Wolfers (1985; London: Zed Books, 1990).

Chapter 6

1. Fernando Coronil, 'Towards a Critique of Globalcentrism: Speculations on Capitalism's Nature', *Public Culture* 12, no. 2 (Spring 2000): 353, 368. Special Issue on 'Millennial Capitalism and the Culture of Neoliberalism', guest ed. Jean Comaroff and John L. Comaroff.
2. Ibid., 368.
3. Timothy Brennan, 'Cosmo-Theory', *South Atlantic Quarterly* 100, no. 3 (Summer 2001): 660, 661.
4. T. S. Eliot, 'Tradition and the Individual Talent', in *Selected Essays*, 3rd enlarged edition (London: Faber and Faber, 1951), 22.
5. A note on the usage of Japanese and Chinese names in the article: by and large, I put the family name first, following the custom of both cultures. The exception will be when a writer is well-known by the inverted use of their names, or when their publications use the reverse order of names.
6. Cited in Kawashima Rondo, 'Exploring New Horizons in Asian Theater: Experimental Play "Lear"', *Fukuoka Arts and Cultural Information* (March 1999), 26.
7. The following accusation was made public: 'KUO PAO KUN, 37, was born in China and was arrested on March 17, 1976. At the time of his arrest, he was an Assistant Secretary of the Chinese Chamber of Commerce. ... His conversion to communist ideology was by self-indoctrination from the books he read in Australia. ... He returned to Singapore in 1965 and set up a Performing Arts Studio to propagate leftist dance and drama. The Performing Arts Studio was renamed the Practice Theatre School .... He was inducted into the MPLL in August 1974, four months ahead of his wife, GOH LAY KUAN' ('The Faces of Subversion', *Straits Times* [Singapore], 28 May 1976, 30).
8. The Chinese-language tradition in theatre in Malaysia and Singapore partook of the modern progressiveness of the May Fourth movement, and Kuo himself further was influenced by the Cultural Revolution and Bertolt Brecht, whose work he introduced to

Singapore in his pre-detention career. Just to read the titles of Kuo's early plays indicate his then-political direction: *Hey, Wake Up* (1968); *The Struggle* (1969); *The Sparks of Youth* (1970); *Sister Lou's New Year Eve* (1972); *The Growth* (1973). The plays can be found — in the original Chinese versions — in Quah Sy Ren (ed.), *The Complete Works of Kuo Pao Kun: Plays in Chinese, the 1960s and the 1970s*, Volume 1 (Singapore: World Scientific, 2005).

9. Yu Yun, 'The Soil of Life and the Tree of Art: A Study of Kuo Pao Kun's Individuality Cultural Through His Playwriting', trans. Kuo Jian Heng, in Kuo Pao Kun, *Images at the Margins: A Collection of Kuo Pao Kun's Plays* (Singapore: Times Books, 2000).
10. For analyses of Kuo's earlier work, see Quah Sy Ren, 'Evolving Multilingual Theatre in Singapore: The Case of Kuo Pao Kun', in *Ethnic Chinese in Singapore and Malaysia: A Dialogue between Tradition and Modernity*, ed. Leo Suryadinata (Singapore: Times Academic Press, 2002), and C. J. W.-L Wee and Lee Chee Keng, 'Introduction: Breaking through Walls and Visioning Beyond — Kuo Pao Kun Beyond the Margins', in *Two Plays by Kuo Pao Kun:* Descendants of the Eunuch Admiral *and* The Spirits Play, ed. C. J. W.-L. Wee and Lee Chee Keng (Singapore: SNP Editions, 2003).
11. See Kuo Pao Kun, *The Coffin Is Too Big for the Hole — And Other Plays* (Singapore: Times Books, 1990) and Kuo, *Images at the Margins*.
12. The musical was written by a Singaporean playwright, Michael Chiang, with music and lyrics by the pop musician Dick Lee. The text of *Beauty World* can be found as part of Chiang's collection, *Private Parts and Other Play Things: A Collection of Popular Singapore Comedies* (Singapore: Landmark Books, 1994).
13. Cited in Mathieu O'Neil, 'The End of the Exotic', http://happening.com.sg/performance/1998/features/november/kengsen.
14. Lim Min Min, *Remembering Through Theatre: Memories and Histories*, BA (Hons.) thesis, Department of Sociology, National University of Singapore, 1998. Also see C. J. W.-L. Wee, 'Creating High Culture in the Globalized "Cultural Desert" of Singapore', *The Drama Review* 47, no. 4 (T180) (Winter 2003): 84–97.
15. Kuo Pao Kun, 'Uprooted and Searching', in *Drama, Culture and Empowerment: The IDEA Dialogues*, ed. John O'Toole and Kate Donelan (Brisbane: IDEA Publications, 1999), 167. Hereafter cited as UP. Further page references to this article will be given within brackets in the main text.
16. Kuo Pao Kun, 'Contemplating an Open Culture: Transcending Multiculturalism', in *Singapore: Re-Engineering Success*, ed. Arun Mahizhnan and Lee Tsao Yuen (Singapore: Oxford University Press, 1998), 61. Hereafter cited as OC. Further page references to this article will be given in brackets in the main text.
17. Intercultural critic Rustom Bharucha is critical of Kuo's 'Open Culture', the ideal implicitly advanced in *Descendants*: 'Instead of concentrating on the dynamics of creation, which is the area of his expertise, Kuo feels obliged to envisage a new genealogy for Singapore itself. … [T]he illusion of this task, which is more a conceptual burden, rests on assumptions of organicity, so that it is assumed that 'other cultures are *naturally* rewarding for the body, mind, and spirit'; and more problematically, that it is the '*natural* trait of creative humankind' to draw energy from new resources' (*Consumed in Singapore: The Intercultural Spectacle of* Lear, Research Paper No. 21 [Singapore: Centre for Advanced Studies, National University of Singapore, 2000], 13). Kuo's position on cultural-identity formation is also in striking contrast to political scientist Partha Chatterjee's response to the same difficulty: 'Now the task [for postcolonial societies] is to trace in their mutually conditioned historicities the specific forms that have appeared, on the one hand, in the domain defined by the hegemonic project of nationalist modernity, and on the other, in the

numerous fragmented resistance to that normalizing project' (*The Nation and Its Fragments: Colonial and Postcolonial Histories* [Princeton, NJ: Princeton University Press, 1993], 13). The difference that arises between Bharucha and Kuo is the result of the different locations the two artist-critics inhabit; it indicates that there should be no single or definite article to the following entity: '*the* postcolonial nation-state'. Instead, what we have are what anthropologists Jean and John L. Comaroff have called 'a labile historical *formation*, a polythetic class of polities-in-motion' ('Naturing the Nation: Aliens, Apocalypse, and the Postcolonial State', *HAGAR: International Social Science Review* 1, no. 1 [2000]: 12). In this regard, differing historical and local specificities are important.

18. Fredric Jameson famously writes, 'Postmodernism is what you have when the modernization process is complete and nature is gone for good. It is a more fully human world than the older one, but one in which "culture" has become a veritable "second nature"' (*Postmodernism, or, the Cultural Logic of Late Capitalism* [Durham, NC: Duke University Press, 1991], ix). But how does one describe a society such as Singapore, then, when 'culture' is not commodified with the same characteristics as the USA's culture industry? Cf. Koichi Iwabuchi: 'Unlike the postmodernity of the West, non-Western postmodernity cannot be conceived of as the subsequent stage of modernity rather, [*sic*] as [Frederick] Buell remarks, it "thrives on incomplete modernization, the result of modernization from the top down. Peripheral sites thus produce cultural situations in which distinct time frames (artificially) constructed by colonialism and Orientalism, and powerfully separated by developmentalism's evolutionary narrative, circulate together". Buell is apt to see the demise of a grand evolutionary narrative in a peripheral postmodernity which articulates "the clash of unevenly coded temporalities", as well as the juxtaposition of many cultures. However this kind of view tends to underestimate the deeply uneven nature of global capitalist modernity. The "always already postmodern" situation of the non-Western periphery should not be celebrated uncritically, as it has been brought about and is still deeply affected by the legacies of colonialism and unequal power relations' (*Recentering Globalization: Popular Culture and Japanese Transnationalism* [Durham, NC: Duke University Press, 2002], 172).
19. Elizabeth A. Kalden, 'All the World's a Stage Now', *Straits Times* (Singapore), 'Life!' section, 21 April 1998.
20. Cited in Kalden, ibid.
21. Mok Wai Yin, 'A Talk with Director Ong Keng Sen', 14 May 1995, in TheatreWorks (Singapore) Programme for *Descendants of the Eunuch Admiral — A Meditation*, Victoria Theatre, Singapore, 3–5 June 1995.
22. There are signs that Ong is broadening his scope. He finished, in June 2002, an intercultural workshop and festival experiment called 'In Transit: Transforming the Arts' at the Haus der Kulturen der Welt. He thus is trying to expand beyond the intercultural staging of the New Asia; Ong says co-curator Johannes Odenthal and he want 'Germans to engage with The Other, The Outsider, and the different biographical, ethnic and political backgrounds of their art production' ('Johannes Odenthal and Ong Keng Sen', http://www.in-transit.de/content/eng/sites/pop_icurators.htm). This statement also carries the implication that the final destination of the New Asia is the journey into the old colonial heartland itself.
23. Bruce Robbins, 'Introduction Part 1: Actually Existing Cosmopolitanism', in *Cosmopolitics: Thinking and Feeling Beyond the Nation State*, ed. Pheng Cheah and Bruce Robbins (Minneapolis: University of Minnesota Press, 1998), 3. For a critique of 'cosmopolitanism' as it appears in recent cultural theorising, see Brennan, 'Cosmo-Theory'.

24. The English-language version of *Descendants* has been published in *Two Plays by Kuo Pao Kun*, ed. Wee and Lee. The quotations that follow in the main text are taken from this edition. The Chinese version of the play will be available in Quah Sy Ren (ed.), *The Collected Works of Kuo Pao Kun: Plays in Chinese, the 1990s*, Volume 3 (Singapore: World Scientific, forthcoming).
25. The Zheng He character functions in critical contrast to the (apparently happy) hybrid, diasporic subject of some postcolonial theorising; this subject is unrooted and seemingly unbound by the limitations of locality. See Pheng Cheah, 'Given Culture: Rethinking Cosmopolitical Freedom in Transnationalism', in *Cosmopolitics*, ed. Cheah and Robbins, for a critique of how metropolitan migrancy is treated within postcolonial cultural criticism.
26. Kuo Pao Kun, *The Evening Climb*, in Kuo, *Images at the Margins*, 334.
27. Recalling pre-Euro-colonial trading systems, and the possibilities of pre-colonial cross-border identities and cosmopolitan transactions, has been a thematic in what might loosely be called Asian fiction in English for some years. See Amitav Ghosh, *In an Antique Land* (London: Granta Books, 1992); and Salman Rushdie, *The Moor's Last Sigh* (London: Jonathan Cape, 1995).
28. Kuo Pao Kun, 'Playwright's Message', in TheatreWorks (Singapore) Programme for *Descendants of the Eunuch Admiral — A Meditation*, Victoria Theatre, Singapore, 3–5 June 1995.
29. What follows is an analysis based on Ong's 1995 production.
30. There are similarities to Robert Wilson's dreamscapes.
31. This clearly is an ironic reference to and comment on Lee Kuan Yew, prime minister from 1959 to 89, and his family — Lee's older son, Lee Hsien Loong, was a deputy prime minister when the play was written. The younger Lee became the premier in 2004, after Goh Chok Tong retired and became 'senior minister'.
32. These represent the four official languages of Singapore, and recall the ending of the day's transmission on the old Radio Television Singapore and later the Singapore Broadcasting Corporation, when four women would say 'good-night' in the four languages.
33. The potential bathos of the last line is offset by the accreted layers of meaning Kuo has built up in the text, and also by Ong's visceral and dramatically visual staging of the last scene.
34. 'First, and most important of all, Asia is not one, but many Asias. ... Some may argue that Europe is also made up of many different countries, but looking at religion for instance, we see immediately that Asia is much more heterogeneous' (Ong Keng Sen, 'Worlds Apart: Europe Still Not Ready for New Asia', *Sunday Times* [Singapore], 3 May 1998).
35. The following discussion is drawn from the notes that I made during the conference. For Ong's earlier position on the need for cultural memory practice in the theatre, see Ong Keng Sen, 'A Theatre of Memory: Reconnection, Regeneration, Rediscovery through Experimentation with Traditional Arts', paper presented at the Singapore Heritage Society's Conference on 'Our Place in Time: Heritage in Singapore', Substation arts centre, Singapore, 17–18 September 1994.
36. Cf. TheatreWorks' informational write-up on the 1998 Programme: 'The Flying Circus Project with its unique, multi-cultural Asian identity, is an expression of Asian dynamism. It is progressive, sophisticated — a space where tradition and modernity, East and West meet and intermingle comfortably. It aims to negotiate the many Asian communities and ultimately, the international community in order to better appreciate this New Asia'. For a recent analysis of the Flying Circus Project, see Helena Grehan, 'Questioning the

Relationship between Consumption and Exchange: TheatreWorks' Flying Circus Project, December 2000', *positions: east asia cultures critique* 12, no. 2 (Fall 2004): 565–86.

37. In 1997, *Lear* also appeared in Osaka and Fukuoka. In 1999, apart from Singapore, it proceeded to Hong Kong, Indonesia, and Australia, and thence to Germany and Denmark.
38. Ong Keng Sen, 'When Bali Mask Gurus Go Ga-Ga Over L[aser] D[isc]s', *Sunday Times* (Singapore), 3 May 1998.
39. See Koh Tai Ann, 'Culture and the Arts', in *The Management of Success: The Moulding of Modern Singapore*, ed. K. S. Sandhu and Paul Wheatley (Boulder, Co.: Westview Press, 1990).
40. Bharucha, *Consumed in Singapore*, 34–42. Kishida unfortunately passed away in Japan in 2003.
41. The analysis pertains to the 1999 Singapore production, though that was broadly similar to the 1997 Japanese production.
42. Bharucha, *Consumed in Singapore*, 21.
43. '*Shenhou zhi ren shi shei?*' (Rio Kishida, '*Lear*: A Production of The Japan Foundation Asia Center. January and February, 1999. Hong Kong, Singapore, Jakarta and Perth'). The script uses five languages, with Japanese and English appearing all the time, mediating in this version of Asia.
44. Bharucha, *Consumed in Singapore*, 42.
45. Lee Weng Choy's position, as discussed by Bharucha in *Consumed in Singapore*, 24. Lee is an art critic and presently an artistic co-director of the independent Substation arts centre, Singapore.
46. Ong Keng Sen, cited in Suzanne Lim, Suzanne, 'Director's Cut: Not for Him the Bright Lights of New York. TheatreWorks' Artistic Director Ong Keng Sen Chooses to Play It Close to Home', *East*, May 2000, 65.
47. Coronil, 'Towards a Critique of Globalcentrism': 368.
48. Chua Beng Huat, *Culture, Multiculturalism and National Identity in Singapore*, Working Paper No. 125 (Singapore: Department of Sociology, National University of Singapore, 1995), 22.
49. Stefan Tanaka, *Japan's Orient: Rendering Pasts into History* (Berkeley: University of California Press, 1993); and Andrew Gordon, *A Modern History of Japan: From Tokugawa Times to the Present* (New York: Oxford University Press, 2003), 94–114.
50. Gavan McCormack and Yoshio Sugimoto (eds.), *The Japanese Trajectory: Modernization and Beyond* (Cambridge: Cambridge University Press, 1988).
51. John Corner and Sylvia Harvey (eds.), *Enterprise and Heritage: Crosscurrents of National Culture* (London: Routledge, 1991).
52. Walter Hatch and Kozo Yamamura, *Asia in Japan's Embrace: Building a Regional Production Alliance* (Cambridge: Cambridge University Press, 1996).
53. David Arase, 'Japan in East Asia', in *Japan in the Posthegemonic World*, ed. Tsuneo Akaha and Frank Langdon (Boulder, Co.: Lynne Rienner, 1993).
54. Yoichi Funabushi, 'The Asianization of Asia', *Foreign Affairs* 72 (November/December 1993).
55. Victor Koschmann, 'Asianism's Ambivalent Legacy', in *Network Power: Japan and Asia*, ed. Peter J. Katzenstein and Takashi Shiraishi (Ithaca: Cornell University Press, 1997).
56. Takashi Shiraishi, 'Japan and Southeast Asia', in *Network Power*, ed. Katzenstein and Shiraishi, 185.
57. For one example of the exhibitions JFAC has undertaken, see Furuichi Yasuko and Nakamoto Kazumi (eds.), *Asian Modernism: Diverse Developments in Indonesia, the Philippines and Thailand* (Tokyo: Japan Foundation Asia Center, [1995]); for one example of the fora

on Asian art JFAC has undertaken, see Furuichi Yasuko (ed.) and Hoashi Aki (assistant ed.), *Symposium: Asian Contemporary Art Reconsidered* (Tokyo: Japan Foundation Asia Center, 1998). The Asia Center, unfortunately, was closed by the Japan Foundation in 2004, following a revamp of the Foundation's development priorities.

58. Japan Foundation Asia Center, *The Japan Foundation Asia Center: Towards Mutual Understanding in Asia in the Twenty-First Century* (Tokyo: Japan Foundation Asia Center, n.d.), 1.
59. Ibid., 2.
60. *Dagong bao* (Hong Kong), 28 July 1998; cited in Lee Chee Keng, 'Intra-Asia Inter-Cultural Theatrical Productions: Looking at Japan Foundation's New Cultural Exchange Efforts', paper presented at the Ninth Annual Graduate Student Conference on East Asia, Columbia University, New York, February 2000, 3.
61. See, for one example, Jenny de Reuck: '*LEAR* remains — for all its multicultural diversity, its celebration of inter-cultural difference — a fugue on the theme of Shakespeare's work. Here, I fear, cultural co-option is cross-dressed as cultural convergence' ('"The Mirror Shattered into Tiny Pieces": Gender and Culture in the Japan Foundation Asia Centre's *LEAR*', *Intersections: Gender History and Culture in the Asian Context* 3 [January 2000] http://www.sshe.murdoch.edu.au/intersections/issue3/jenny3.html).
62. Yuki Hata, 'Children Who Kill Their Fathers: The Creation of Lear' (Producer's Message), in the JFAC Programme for *Lear*. For an illuminating comparison of a slightly earlier consumption of the modern Asian Other in Japan in the late 1980s to the mid-1990s — here of yet another Singaporean, the pop musician Dick Lee — see chapter 5, 'Popular Asianism in Japan: Nostalgia for (Different) Asian Modernity', of Iwabuchi's *Recentering Globalization*.
63. Hata, 'Children Who Kill Their Fathers'.
64. Ong Keng Sen, '*LEAR*: Linking Night and Day' (Director's Message), in JFAC Programme for *Lear*, Kallang Theatre, Singapore, 28–31 January 1999.
65. It is worthwhile citing Rey Chow at this juncture, though the quotation is taken out of its original context: 'In an era in which the critique of the West has not only possible but mandatory, where does this critique leave those ethnic peoples whose entry into culture is, precisely because of the history of Western imperialism, already "Westernized"?' (*Woman and Chinese Modernity* [Minneapolis: University of Minnesota Press, 1991], xi).

Epilogue

1. Anwar Ibrahim, *The Asian Renaissance* (Singapore: Times Books International, 1996).
2. Lisa Rofel, *Other Modernities: Gendered Yearnings in China after Socialism* (Berkeley: University of California Press, 1999), 12.
3. Stuart Hall, 'When was "the Post-Colonial"? Thinking at the Limit', in *The Post-Colonial Question: Common Skies, Divided Horizons*, ed. Iain Chambers and Lidia Curti (London: Routledge, 1996), 247.
4. Aihwa Ong, *Neoliberalism as Exception: Mutations in Citizenship and Sovereignty* (Durham, NC: Duke University Press, 2006), 178. For Ong, Singapore is a representative if 'emerging site of globality' in Southeast Asia; in the region, she adds, 'we find an innovative use of neoliberal logic at three registers: the transformation of links between internal and external spaces, the orchestration of knowledge flows, and the linking of knowledge and entitlements. First, a site like Singapore redefines itself not within an established urban system but in relation to an emerging network of symbiotic flows. Second, by pulling together elements from disparate sites, the hub intertwines its future with that of global

organizations. Third, network participants — technologies, firms, and experts — set new norms of innovation and flexibility for citizens. At stake is the fabrication of a niche of technoethical diversity is the reorganization of society and of citizens' (178, 179).

5. Geraldine Heng and Janadas Devan, 'State Fatherhood: The Politics of Nationalism, Sexuality, and Race in Singapore', in *Nationalisms and Sexualities*, ed. Andrew Parker, Mary Russo, Doris Sommer and Patricia Yaegar (New York: Routledge, 1992), 343.
6. Talks collapsed at the Seattle meeting in December 1999. As one journalist succinctly puts it, 'The basic gripes of the developing world is that, when it comes to trade, the West says one thing and does another. While protecting its own vulnerable sectors from competition, it demands that southern countries open up theirs' (Charlotte Denny, 'Qatar Could See a First-Class Beef', *Guardian Weekly*, 19–25 April 2001, 10).
7. Arnold I. Davidson, 'Ethics as Ascetics: Foucault, the History of Ethics, and Ancient Thought', in *The Cambridge Companion to Foucault*, ed. Gary Gitting (Cambridge: Cambridge University Press, 1994), 118–19.
8. Michel Foucault, 'Governmentality', in *Ideology and Consciousness* 6 (Autumn 1979): 10.
9. Michel Foucault, *The History of Sexuality: An Introduction*, vol. 1, trans. Robert Hurley (New York: Pantheon, 1978), 88.
10. Michel Foucault has animated a fair amount of significant critical cultural analyses since the late 1980s, especially (but not only) in the emerging area of an anthropology of modernity. As anthropologist of China Lisa Rofel observes: 'For Foucault, modernity ushers in a novel regime of disciplinarity. Far from offering a mode of greater individual freedom and progress, this regime signals an ever more thorough form of domination' (*Other Modernities*, 11). She contends that work such as Paul Rabinow's *French Modern: Norms and Forms of the Social Environment* (Cambridge, Mass.: MIT Press, 1989), which 'scrupulously follows Foucault', also 'assumes the universality of Foucault's vision of modernity and the heterogeneity of its effects, while ignoring the larger (neo)colonial world and relations of marginalization that might indicate dissident interpretations' (*Other Modernities*, note 11, 287). Rofel's own critical stance — one that still incorporates a Foucauldian dimension — is that: 'Modernity is ... fissured with paradox and incompleteness, not simply because all categories implode on their own unstable differences but because of distinctive social histories within a global imperialism' (ibid., 15). This is a position that I broadly agree with, and the ongoing presence of the 'monarch' I indicate is part of the city-state's distinctive social history within this 'global imperialism'.
11. In August 2004, Lee Hsien Loong, Lee Kuan Yew's oldest son, became the third prime minister in post-independence history. Retiring Prime Minister Goh Chok Tong was appointed the 'senior minister', replacing the senior Lee, and Lee Kuan Yew was appointed to the newly created position, the 'minister mentor'. These are both cabinet-level appointments.
12. Lee Kuan Yew, 'Democracy and Human Rights for the World.' Speech at the 'Create 21' Asahi forum, Tokyo, 20 November 1992; cited in Linda Low, *The Political Economy of a City-State: Government-Made Singapore* (Singapore: Oxford University Press, 1998), 31–32.
13. Low, *Political Economy of a City-State*.
14. George Yeo, 'Worldwide Web: Strengthening the Singapore Network', 16. Opening speech at the Institute of Policy Studies conference on 'Civil Society: Harnessing State-Society Synergies', Orchard Hotel, Singapore, 6–7 May 1998.
15. For a general discussion of Southeast Asian authoritarian capitalist development, see Richard Robison, Kevin Hewison and Garry Rodan, 'Political Power in Industrialising Capitalist Societies: Theoretical Approaches', in *Southeast Asia in the 1990s: Authoritarianism,*

Democracy and Capitalism, ed. Kevin Hewison, Richard Robison and Garry Rodan (St. Leonards, NSW: Allen & Unwin, 1993). The authors observe: 'Where capitalist growth is vigorous and where the national economy becomes increasingly integrated with the world economy, ... pressure [for the state to be less interventionist] becomes more difficult for regimes to resist. ... [T]he new relationship between market capitalism and the state requires mechanisms of accountability inimical to the most authoritarian regimes, with Singapore's notable exception' (29). The term 'authoritarian' suggests a category of state brutality that Singapore does not quite fit into — it is here that perhaps we can see how 'government', 'governmentality' and, indeed, Gramscian 'hegemony' all simultaneously operate in the city-state.

16. The best-known argument may be Kenichi Ohmae, *The End of the Nation State: The Rise of Regional Economies* (New York: Free Press, 1995).
17. Cf. Paul Hirst and Grahame Thompson, *Globalization in Question: The International Economy and the Possibilities of Governance* (Cambridge: Polity Press, 1996): '[Asian Newly Industrialising Countries, including Singapore,] show the value of determined national economic management and solidaristic public policies in producing international competitiveness' (114–15).
18. Michael Hardt and Antonio Negri, *Empire* (Cambridge, Mass.: Harvard University Press, 2000), 247. The authors also suggest that with the new Information Economy, 'the disciplinary system has become obsolete and must be left behind. Capital must accomplish a negative mirroring and an inversion of the new quality of [immaterial] labor power; it must adjust itself so as to be able to command once again. We suspect that for this reason the industrial and political forces that have relied most heavily and with the most intelligence on the extreme modernization of the disciplinary model (such as the major elements of Japanese and East Asian capital) are the ones that will suffer most severely in this passage' (276). I will return to this question in the next section.
19. 'Q. If You Were Starting to Build Up a Nation, What Would be the Challenge?' [edited transcript of interview], *Straits Times Interactive*, 1 July 1999, <http://straitstimes.asia1.com.sg/sin/sin24_0701.html>.
20. Kanishka Jayasuriya, 'Authoritarian Liberalism, Governance and the Emergence of the Regulatory State in Post-Crisis East Asia', in *Politics and Markets in the Wake of the Asian Crisis*, ed. Richard Robison, Mark Beeson, Kanishka Jayasuriya and Hyuk-Rae Kim (London: Routledge, 2000), 319.
21. See, for example, Ben Dolveen, 'Less Than a Lion's Share', *Far Eastern Economic Review*, 5 November 1998, 46–47, for one viewpoint of this.
22. Cited in Zuraidah Ibrahim, 'S'pore Focus on Key Areas for Growth', *Straits Times Interactive*, 13 October 1998, <http://straitstimes.asia1.com.sg/pages/sin1_1013.html>.
23. Cited in 'Twin Engines to Boost Economy', *Straits Times Interactive*, 12 November 1998, <http://web3.asia1.com/archive/st/4/pages/sin9_1112.html>. Never could you find a stronger statement regarding how the semi-periphery must struggle to stay within the globalised sphere it deems necessary for development.
24. 'Staying Ahead: Business', *Straits Times Interactive*, 13 November 1998, <http://web3.asia1.com.sg/archive/st/4/pages/sin11_1112.html>.
25. See C. J. W.-L. Wee, 'National Identity, the Arts, and the Global City', in *Singapore in the New Millennium: Challenges Facing the City-State*, ed. Derek da Cunha (Singapore: Institute of Southeast Asian Studies, 2002).
26. 'Q. If You Were Starting to Build Up a Nation, What Would be the Challenge?'

27. Geoffrey Pereira, 'Search for High-Tech Model for S'pore', *Straits Times Interactive*, 17 April 1999, <http://web3.asia1.com.sg/archive/st/6wrld/wrld6_0417.html>.
28. The state has since increasingly financed and supported the research development of the biomedical sciences. The science hub in the Buena Vista area has become called 'Biopolis'. The undergraduate study of the biological sciences has also been boosted at the two major local universities, the National University of Singapore and the Nanyang Technological University.
29. Lee Hsien Loong, 'America's Rising Stakes in Asia', *Straits Times* (Singapore), 8 May 1998, 67.
30. There have been some gestures that globalisation could have been be more carefully undertaken during the period leading up to the crisis — from no less than Lee Kuan Yew. Lee said in a talk to the US Council of Foreign Relations in New York City in 1998 that the liberalisation of capital accounts, now seen in hindsight, should have been calibrated to match the level of sophistication of the various banking supervisory systems and banking laws (Lee Siew Hwa, 'Liberalisation of Capital Accounts Left Economies Exposed, Says S[senior] M[inister]', *Straits Times Interactive*, 22 October 1998, <http://www.straitstimes.asia1.com/pages/wrld14_1022.html>.
31. Lee Kuan Yew, 'I'm Convinced We're Headed Down the Hill', *Straits Times Interactive*, 5 August 1999, <http://www.straitstimes.asia1.com.sg/sin/sin39_0507.html>.
32. StarHub is owned by Singapore Technologies, Singapore Power, British Telecom and Nippon Telegraph & Telephone. Communications and Information Technology Minister Yeo Cheow Tong said that they would be compensated (Tammy Tan, 'Telecoms Market to Be Freed Up Fully from April', *Straits Times Interactive*, 22 January 2000 <http://straitstimes.asia1.com.sg/one1/one1.html>.
33. Cited in 'Singaporeans Come First, But…', *Straits Times Interactive*, 27 March 1999, <http://web3.asia1.com.sg/archive/st/1/one1/one1.html>. In 2001, two out of the four major local banks had non-Singaporean chief executive officers, as did the state-owned shipping company, Neptune Orient Lines, and the largest local electronics manufacturer, Chartered Semiconductor. The PAP government now under Lee Hsien Loong remains true to this commitment. The need for immigrant 'talent' was part of his independence day address to the city-state in 2006 ('National Day Rally: Embrace Talent, Technology to Secure S'pore's Future: PM', *Straits Times* [Singapore], 21 Aug. 2006, 1).
34. Cf. University of Michigan's Linda Lim: 'The role of the state in business has become at best unnecessary and at worst dysfunctional. It has warped the development of the private sector. For a bright young person, the system has been totally biased against entrepreneurship' (quoted in William Mellor, 'The Risks of Playing It Safe', *Asiaweek*, 4 May 2001).

    DBS Bank — already the leader in Southeast Asia — purchased Hong Kong's Dao Heng Bank in April 2001 for over US$5 billion, making DBS Hong Kong's fourth biggest lender and thrusting it into competition with global heavyweights such as the Hongkong and Shanghai Banking Corporation. In March of the same year, SingTel announced that it had bought Australia's number two telecommunication company, Cable & Wireless Optus for US$9 billion. Both purchases, however, were considered overpriced and the stock value of both companies fell. This, then, is the cost to be paid for the modest and — the government hopes — only an initial expansion of the island's 'global reach' into the region. The SingTel deal itself followed two high-profile flops. The GLC, then run by Lee Kuan Yew's younger son, Lee Hsien Yang, failed in its attempts to buy Hongkong Telecom in early 2000 and then, shortly thereafter, Malaysia's Time Engineering. The connection of the PAP to GLCs is a major image problem for them, whether fairly or otherwise, when it comes to the purchase of companies sensitive to a country's economy or security. Cf. Patrick Smith, 'Singapore

Companies Pay High Entry Fees', *Sydney Morning Herald*, 17 April 2001: 'Singapore's blue chips tend to draw their guiding executives from the same pool that feeds the bureaucracy. ... These executives may be having a trouble distinguishing between a policy (imposed from the outside) and a corporate strategy (developed within).'

35. 'The Brain Game: Can Creativity Be Created — and Will This Quest Threaten Social Order? Asia Needs to Encourage Innovation in Order to Be Competitive, *Asia Magazine*, 19–21 December 1997, 10.
36. Anthony Giddens, *The Third Way* (Cambridge: Polity Press, 1998).
37. Alison de Souza, '8 in 10 have Faith in Govt.' and 'Govt.: How Public Sees It', *Straits Times Interactive*, 20 June 1998, <http://web3.asia1.com/archive/st/6/pages/sin4_0620.html>. The *Straits Times* tried to make the poll representative of the post-independence middle-class. Cf. Andrea Hamilton, 'Let's Talk About Openness: A Debate Begins on the Benefits of Criticism', *Asiaweek*, 26 June 1998.
38. Asia observers note how Singapore remains resistant to regional democratic urges: 'For a region in which everyone is supposed to be more interested in making money than playing politics, Asia is showing a remarkable burst of political activity. ... Singapore's latest event[, however,] seemed to belong to the old Asian kind when its new president, S. R. Nathan, made his maiden speech to parliament. Press coverage was not exactly critical: "People will be at the heart of government policy in the Singapore of the next millennium," is how the *Straits Times* began a faithful echo of Nathan's "bold vision". But at least his policy address (written by the prime minister's office) endorsed the need for more "robust" discussions of important issues' (John Gittings, 'Inside Asia: China Still Out of Step as Asians Stumble Towards Democracy', *Guardian Weekly*, 14–20 October 1999, 6).
39. Quoted in Assis Shameen and Alejandro Reyes, 'Creative Destruction City', *Asiaweek*, 24 March 2000 <http://www.cnn.com/ASIANOW/asiaweek/magazine/2000/0324/cover1.html>.
40. Quoted in Assis Shameen and Alejandro Reyes, ibid.
41. Bruce Cumings, 'End of Japanese Honeymoon: Old Partnership with US Turns Sour', *Le Monde Diplomatique*, April 1999, supplement to *Guardian Weekly*, 3.
42. Francis Fukuyama, 'The End of History?', in *The New Shape of World Politics*, ed. Fareed Zakaria (New York: Norton, 1997), 1; the essay first appeared in *The National Interest* issue of summer 1989. It needs to be added that the Cold War was not only thought of as being ideological — there were many variants as to what the participants at different points thought it was; the simple point here, though, is that whatever the Cold War may have been, the year 1989 afforded the opportunity for the announcement of the ending of ideological conflict.
43. Walter Benn Michaels, *The Shape of the Signifier: 1967 to the End of History* (Princeton, NJ: Princeton University Press, 2004), 29.
44. Samuel P. Huntington, 'The Clash of Civilizations?' in *New Shape of World Politics*, ed. Zakaria, 67.
45. Michaels, *Shape of the Signifier*, 31.
46. Cf. Peter J. Taylor, D. R. F. Walker and J. V. Beaverstock: 'Although [Hong Kong and Singapore] ... are [business] centers for their own regions, Northeast and Southeast Asia respectively, when no division is made (for instance as in Asian or Asia-Pacific office designations) Hong Kong edges out Singapore only by 3 to 2 [firms] for the larger regional responsibility. It should be noted when [premier world city] Tokyo appears as a regional headquarters [though "superior" to the other two cities], its region is limited to Japan; this city seems not to have developed responsibilities beyond its own state' ('Firms and Their

Global Service Networks', in *Global Networks, Linked Cities,* ed. Saskia Sassen [New York: Routledge, 2002], 102). The authors categorise Singapore as part of an 'alpha world city' band, though at a level within the band just under that occupied by London, Paris, Tokyo and New York. Chicago, Frankfurt, Hong Kong, Los Angeles and Milan occupy the same level as Singapore within that premium band.

47. Formerly the ministry of information and the arts (MITA).
48. Tan Chin Nam, 'Let Us Co-Create Our Nation's Brand', *Fusion@MICA* 10 (April–June 2006).
49. Thomas Cromwell, 'Why Nation Branding Is Important for Singapore', *Fusion@MICA* 10 (April– June 2006).
50. Goh Chin Lian, 'Wanted: A Single Brand for S'pore', *Straits Times* (Singapore), 2 September 2006, 1.
51. 'Singapore 2006 Showcases Cosmopolitan Singapore', *Fusion@MICA* 10 (April–June 2006).
52. *Belief: Singapore Biennale 2006*, 4 September–12 November 2006, visitor's guide.
53. See chapter 4, note 34.
54. Mark W. Rectanus, *Culture Incorporated: Museums, Artists, and Corporate Sponsorships* (Minneapolis: University of Minnesota Press, 2002), 7. While arts censorship still is exercised in Singapore, the state seems willing to allow a little more latitude for 'critical reflection', if not quite 'subversion', as part of a more 'relaxed' image.
55. Zara Stanhope, 'Home Truths', in *Zones of Contact — 2006 Biennale of Sydney: A Critical Reader*, ed. Natasha Bullock and Reuben Keehan (Sydney: Artspace Visual Arts Centre, 2006), 66.
56. John Urry, *Consuming Places* (London: Routledge, 1995).
57. Apinan Poshyananda, 'Asian Art and the New Millennium: From Glocalism to Techno-Shamanism', in *International Symposium 1999: 'Asian Art: Prospects for the Future' Report*, ed. Furuichi Yasuko and asst. ed., Hoashi Aki (Tokyo: Japan Foundation Asia Center, 2000), 165. Apinan is a noted Thai curator and academic who curated the 'Contemporary Art in Asia: Traditions/Tensions' show in 1996 by the Asia Society Galleries in New York City.
58. Arjun Appadurai, *Modernity at Large: Cultural Dimensions of Globalization* (Minneapolis: University of Minnesota Press, 1996), 3.
59. Ibid., 11, 15.
60. Arjun Appadurai, *Fear of Small Numbers: An Essay on the Geography of Anger* (Durham, NC: Duke University Press, 2006), ix–x; 22–23.
61. Appadurai, *Modernity at Large*, 27–48.
62. Martin Jacques, 'Globalisation Has Had Its Day', *Guardian Weekly*, 21–27 July 2006, 27.
63. Karl Manheim, *Ideology and Utopia* (New York: Harcourt, Brace, and World, n.d.), 262.

Selected Bibliography

Abbas, Ackbar. *Hong Kong: Culture and the Politics of Disappearance.* Minneapolis: University of Minnesota Press, 1997.

Adorno, Theodor W. and Max Horkheimer. *Dialectic of Enlightenment.* New York: Herder, 1972.

Alexander, Christopher. 'A City Is Not a Tree', *Architectural Forum* 122, no. 1 (April 1965): 58–61.

Amin, Samir. *Delinking: Towards a Polycentric World*, trans. Michael Wolfers. 1985; London: Zed Books, 1990.

Amsden, Alice H. *Asia's Next Giant: South Korea and Late Industrialization.* New York: Oxford University Press, 1989.

Anderson, Benedict. *Imagined Communities: Reflections on the Origin and Spread of Nationalism.* London: Verso, 1983.

__________. *Language and Power: Exploring Political Cultures in Indonesia.* Ithaca, NY: Cornell University Press, 1990.

__________. *The Spectre of Comparisons: Nationalism, Southeast Asia, and the World.* London: Verso, 1998.

Anwar Ibrahim. *The Asian Renaissance.* Singapore: Times Books International, 1996.

Apinan Poshyananda. 'Asian Art and the New Millennium: From Glocalism to Techno-Shamanism.' In *'Asian Art: Prospects for the Future' Report*, ed. Furuichi Yasuko and asst. ed. Hoashi Aki. Tokyo: Japan Foundation Asia Center, 2000.

Appadurai, Arjun. *Fear of Small Numbers: An Essay on the Geography of Fear.* Durham, NC: Duke University Press, 2006.

__________. *Modernity at Large: Cultural Dimensions of Globalization.* Minneapolis: University of Minnesota Press, 1996.

Arase, David. 'Japan in East Asia.' In *Japan in the Posthegemonic World*, ed. Tsuneo Akaha and Frank Langdon. Boulder, Co.: Lynne Rienner, 1993.

Balibar, Etienne. 'The Nation Form: History and Ideology.' In Etienne Balibar and Immanuel Wallerstein, *Race, Class, Nation: Ambiguous Identities.* London: Verso, 1991.

Bauman, Zygmunt. *Modernity and Ambivalence.* Cambridge: Polity Press, 1991.

Benjamin, Geoffrey. 'The Cultural Logic of Singapore's "Multiracialism".' In *Singapore: Society in Transition*, ed. Riaz Hassan. Kuala Lumpur: Oxford University Press, 1976.

Berman, Marshall. *All that Is Solid Melts into Air: The Experience of Modernity*. 1982; New York: Penguin, 1988.

Bharucha, Rustom. *Consumed in Singapore: The Intercultural Spectacle of* Lear, Research Paper No. 21. Singapore: Centre for Advanced Studies, National University of Singapore, 2000.

Birch, David. 'Singapore English Drama: A Historical Overview 1958–1985.' In *9 Lives: 10 Years of Singapore Theatre 1987–1997*, ed. Sanjay Krishnan. Singapore: The Necessary Stage, 1996.

Bloodworth, Dennis. *The Tiger and the Trojan Horse*. Singapore: Times Books International, 1986.

Bradbury, Malcolm and James McFarlane (eds.). *Modernism: A Guide to European Literature 1890–1930*. 1976; London: Penguin, 1991.

Branegan, Jay. 'Is Singapore a Model for the West?' *Time*, 18 January 1993, 36–37.

Brennan, Timothy. 'Cosmo-Theory', *South Atlantic Quarterly* 100, no. 3 (Summer 2001): 659–92.

Brown, David. *The State and Ethnic Politics in Southeast Asia*. London: Routledge, 1994.

Burrow, J. W. *A Liberal Descent: Victorian Historians and the English Past*. Cambridge: Cambridge University Press, 1981.

Castell, Manuel. 'Four Asian Tigers with a Dragon Head: A Comparative Analysis of the State, Economy and Society in the Asian Pacific Rim.' In *States and Development in the Asian Pacific Rim*, ed. Richard P. Appelbaum and Jeffrey Henderson. London: Sage Publications, 1992.

Chan Heng Chee. 'Political Developments.' In *A History of Singapore*, ed. Ernest C. T. Chew and Edwin Lee. Singapore: Oxford University Press, 1991.

_________. *The Politics of Survival*. Singapore: Oxford University Press, 1971.

Chan Heng Chee and H.-D. Evers. 'Nation Building and National Identity in Southeast Asia.' In *Buildings States and Nations*, Vol. 2, ed. S. N. Eisenstadt and Stein Rokkan. Beverly Hills: Sage, 1973.

Chatterjee, Partha. *The Nation and Its Fragments: Colonial and Postcolonial Histories*. Princeton, NJ: Princeton University Press, 1993.

_________. *Nationalist Thought in the Colonial World: A Derivative Discourse?* London: Zed Books, 1986.

Cheng Siok Hwa. 'Economic Change and Industrialization.' In *A History of Singapore*, ed. Ernest C. T. Chew and Edwin Lee. Singapore: Oxford University Press, 1991.

Chew, Ernest C. T. and Edwin Lee (eds.). *A History of Singapore*. Singapore: Oxford University Press, 1991.

Ching, Leo. 'Globalizing the Regional, Regionalizing the Global: Mass Culture and Asianism in the Age of Late Capital.' In *Globalization*, ed. Arjun Appadurai. Durham, NC: Duke University Press, 2001.

Chow, Rey. *Woman and Chinese Modernity*. Minneapolis: University of Minnesota Press, 1991.

Chua Beng Huat. '"Asian Values" Discourse and the Resurrection of the Social', *positions: east asia cultures critique* 7, no. 2 (Fall 1999): 573–92.

_________. *Communitarian Ideology and Democracy in Singapore*. London: Routledge, 1995.

_________. 'Culture, Multiracialism and National Identity in Singapore.' In *Trajectories: Inter-Asia Cultural Studies*, ed. Kuan-Hsing Chen. London: Routledge, 1998.

_________. *Political Legitimacy and Housing: Stakeholding in Singapore*. London: Routledge, 1997.

_________. 'Taiwan's Present/Singapore's Past Mediated by Hokkien Language.' In *Rogue Flows: Trans-Asian Cultural Traffic*, ed. Koichi Iwabuchi, Stephen Muecke and Mandy Thomas. Hong Kong: Hong Kong University Press, 2004.

Cohn, Bernard S. *Colonialism and Its Forms of Knowledge: The British in India.* Princeton, NJ: Princeton University Press, 1996.

Collini, Stefan. *Liberalism and Sociology: L. T. Hobhouse and Political Argument in England 1880–1914.* Cambridge: Cambridge University Press, 1979.

Comaroff, Jean and John L. 'Naturing the Nation: Aliens, Apocalypse, and the Postcolonial State', *HAGAR: International Social Science Review* 1, no. 1 (2000): 7–40.

Coronil, Fernando. 'Towards a Critique of Globalcentrism: Speculations on Capitalism's Nature', *Public Culture* 12, no. 2 (Spring 2000): 351–74. Special Issue, 'Millennium Capitalism and the Culture of Neoliberalism.'

Cromwell, Thomas. 'Why Nation Branding Is Important for Singapore.' *Fusion@MICA* 10, April–June 2006.

Davidson, Arnold I. 'Ethics as Ascetics: Foucault, the History of Ethics, and Ancient Thought.' In *The Cambridge Companion to Foucault*, ed. Gary Gitting. Cambridge: Cambridge University Press, 1994.

De Reuck, Jenny. '"The Mirror Shattered into Tiny Pieces": Gender and Culture in the Japan Foundation Asia Centre's *LEAR*', *Intersections: Gender History and Culture in the Asian Context* 3 (available at http://www.sshe.murdoch.edu.au/intersections/issue3/jenny3.html/, accessed January 2000).

Dirks, Nicholas. 'History as a Sign of the Modern.' *Public Culture* 2, no. 2 (1990): 25–32.

Dirlik, Arif. 'Globalisation and the Politics of Place.' In *Globalisation and the Asia-Pacific: Contested Territories*, ed. Kris Olds, Peter Dicken, Philip F. Kelly, Lily Kong and Henry Wai-chung Yeung. London: Routledge, 1999.

Doshi, Tilak and Peter Coclanis. 'The Economic Architect: Goh Keng Swee.' In *Lee's Lieutenants: Singapore's Old Guard*, ed. Lam Peng Er and Kevin Y. L. Tan. St. Leonards, NSW: Allen & Unwin, 1999.

Drysdale, John. *Singapore: Struggle for Success.* Singapore: Times Books International, 1984.

Elegant, Robert. 'The Singapore of Mr Lee: "Confucian" Ethics, Asian Values.' *Encounter*, June 1990: 21–29.

Eliot, T. S. 'Tradition and the Individual Talent.' In T. S. Eliot, *Selected Essays*, 3rd enlarged edition. London: Faber and Faber, 1951.

Enright, D. J. *Memoirs of a Mendicant Professor*. London: Chatto and Windus, 1969.

Fukuyama, Francis. 'The End of History.' In *The New Shape of World Politics*, ed. Fareed Zakaria. New York: Norton, 1997.

Furuichi Yasuko (ed.) and Hoashi Aki (assistant ed.). *Symposium: Asian Contemporary Art Reconsidered.* Tokyo: Japan Foundation Asia Center, 1998.

Gamer, Robert E. *The Politics of Urban Development in Singapore.* Ithaca, NY: Cornell University Press, 1972.

García Canclini, Néstor. *Hybrid Cultures: Strategies for Entering and Leaving Modernity*, trans. Christopher L. Chiappari and Silvia L. López. Minneapolis: University of Minnesota Press, 1995.

Geertz, Clifford. 'The Integrative Revolution: Primordial Sentiments and Civil Politics in the New States.' In *Old Societies and New States*, ed. Clifford Geertz. New York: Free Press, 1963.

Gellner, Ernest. *Nations and Nationalism*. Oxford: Basil Blackwell, 1983.

Goh Chok Tong. 'Prepare Our Children Well for the New Century', *Contact* (September 1996): 2.

Goh Keng Swee. *The Economics of Modernization and Other Essays*. Singapore: Asia Pacific Press, 1972.

__________. *Urban Incomes and Housing: A Report of the Social Survey of Singapore 1953–54.* Singapore: Government Printing Office, 1956.

Goh Keng Swee and the Education Study Team. *Report on the Ministry of Education 1978.* Singapore: Singapore National Printers, 1979.

Grehan, Helena. 'Questioning the Relationship between Consumption and Exchange: TheatreWorks' Flying Circus Project, December 2000', *positions: east asia cultures critique* 12, no. 2 (Fall 2004): 565–86.

Gupta, Akhil. 'The Song of the Nonaligned World: Transnational Identities and the Reinscription of Late Capitalism.' *Cultural Anthropology* 7, no. 1 (February 1992): 63–79.

Gupta, Akhil, and James Ferguson. 'Beyond "Culture": Space, Identity, and the Politics of Difference.' *Cultural Anthropology* 7, no. 1 (February 1992): 6–23.

Habermas, Jürgen. *The Philosophical Discourse of Modernity,* trans. Frederick Lawrence. Cambridge, Mass.: MIT Press, 1987.

_________. *The Postnational Constellation,* trans. Max Pensky. Cambridge, Mass.: MIT Press, 2001.

Hack, Karl. 'Theories and Approaches to British Decolonization in Southeast Asia.' In *The Transformation of Southeast Asia: International Perspectives on Decolonization,* ed. Marc Frey, Ronald W. Pruessen and Tan Tai Yong. Armonk, NY: M. E. Sharpe, 2003.

Hall, Donald E. (ed.). *Muscular Christianity: Embodying the Victorian Age.* Cambridge: Cambridge University Press, 1994.

Hall, Stuart. 'The Local and the Global: Globalization and Ethnicity.' In *Dangerous Liaisons: Gender, Nation, and Postcolonial Perspectives,* ed. Anne McClintock, Aamir Mufti and Ella Shohat. Minneapolis: University of Minnesota Press, 1997.

_________. 'When Was the "Post-Colonial"? Thinking at the Limit.' In *The Post-Colonial Question: Common Skies, Divided Horizons,* ed. Iain Chambers and Lidia Curti. London: Routledge, 1996.

Hardt, Michael, and Antonio Negri. *Empire.* Cambridge, Mass.: Harvard University Press, 2000.

Harper, T. N. *The End of Empire and the Making of Malaya.* Cambridge: Cambridge University Press, 1999.

_________. 'Lim Chin Siong and the "Singapore Story".' In *Comet in Our Sky: Lim Chin Siong in History,* ed. Tan Jing Quee and Jomo K. S. Kuala Lumpur: Insan, 2001.

Harootunian, Harry. *History's Disquiet: Modernity, Cultural Practice, and the Question of Everyday Life.* New York: Columbia University Press, 2000.

Harvey, David. *The Condition of Postmodernity: An Enquiry into the Conditions of Cultural Change.* Cambridge, Mass.: Blackwell, 1990.

Hatch, Walter and Kozo Yamamura. *Asia in Japan's Embrace: Building a Regional Production Alliance.* Cambridge: Cambridge University Press, 1996.

Hatta, Yuki. 'Children Who Kill Their Fathers: The Creation of *Lear*' (Producer's Message). In Japan Foundation Asia Center Programme for *Lear,* Kallang Theatre, Singapore, 28–31 January 1999.

Heng, Geraldine and Janadas Devan. 'State Fatherhood: The Politics of Nationalism, Sexuality, and Race in Singapore.' In *Nationalisms and Sexualities,* ed. Andrew Parker et al. New York: Routledge, 1992.

Hill, Michael and Lian Kwen Fee. *The Politics of Nation Building and Citizenship in Singapore.* London: Routledge, 1995.

Hirst, Paul, and Grahame Thompson. *Globalization in Question: The International Economy and the Possibilities of Governance.* Cambridge: Polity Press, 1996.

Ho Rih Hwa. *Eating Salt: An Autobiography.* Singapore : Times Books International, 1991.

Hobhouse, L. T. 'The Career of Fabianism', *Nation* (30 March 1907).

Hobsbawm, E. J. *Age of Extremes: The Short Twentieth Century 1914–1991*. London: Abacus, 1995.

_________. 'Ethnicity and Nationalism in Europe Today.' *Anthropology Today* 8, no. 1 (February 1992): 3–13.

_________. *Nations and Nationalism since 1780: Programme, Myth, Reality*. Cambridge: Cambridge University Press, 1990.

Hobsbawm, E. J. and Terence O. Ranger (eds.). *The Invention of Tradition*. Cambridge: Cambridge University Press, 1983.

Hofheinz, Jr., Roy and Kent Calder. *The Eastasia Edge*. New York: Basic Books, 1982.

Holden, Philip J. 'The Free Market's Second Coming: Monumentalising Raffles.' In *Reading Culture: Textual Practices in Singapore*, ed. Phyllis G. L. Chew and Anneliese Kramer-Dahl. Singapore: Times Academic Press, 1999.

Hong Lysa. 'Making the History of Singapore: S. Rajaratnam and C. V. Devan Nair.' In *Lee's Lieutenants: Singapore's Old Guard*, ed. Lam Peng Er and Kevin Y. L. Tan. St. Leonards, NSW: Allen & Unwin, 1999.

Huff, W. G. *The Economic Growth of Singapore: Trade and Development in the Twentieth Century*. Cambridge: Cambridge University Press, 1994.

Huntington, Samuel. 'The Clash of Civilizations.' In *The New Shape of World Politics*, ed. Fareed Zakaria. New York: Norton, 1997.

Ivy, Marilyn. *Discourses of the Vanishing: Modernity, Phantasm, Japan*. Chicago: University of Chicago Press, 1995.

Iwabuchi, Koichi. *Recentering Globalization: Popular Culture and Japanese Transnationalism*. Durham, NC: Duke University Press, 2002.

Iwabuchi, Koichi (ed.). *Feeling Asian Modernities: Transnational Consumption of Japanese TV Dramas*. Hong Kong: Hong Kong University Press, 2004.

Jameson, Fredric. *A Singular Modernity: Essay on the Ontology of the Present*. London: Verso, 2002.

_________. *Postmodernism, or, the Cultural Logic of Late Capitalism*. Durham, NC: Duke University Press, 1991.

Japan Foundation Asia Center. *The Japan Foundation Asia Center: Towards Mutual Understanding in Asia in the Twenty-First Century*. Tokyo: Japan Foundation Asia Center, n.d.

Jayasuriya, Kanishka. 'Authoritarian Liberalism, Governance and the Emergence of the Regulatory State in Post-Crisis East Asia.' In *Politics and Markets in the Wake of the Asian Crisis*, ed. Richard Robison, Mark Beeson, Kanishka Jayasuriya and Hyuk-Rae Kim. London: Routledge, 2000.

Johnson, Chalmers. *MITI and the Japanese Miracle: The Growth of Industrial Policy, 1925–1975*. Stanford: Stanford University Press, 1982.

Josey, Alex. *Lee Kuan Yew*. Singapore: Donald Moore Press, 1968.

Khoo, Eric (director). *Mee Pok Man*. Singapore: Zhao Wei Films, 1995.

_________ (director). *Twelve Storeys* (Mandarin-Chinese: *Shi'er lou*). Singapore: Zhao Wei Films, 1997.

Kinsella, Sharon. *Adult Manga: Culture and Power in Contemporary Japanese Culture*. Honolulu: University of Hawai'i Press, 2000.

Koh Tai Ann. 'Culture and the Arts.' In *The Management of Success: The Moulding of Modern Singapore*, ed. K. S. Sandhu and Paul Wheatley. Boulder, Co.: Westview Press, 1990.

Koolhaas, Rem. *Project for Prada Part 1*. Milan: Fondazione Prada Edizioni, 2001.

_________. 'Singapore Songlines: Portrait of a Potemkin Metropolis ... or Thirty Years of Tabula Rasa.' In Rem Koolhaas and Bruce Mau, *Small, Medium, Large, Extra-Large*, ed. Jennifer Sigler. Rotterdam: 010 Publishers, 1995.

Koschmann, Victor. 'Asianism's Ambivalent Legacy.' In *Network Power: Japan and Asia*, ed. Peter J. Katzenstein and Takashi Shiraishi. Ithaca: Cornell University Press, 1997.

Krishna, Sanjay, Sharaad Kuttan, Lee Weng Choy, Leon Perrera and Jimmy Yap (eds.). *Looking at Culture*. Singapore: Artres Design & Communications, 1996.

Kuo Pao Kun. *The Complete Works of Kuo Pao Kun: Plays in Chinese, the 1960s and the 1970s*, Vol. 1, ed. Quah Sy Ren. Singapore: World Scientific, 2005.

_________. 'Contemplating an Open Culture: Transcending Multiculturalism.' In *Singapore: Re-Engineering Success*, ed. Arun Mahizhnan and Lee Tsao Yuen. Singapore: Oxford University Press, 1998.

_________. *Images at the Margins: A Collection of Kuo Pao Kun's Plays*. Singapore: Times Books, 2000.

_________. 'Playwright's Message.' In TheatreWorks (Singapore) Programme for *Descendants of the Eunuch Admiral — A Meditation*, Victoria Theatre, Singapore, 3–5 June 1995.

_________. *Two Plays by Kuo Pao Kun:* Descendants of the Eunuch Admiral *and* The Spirits Play, ed. C. J. W.-L. Wee and Lee Chee Keng. Singapore: SNP Editions, 2003.

_________. 'Uprooted and Searching.' In *Drama, Culture and Empowerment: The IDEA Dialogues*, ed. John O'Toole and Kate Donelan. Brisbane: IDEA Publications, 1999.

Kusno, Abidin. *Beyond the Postcolonial: Architecture, Urban Space and Political Cultures in Indonesia*. London: Routledge, 2000.

Kwok Kian Chow. *Channels and Confluences: A History of Singapore Art*, exhibition catalogue. Singapore: Singapore Art Museum, 1996.

Kwok Kian Woon. 'The Problem of "Tradition" in Contemporary Singapore.' In *Heritage and Contemporary Values in Singapore*, ed. Arun Mahizhnan. Singapore: Institute of Policy Studies, 1993.

Kwok Kian Woon and Low Kee Hong. 'Cultural Policy and the City-State: Singapore and the "New Asian Renaissance".' In *Global Culture: Media, Arts, Policy, and Globalization*, ed. Diana Crane, Nobuko Kawashima and Ken'ichi Kawasaki. New York: Routledge, 2002.

Lam Peng Er and Kevin Y. L. Tan (eds.). *Lee's Lieutenants: Singapore's Old Guard*. St. Leonards, NSW: Allen & Unwin, 1999.

Langenbach, Ray. *Performing the Singapore State, 1988–1995*. Ph.D. dissertation, University of Western Sydney, 2003.

Lee Chee Keng. 'Intra-Asia Inter-Cultural Theatrical Productions: Looking at Japan Foundation's New Cultural Exchange Efforts.' Paper presented at the Ninth Annual Graduate Student Conference on East Asia, Columbia University, New York, February 2000.

Lee, Edwin. 'The Colonial Legacy.' In *Management of Success: The Moulding of Modern Singapore*, ed. Kernial Singh Sandhu and Paul Wheatley. Boulder, Co.: Westview Press, 1990.

Lee Kuan Yew. 'Preface.' In Goh Keng Swee and the Education Study Team, *Report on the Ministry of Education 1978*. Singapore: Singapore National Printers, 1979.

_________. *Towards a Malaysian Malaysia*. Singapore: Government Printing Office, 1965.

_________. *The Singapore Story: Memoirs of Lee Kuan Yew*. Singapore: Times Editions, 1998.

Leifer, Michael. *Singapore's Foreign Policy*. London: Routledge, 2000.

Lien Ying Chow with Louis Kraar. *From Chinese Villager to Singapore Tycoon: My Life Story*. Singapore: Times Books International, 1992.

Lim Min Min. *Remembering through Theatre: Memories and Histories*. BA (Hons.) thesis, Department of Sociology, National University of Singapore, 1998.

Lim, Richard. *Building a Singapore Bank: The OUB Story*. Singapore: Overseas Union Bank Limited, 1999.

Lim, Shirley Geok-lin. 'The English-Language Writer in Singapore.' In *Singaporean Literature in English: A Critical Reader*, ed. Mohammad A. Quayum and Peter Wicks. Serdang: Universiti Putra Malaysia Press, 2002.

Lim, William S. W. *Asian New Urbanism.* Singapore: Select Books, 1998.

Lodge, George C. and Ezra Vogel (eds.). *Ideology and National Competitiveness: An Analysis of Nine Countries.* Boston: Harvard Business School, 1987.

Loh Kah Seng. 'Within the Singapore Story: The Use and Narrative of History in Singapore', *Crossroads* 12, no. 2 (1998): 1–21.

Low, Linda. *The Political Economy of a City-State: Government Made Singapore.* Singapore: Oxford University Press, 1998.

Maki, Fumihiko. *Investigations in Collective Form.* St. Louis, Mo.: Washington University School of Architecture, 1964.

Mannheim, Karl. *Ideology and Utopia.* Harcourt, Brace, and World, n.d.

McCormack, Gavan and Yoshio Sugimoto (eds.). *The Japanese Trajectory: Modernization and Beyond.* Cambridge: Cambridge University Press, 1988.

Michaels, Walter Benn. *The Shape of the Signifier.* Princeton: Princeton University Press, 2004.

Milner, Alfred. 'Credo', *Times* (London), 27 July 1925.

Ministry of Culture. *Singapore 1984.* Singapore: Information Division, Ministry of Culture, 1984.

Nair, C. V. Devan (compiler and ed.). *Socialism that* Works ... *the Singapore Way.* Singapore: Federal Publications, 1976.

Ohmae, Kenichi. *The End of the Nation State: The Rise of Regional Economies.* New York: Free Press, 1995.

Oliver, F. S. *The Endless Adventure: Personalities and Practical Politics in Eighteenth-Century England.* London: Macmillan, 1930.

Ong, Aihwa. *Flexible Citizenship: The Cultural Logics of Transnationality.* Durham, NC: Duke University Press, 1999.

_________. *Neoliberalism as Exception: Mutations in Citizenship and Sovereignty.* Durham, NC: Duke University Press, 2006.

Ong Keng Sen. '*LEAR*: Linking Night and Day' (Director's Message). In Japan Foundation Asia Center Programme for *Lear*, Kallang Theatre, Singapore, 28–31 January 1999.

_________. 'A Theatre of Memory: Reconnection, Regeneration, Rediscovery through Experimentation with Traditional Arts.' Paper presented at the Singapore Heritage Society Conference, 'Our Place in Time: Heritage in Singapore', Substation arts centre, Singapore, 17–18 September 1994.

Pandey, Gyanendra. *The Construction of Communalism in Colonial India.* Delhi: Oxford University Press, 1990.

PuruShotam, Nirmala S. *Negotiating Language, Constructing Difference: Disciplining Difference in Singapore.* Berlin: Mouton de Gruyter, 1998.

Quah Sy Ren. 'Evolving Multilingual Theatre in Singapore: The Case of Kuo Pao Kun.' In *Ethnic Chinese in Singapore and Malaysia: A Dialogue between Tradition and Modernity*, ed. Leo Suryadinata. Singapore: Times Academic Press, 2002.

Rabinow, Paul. *French Modern: Norms and Forms of the Social Environment.* Cambridge, Mass.: MIT Press, 1989.

Rajaratnam, S. 'An Epistle to the Synod of the Socialist Orthodox Church.' In *Socialism that* Works ... *the Singapore Way*, compiled and ed. C. V. Devan Nair. Singapore: Federal Publications, 1976.

_________. *The Prophetic and the Political: Selected Speeches and Writings of S. Rajaratnam*, ed. Chan Heng Chee and Obaid ul Haq. Singapore: Graham Brash, 1987.

_________. 'Raja Wants Revival of a "Singaporean Singapore".' *Straits Times Weekly Overseas Edition*, 17 March 1990, 3.

Ratnam, K. J. *Communalism and the Political Process in Malaya*. Kuala Lumpur, 1965.

Rectanus, Mark W. *Culture Incorporated: Museums, Artists, and Corporate Sponsorships*. Minneapolis: University of Minnesota Press, 2002.

Robbins, Bruce. 'Introduction Part 1: Actually Existing Cosmopolitanism.' In *Cosmopolitics: Thinking and Feeling Beyond the Nation State*, ed. Pheng Cheah and Bruce Robbins. Minneapolis: University of Minnesota Press, 1998.

Robison, Richard, Kevin Hewison and Garry Rodan. 'Political Power in Industrialising Capitalist Societies: Theoretical Approaches.' In *Southeast Asia in the 1990s: Authoritarianism, Democracy and Capitalism*, ed. Kevin Hewison, Richard Robison and Garry Rodan. St. Leonards, NSW: Allen & Unwin, 1993.

Rofel, Lisa. *Other Modernities: Gendered Yearnings in China after Socialism*. Berkeley: University of California Press, 1999.

Rosaldo, Renato. *Culture and Truth: The Remaking of Social Analysis*. Boston: Beacon Press, 1979.

Sardar, Ziauddin. *The Consumption of Kuala Lumpur*. London: Reaktion Books, 2000.

Siddique, Sharon. 'Culture and Identity in the Public Housing Environment.' In *The City and the State: Singapore's Built Environment Revisited*, ed. Ooi Giok Ling and Kenson Kwok. Singapore: Oxford University Press, 1997.

_________. 'Singaporean Identity.' In *Management of Success: The Moulding of Modern Singapore*, ed. K. S. Sandhu and Paul Wheatley. Singapore: Institute of Southeast Asian Studies, 1989.

Skinner, Quentin. 'Meaning and Understanding in the History of Ideas', *History and Theory* 8 (1969): 3–53.

Steward, Julian (ed.). *Contemporary Change in Traditional Societies*. Urbana: University of Illinois Press, 1967.

Tan Chin Nam. 'Let Us Co-Create Our Nation's Brand.' *Fusion@MICA* 10, April–June 2006.

Tanaka, Stefan. *Japan's Orient: Rendering Pasts into History*. Berkeley: University of California Press, 1993.

Tay Kheng Soon with Robbie B. H. Goh. 'Reading the Southeast Asian City in the Context of Rapid Economic Growth.' In *Theorizing the Southeast Asian City as Text*, ed. Robbie B. H. Goh and Brenda S. A. Yeoh. Singapore: World Scientific, 2003.

Tay Teck Lock (director). *Money No Enough*. Singapore: JSP Entertainment, 1998.

Taylor, Peter J., D. R. F. Walker and J. V. Beaverstock. 'Firms and Their Global Service Networks.' In *Global Networks, Linked Cities*, ed. Saskia Sassen. New York: Routledge, 2002.

Toh Chin Chye. 'Cultural Heritage versus Technological Development: Challenges to Education.' In *Cultural Heritage versus Technological Development*, ed. R. E. Vente, R. S. Bhatal and R. M. Nakhoda. Hong Kong: Maruzen Asia, 1981.

Tong Chee Kiong. 'The Rationalization of Religion.' In *Imagining Singapore*, ed. Ban Kah Choon, Anne Pakir and Tong Chee Kiong. Singapore: Times Academic Press, 1992.

Tong, Kelvin and Jasmine Ng (directors). *Eating Air*. Singapore: Multi-Story Complex, 1999.

Tsuzuki, Etsuko. 'Between Ethnic Culture and Intimidated Culture.' In Fukuoka Art Museum, *Annual Artist Today — Fukuoka Annual V: Tang Da Wu*, exhibition catalogue. Fukuoka: Fukuoka Art Museum, 1991.

Tu Wei-ming. *Confucian Ethics Today: The Singapore Challenge*. Singapore: Curriculum Development Institute of Singapore / Federal Publications, 1984.

_________. *Confucianism in an Historical Perspective*. Singapore: Institute of East Asian Philosophies, 1989.

Tu Wei-ming (ed.). *Confucian Traditions in East Asian Modernity: Moral Education and Economic Culture in Japan and the Four Mini-Dragons.* Cambridge, Mass.: Harvard University Press, 1996.

_________ (ed.). *The Living Tree: The Changing Meaning of Being Chinese Today.* Stanford: Stanford University Press, 1994.

_________ (ed.). *The Triadic Chord: Confucian Ethics, Industrial East Asia and Max Weber: Proceedings of the 1987 Singapore Conference on Confucian Ethics and the Modernisation of Industrial East Asia.* Singapore: Institute of East Asian Philosophies, 1991.

Uhde, Jan and Yvonne Ng Uhde. *Latent Images: Film in Singapore.* Singapore: Oxford University Press, 2000.

Urry, John. *Consuming Places.* London: Routledge, 1995.

Vasil, Raj K. *Asianising Singapore: The PAP's Management of Ethnicity.* Singapore: Heinneman, 1995.

Vogel, Ezra F. *Japan as Number One: Lessons for America.* Cambridge, Mass.: Harvard University Press, 1979.

Von Vorys, Karl. *Democracy without Consensus: Communalism and Political Stability in Malaysia.* Princeton: Princeton University Press, 1975.

Wade, Robert. *Governing the Market: Economic Theory and the Role of Government in East Asian Industrialization.* Princeton, NJ: Princeton University Press, 1990.

Warren, James F. *Ah Ku and Karayuki-San: Prostitution in Singapore, 1870–1940.* Singapore: Oxford University Press, 1993.

_________. *Rickshaw Coolie: A People's History of Singapore, 1880–1940.* Singapore: Oxford University Press, 1986.

Webster, Anthony. *Gentlemen Capitalists: British Imperialism in South East Asia 1770–1890.* London: Tauris Academic Studies, 1998.

Wee, C. J. W.-L. 'Buying Japan: Singapore, Japan and an "East Asian" Modernity', *Journal of Pacific Asia* 4 (1997): 21–46.

_________. 'Creating High Culture in the Globalized "Cultural Desert" of Singapore', *The Drama Review* 47, no. 4 (Winter 2003): 84–97.

_________. 'The "Clash" of Civilizations? Or an Emerging "East Asian Modernity"?', *SOJOURN: Journal of Social Issues in Southeast Asia* 11, no. 2 (1996): 211–30.

_________. *Culture, Empire, and the Question of Being Modern.* Lanham, Md.: Lexington Books, 2003.

_________. 'Framing the "New" East Asia: Anti-Imperialist Discourse and Global Capitalism.' In *'The Clash of Civilizations?' Asian Responses*, ed. Salim Rashid. Dhaka: University Press, 1997.

_________. 'National Identity, the Arts, and the Global City.' In *Singapore in the New Millennium: Challenges Facing the City-State*, ed. Derek da Cunha. Singapore: Institute of Southeast Asian Studies, 2002.

_________. 'The Vanquished: Lim Chin Siong and a Progressivist National Narrative.' In *Lee's Lieutenants: Singapore's Old Guard*, ed. Lam Peng Er and Kevin Y. L. Tan. St. Leonards, NSW: Allen & Unwin, 1999.

Wee, C. J. W.-L. (ed.). *Local Cultures and the 'New Asia': The State, Culture, and Capitalism in Southeast Asia.* Singapore: Institute of Southeast Asian Studies, 2002.

Wee, C. J. W.-L. and Lee Chee Keng. 'Introduction: Breaking through Walls and Visioning Beyond — Kuo Pao Kun Beyond the Margins.' In *Two Plays by Kuo Pao Kun:* Descendants of the Eunuch Admiral *and* The Spirits Play, ed. C. J. W.-L. Wee and Lee Chee Keng. Singapore: SNP Editions, 2003.

Weiss, Linda. 'Sources of the East Asian Advantage: An Institutional Analysis.' In *Pathways to Asia: The Politics of Engagement*, ed. Richard Robison. St. Leonards, NSW: Allen & Unwin, 1996.

Williams, Raymond. *Culture and Society, 1780–1950.* London: Chatto & Windus, 1958.

Wilson, H. E. *Social Engineering in Singapore: Educational Policies and Social Change, 1819–1972.* Singapore: Singapore University Press, 1978.

Wong, John and Aline K. Wong. 'Confucian Values as a Social Framework for Singapore's Economic Development.' In *Conference on Confucianism and Economic Development in East Asia.* Taipei: Chung-Hua Institution for Economic Research, 1989.

Wong Lin Ken. 'Commercial Growth Before the Second World War.' In *A History of Singapore*, ed. Ernest C. T. Chew and Edwin Lee. Singapore: Oxford University Press, 1991.

World Bank. *The East Asian Miracle: Economic Growth and Public Policy.* New York: Oxford University Press, 1993.

Yeoh, Brenda S. A. *Contesting Space: Power Relations and the Urban Built Environment in Colonial Singapore.* Kuala Lumpur: Oxford University Press, 1996.

Yong, C. F. *Chinese Leadership and Power in Colonial Singapore.* Singapore: Times Academic Press, 1992.

__________. *Tan Kah-Kee: The Making of an Overseas Chinese Legend.* Singapore: Oxford University Press, 1989.

Yu Yun. 'The Soil of Life and the Tree of Art: A Study of Kuo Pao Kun's Individuality Cultural through His Playwriting', trans. Kuo Jian Heng. In Kuo Pao Kun, *Images at the Margins: A Collection of Kuo Pao Kun's Plays.* Singapore: Times Books, 2000.

Index